Justice, the Digital Revolution, Society and the Individual

Justice, the Digital Revolution, Society and the Individual

By

Bruno Zeller and Mirella Atherton

BRILL | NIJHOFF

LEIDEN | BOSTON

Library of Congress Cataloging-in-Publication Data

Names: Zeller, Bruno, author. | Atherton, Mirella, author.
Title: Justice, the Digital Revolution, Society and the Individual / By Bruno Zeller and Mirella Atherton.
Description: Boston : Brill, 2025. | Includes bibliographical references and index. | Summary: "The effects that the digital revolution is having on the threads that make up the fabric of our society are significant. Methods of communication and the ways in which individuals interact are changing. This has led to changes to our institutions, our well known structures and our trusted hierarchies. In this book we investigate the instruments of change in order to grasp how justice, the construct of society and the individual can be understood. The innovations brought forward by the digital revolution are inevitable and are here to stay, indeed at times they will cause conflict. This book recognises that changes to institutions such as the law must occur for us to adapt to a new and changing environment"– Provided by publisher.
Identifiers: LCCN 2024042976 | ISBN 9789004702684 (hardback) | ISBN 9789004702691 (ebook)
Subjects: LCSH: Technology and law. | Internet–Law and legislation. | Online social networks–Law and legislation. | Artificial intelligence–Law and legislation.
Classification: LCC K487.T4 Z45 2025 | DDC 343.09/99–dc23/eng/20240916
LC record available at https://lccn.loc.gov/2024042976

Typeface for the Latin, Greek, and Cyrillic scripts: "Brill". See and download: brill.com/brill-typeface.

ISBN 978-90-04-70268-4 (hardback)
ISBN 978-90-04-70269-1 (e-book)
DOI 10.1163/9789004702691

Contents

Foreword

The digital economy is changing the way we live and work. There is a significant change happening across every sector of society, from government to the private sector. That is, the world is experiencing digital transformation, whereby, the digitalisation is traversing national borders. However, this is not a new phenomenon. Governments are grappling with how to assess, let alone regulate and keep pace with its impact upon their domestic-sovereign economies. The development of an international regulatory regime remains wholly elusive and complex. There appears to be a lack of transnational appetite to develop international principles and concepts to guide nation states.

This book addresses these fundamental issues and more. The aim of this book is to promote an understanding of evolving digital revolution. The authors provide an excellent account and outline of the challenges facing the world, by identifying the changes that are observable to the conception of justice itself. Significantly, the authors have focused on the concept of Justice, which is subject to many mechanisms and factors, and we show that the very heart of the institutions of justice we value are at risk of destabilisation. In doing so, the authors have highlights how by not getting this right, the overall stability of a society is dependent on the wellbeing and contentment of the individuals that make up the structures within society. Put another way, when the structural social connections are lost and economic gains are concentrated in the elite the stability of a society is compromised and inequality, discontentment, breakdowns, and conflicts occur. More importantly, the book argues that the current day analysis requires researchers, governments, and regulators, along with practitioners to look back, and that is to ask the question what has history taught us? In taking this a step further, and by adopting this approach, this is not different to that of undertaking a complex investigation. That is precisely what this book does, augments an investigation that is much needed for the current times as technology continues to challenge everyone.

By studying and acquiring the knowledge and contemporary views on the social construction of what we consider to be real, people are able to, and will be better equipped to be able to predict what will happen next. Our thinking needs to change. The book acknowledges that any user of an integrated system such as the online environment needs to be protected. Finally, the book draws upon, and makes the case how data protection laws have been implemented by nearly every country. However, when looking deeper into the regulation of data, a level of symbolism has emerged, which is largely detached from the practical reality of protecting personal data. The book asks the relevant question – is and should this change? This book is a fascinating and important read and is recommended to anyone interested in technology and its future impact to the world.

Dr. Robert Walters
International Arbitrator – Solicitor
Director Digital Finance Law Project – Victoria University
Adjunct Senior Research Fellow – University Western Australia
Adjunct Professor European Faculty of Law, Slovenia Europe
Advisor to the Corporate and Insolvency Centre – Gujarat National Law University India

Acknowledgements

With special thanks and acknowledgement to Professor Tania Sourdin, Professor John Anderson and Associate Professor Neil Foster for their expert guidance on writing books. Thank you to all of the staff at the University of Western Australia's Law School and the University of Newcastle's School of Law and Justice for their ongoing support and assistance. It is humbling to be able to converse with such interesting and diverse academics on a wide range of topics. Our valued colleagues and the wonderful students we teach will have the greatest impact on the success of this book, so we do hope it provides some insights. A special thank you to Dr. Suzana Nashcova and Dr. Robert Walters for their helpful contributions and feedback.

PART 1

The Legal Theories

CHAPTER 1

Introduction

The starting point to this book is the observation by Wittgenstein in 1958 where he noted:

> If we want to study the problems of truth and falsehood, of the disagreements of propositions with the reality, of the nature of assertion, assumption and question, we shall with great advantage at primitive forms of language in which these forms of thinking appear without the confusing background of highly complicated process of thought.[1]

This book is arguing that as the digital revolution today is the modern industrial revolution of yesterday, a process of inventions which has not yet run its course. It is affecting the economy by increasing efficiency and hence profitability. It has given rise to multinational businesses namely the technology giants which control the digital systems and hence control information. This in itself is not new and as an example, in the Middle Ages the church controlled the information and hence society. But the digital systems have also changed the way we live and interact with each other. By analogy the visitor in an art show has moved from the landscape section into the abstract collection and needs to make sense of what they are looking at.

Therefore, this book is concerned with the effects of the digital revolution has on the fabric of society. As reality is socially constructed, the communication, that is how people interact is of paramount importance. The most obvious fact is that we have moved from face-to-face social intercourse to communication via machines. A specific example is the mobile phone. We are attempting to indicate and discuss some of the important instruments of change only insofar as needed in order to understand the main theme of this book namely how is justice and the construct of society understood? This is important as the inevitable fact is that the digital revolution is here to stay, indeed it has not run its course yet. This book also recognises that an understanding of the changes in the social construction of reality would never be successful if institutions such as the law would not adapt to the changing landscape. The focus of this book

1 See L. Wittgenstein. 1958. *Preliminary Studies for the "philosophical investigations" generally known as the blue and brown book*. Harper Torchbooks.

 | DOI:10.1163/9789004702691_002

is on societal change but references to the significant work by Hildebrandt and Brownsword is important and will be made where necessary.

These facts as noted above makes it valuable to understand how our socially perceived reality is constructed and where it leads to. This is specifically important as we are living in turbulent times. The "gentil" hippy days of the 1960's have been replaced by political uncertainties, armed conflicts, massive people migrations and a shift of the radical right.

However to understand the future we also need to understand the past and hence this book will be – where appropriate – looking back in history and piecing together important theories and events. It will allow us to isolate and find what institutions are of importance to recreate a viable socially constructed reality as after all justice the cornerstone of a well-functioning society. It is a legal construct that requires dedication and faith for implementation. It requires efforts of institution in order to protect not only today's society but those who come after us.

To further explain, personal observations are useful. People who lived or are living in small country towns and those who are in their 70's remember when we all knew our neighbours in the street and when we shopped at the cornerstone where the owner was the fountain of knowledge what whatever happened in the neighbourhood. Specifically those who worked in schools to shop at the supermarket for a loaf of bread would take an hour as stopping and talking a few minutes with each person one knew would take up the time.

The same people today do not even know the few people living in the same street. There is an exception to the above namely among people who own dogs. Why is this so? The reason is simple if a dog meets another one, they need to meet and greet and hence the owners of the dog take the opportunity to converse as well. The dog is the connection in a social setting like the people we used to know. The fact which connects the people above is that they were actively involved in social events before the digital revolution.

Young computer savvy adults today are increasingly concerned with the dark side of the new technology and the harms that may be caused to children and young adults. Since the public release of tools such as "Dall-E" and "Midjourney", artificial intelligence-generated images produced have stoked confusion about breaking news, fashion trends and Taylor Swift.[2] Arguably regulation is extremely important to bring the applications of new technology out of the shadows.

---

2 Sydney Morning Herald. 2024. "*Is this face made by AI, or is it real? We bet you can't tell*", https://www.smh.com.au/world/north-america/is-this-face-made-by-ai-or-is-it-real-we-bet-you-can-t-tell-20240201-p5fiqw.html.

For teenagers the mobile phone is an essential part of social space, and many cannot imagine life without it. It is not necessary to have face to face conversation as texting is an adequate substitute anymore. Also because the immense volume of information all needs to be in small grabs. The most telling observation of today's society is that the digital systems rule our lives. It is common to see people at dinner in a restaurant playing with the mobile phones instead of engaging in conversations or a room with people where silence rules as everybody plays with the digital gadgets. Even young children are technology savvy and gadgets have become the modern babysitters.

It is not difficult to see that the current digital revolution has been the game changer. But at the same time it must never be forgotten that the present has been shaped by the past and the present will be shaping the future. We will therefore attempt to explain the present by also looking at the past. So what is this book about?

This book is concerned that the current digital revolution has brought about a major change or shift in society at large. This in itself is not new as society is always in a gradual state of change, but these changes have never been as quick as those currently observable. This book identifies the changes that are noticeable to the conception of justice itself. Justice is subject to many mechanisms and factors, and we show that the very heart of the institutions of justice that we value are at risk of destabilisation. Stability of a society is dependent on the wellbeing and contentment of the individuals that make up the structures within society. When the social connections are lost and economic gains are concentrated in the hands of the elite, the stability of a society is compromised and inequality, discontentment, breakdowns, and conflicts occur.

The roles of individuals, groups and subgroups within society as well as the role of institutions are examined. The richness of opportunities still present because of and even in despite of online access is recognised, as is, those embraced by subgroups such as the revival of choirs as a means to socialise. Also, classical music such as composed by Bach, Monteverdi and Vivaldi just to note a few are now played with non-western instruments such as the Japanese flute and the Digeridoo to note two. To understand music, it is crucial to appreciate the culture and society in which it was written. We need to go back to the Middle Ages starting with Hildegard von Bingham via Monteverdi, Vivaldi, Bach, Beethoven,[3] and not to be forgotten the Beatles to name a few. Each of these composers learned from the previous composers and these and other

3 Readers not familiar with classical music might even be tempted to investigate and familiarise themselves with the power of music.

arts such film music has its origin in the classics. What is valid in the structure and history of music is equally valid in the structure and history of society, the very purpose of this book. It will only be at the end where all the learned historical developments are studied will it be possible to draw a conclusion and answer the question posed by this book namely how has and will the digital revolution change society and how can it be brought back into equilibrium.

In brief therefore this book attempts through the application and discussion of legal and political theory around technology to better understand the need for and how to achieve 'justice' and 'equality' in the context of the digital revolution.[4] The discussions in this book are not concerned with the technical aspect of digital systems. This first chapter is in part based on observations, questions and discussions with colleagues. Subsequent chapters will critically examine the observations considering extensively existing literature and history.

1 Drivers of Change

We argue that the quality of political and legal leadership together with vigilance to uphold justice are imperative for stability of social structures. In the context of a digital revolution progress occurs at lightning speed and construction of the universe is brought about by the actions of a few individuals especially those in charge of the technology giants. Legal institutions are important in shaping the new digitally constructed reality.

As the world is always in a flux the reshaping of identities and cultures as well as a class divide have again become more evident and demonstrates the force of the technological changes that are taking place. Communication methods are now based on platforms and in public view like never seen before. Arguably changes are not often chance occurrences, they require leadership to shape and guide developments into desirable well-planned directions. This book argues that an analysis of current problems requires looking back at moments in time and that is to ask the question what has history taught us? With that knowledge and study on contemporary views on the social construction of what we consider to be real, we should be able to predict what will happen next.

4 It must be noted that this book does not comment nor rely specifically on the work of Y. Harari. 2014. *Sapiens: A Brief History of Humankind.* London: Harvill Secker.

Equality and justice were benchmarks for legal thinkers such as Aristotle and other Greek philosophers as well as later Kant, Hegel and Marx and today Rawls and Berger and Luckmann. Their importance is that they provide a solution to restoring justice in our institutions, our societies and in individuals. Rawls as an example, defined the social contract in a well-ordered society where there is cooperation between individuals to choose what is fair. Ultimately an unbiased collective vision culminates in a working democracy which promotes equality between individuals who can participate by their own free will. History has shown that a democracy can deteriorate when voters are polarised. False information can exacerbate polarisation and threaten democracy by removing power from individuals. De-humanisation, de-personalisation or perhaps hyper-personalisation have become part of the on-demand economy where power is concentrated in corporations who operate and control what is online.

Not surprisingly power and power structures are an inevitable part of past and present reality. Foucault recognised anti-authority struggles existed within a hierarchy where power processes exist. Once institutions who have power are legitimised, inequality can result, and it is very difficult to break free from the subjective and objective restrictions of a power imbalance. The power of the law is in these times the only beacon of light correcting the power imbalance and hence maintain justice for all.

Knowledge carries power and the way in which individuals view and understand their world shapes an understanding of what is real. Unplanned events and unplanned functions are still possible and are a feature of the new and uncontrolled technology. What we are observing now is that new technology has spread its' tentacles far into the lives of every individual and this new technology has become entangled in not only culture but the undesirable effect of reshaping what was once considered a private life. The level of explainability and transparency of new technology is diminishing as time goes on and the belief that humanity can evolve beyond the current limitations is becoming more and more inevitable. This is bringing the legal definition of personhood, autonomy, and the notion of identity in the coming era into question and requires a reconstruction.

There is no doubt that the internet like any other invention has brought about significant innovations and progress. It is comparable to the inventions of the past such as the printing press, the calculator and the mobile device. Access to information is faster and more readily available to the public at large as the internet is a vast library. Long gone are the days where academics and other researchers waited for printed copies sourced from other libraries which took weeks. Instant access to information is now a normal part of the on-demand economy. Simply put, it used to be difficult and time consuming to source information. Now, some of this information is controlled by a small number of elites – and as we have seen in history before – its veracity cannot be verified.

The biggest difference between information sources from books and articles is the fact that the authors were well known, and the information was identifiable and authenticated. This important detail has become problematic. The point really is what is real now? And how is one to know what is real now? These are important questions as today there are simply no reliable methods to separate real news from fake news and false information. Information affects the way we react to change. The problem is that digital technology is an all-absorbing system like a sponge soaking up all of our information. It doesn't seem to matter whether the information is real or otherwise. The most important difference between the printing press and digital media is that the digital media has the capacity to absorb private and personal data and this capability introduces risks of surveillance ability.

In addition, social reality has changed from personal contacts to social connections operated via machines, the result is that the personal factor in personal contact is diminishing. However, this might be true but how does one analyse this and how do we know what is real and what is virtual? Berger and Luckmann in their introduction make a pertinent comment namely, "The ordinary man in the street does not trouble himself about what is real to him and what he knows about unless he is stopped short by some sort of problem. He takes his reality and knowledge for granted."[5] This book is testing this hypothesis and extrapolating this hypothesis to include not only the man in the street but how society experiences reality and knowledge. The next sections will set out the parameters in the way the communication channels have changed and influence how problems are created due to the way we communicate.

2 The Communication Dilemma

It is an obvious statement to note that the Internet of Things (IoT) has changed the way we interact with each other. The face-to-face communication that used to predominantly exist has given way to texting, e-mails and a virtual feeling rather than real feeling of connection.

5 Peter L. Berger and Thomas Luckmann. 1966. *The social construction of reality: A treatise in the sociology of knowledge*. First Anchor, 14.

It is useful to note some basic issues in relation to communication. Successful communication in whatever form is dependent on the sender's and the recipient's experience of the relevant topic matter. It is also obvious that the experience of each other depends on the social and proximal distance between the sender and recipient. One fact is clear, that an individual is or at least should be able to understand himself at a given moment. However, anything written or recorded many years ago may need to be reconstructed. Attempting to reconstruct written records of the past may not always be accurate as social reality may have changed. It is however obvious that people in a closely knit social group will not face the same issue as these individuals can rely on a shared experience. Culturally homogenous societies find it easier to fix meanings and to understand what is objectively valuable compared with multicultural societies. Given the fact that the world is experiencing a wave of migration specially from underdeveloped nations culturally homogenous society are not the norm anymore and hence the issue of communication has become a real issue for governments, business and individuals.

Berger and Luckmann in *The Social Construction of Reality* 1966 before the digital revolution took hold, did and could argue that only in face-to-face encounters is the other person real or put in another way by Turchin "the others mind is an enigma wrapped in darkness". It is interesting to note that Berger and Luckmann wrote that it is impossible for man to develop as man in isolation as a "solitary human being is being on the animal level".[6] The question is at what level is a human being communicating in the virtual world online?

In addition, and not necessarily only due to the internet we have also seen a gradual decline in the Western World of living within the clan, that is grandparents and children live in the same household or next door. Grandparents looked after the children while the parents are out working. In effect old people's homes and kindergartens were not needed and the socialisation process took place within the extended kinship group. The close living with the clan has given way to single flat dwelling where not even the people on the same floor talk to each other. Instead of eating together like we once did we often see isolated people staring at their phones while they eat. The point is that many migration groups still live within clans and hence assimilation is difficult. One could even argue that it creates cultural divides which are not conducive to formulating legal and culturally based directives to a society.

Not surprising there is very little communication between strangers. In effect society is slowly forgetting how to interact in the real world but we all

6 Berger and Luckmann, 1966, 69.

have become versed in the digital or virtual world. Arguably the intellectual and physical stimulus of connection has diminished in the big cities.

That said the aim of this book, as already stated, is to focus on the often-forgotten effect of the digital revolution on society. To that end an understanding of the social construction of reality and in our context a re-construction of reality is essential. Specifically a look backward in time will assist in the untangling and understanding of the changes that the digital revolution has brought about. The importance of looking backwards is that based on the fact that if we do not understand history, we do not fully understand the present and miss the opportunity to adapt to future trends in order to maintain a well-functioning society. This is confirmed by Berger and Luckmann arguing that:

> The symbolic universe orders history. It locates all collective events in a cohesive unity that includes past, present and future. With regard to the future, it establishes a common frame of reference for the projection of individual actions. Thus, the symbolic universe links men with their predecessors and their successors in a meaningful totality.[7]

The observation by Berger and Luckmann brings to the fore the question whether the universe really orders history. As the digital revolution has brought many changes which have enriched our culture, the question is how can we detect and then use a common frame of reference to protect individuals?

One common universal fact as noted before is that we learn from history. At best we learn from the past or as it can be argued we perfect the mistakes we made. Turchin correctly noted that "a science of history is not only possible but also useful: it helps us anticipate how the collective choices we make in the present can bring us a better future."[8] The importance at looking at the past is that recurring patterns emerge one being that every society in history at one time has or will run into problems. Issues among others such as an overproduction of young graduates as well as a declining public trust are becoming more obvious and need to be understood.

The next part will briefly analyse (but only as required by the overall aim of the book) the effects of elites on the construction of a social understanding. The importance lies in the fact that elites after all are the decision makers and how they react to events will shape the path of the society.

7 Berger and Luckmann, 1966, 120.

8 Peter Turchin. 2023. *End Times*. Penguin Press, at ix.

3 The Effects of Elites

A social change has taken place in the functioning and overproduction of elites. Elites are not simply those people who are better than others due to hard work or intelligence but are a select group who have social power that is they influence other people such as politicians and leaders of big corporations such as the technology giants and influencers, the new phenomenon created by social media. Power is and always has been executed by those who have wealth, and the powerful hire people who do their bidding. The fact is that there has always been an elite group which governs society whether in a democratic or dictatorial leadership model. The elite overproduction has changed now and has altered the social structure of society. Turchin explains it in the following way by using the example of musical chairs.

There are a number of chairs but a greater number of people. When the music stops the player without a chair is eliminated. He or she is the frustrated looser the others are the leaders. In the next round the chairs are the same but the number of players is increased producing an increased number of frustrated losers increasing the degree of chaos and frustration as with increasing times players start to break the rules and in the end more catch on.[9] Some observers see Former President Trump in the United States coming to mind as being an example of a promoter of the elite overproduction game. The issue is not the production of the elite but the production of an increased number of frustrated losers.

Aside from the fact that we cannot all be winners, the second factor which is a result of the digital revolution is the uneven distribution of wealth. This has resulted in a change in the thinking of the stabilising force in society namely the middle class. Simply put the losers of the overproduction game have landed in the lower class. After the steady growth of wages since the middle 1970's, real wages stopped growing despite the continuous growth of the economy. The effect is that the rich were getting richer, and this bred discontent and in effect a combustible combination of conflict.

Another factor contributing to the creation of elites is that the digital revolution has not been static either. New systems are being invented and currently – and a concern this book will address later – is the emergence of Artificial Intelligence (AI) a yet untested phenomenon which as the saying goes "the genie has been let out of the bottle, but we do not know how to put it back". One of the issues this book tries to understand is whether society

9 Turchin, 2023, 9.

directs the online systems rather than being directed by the online systems? Importantly due to the capability of these new digital systems a new question emerges, namely the distinction of what is real and what is generated that is only virtual? The distinction has been blurred. The question why we need to live in a virtual reality needs to be addressed as it appears that society is not the Master of Technology anymore.

Are the technology giants the new ruling class? If they are, do they control the media which controls the information, the social interactions, shapes opinions and which then shapes government actions? The question is whether our democratic structures and societies are still successful or are we in a state of fragmentation and decline? It appears to be more likely that we are showing signs of fragmentation as we are experiencing internal warfare and discord. Turchin suggested that a study of how states are breaking down is essential as it acts as a warning so mistakes can still be corrected.[10]

4 A Look Back into History

This book contends that the importance in understanding society is to understand how society constructs and understands reality. The fact is that every society changes and our society again is in a period of rapid change. In order to understand how a society constructs its living reality we rely principally on Berger and Luckmann, *The Social Construction of Reality*. As justice is another important factor of stability within a society the work of Rawls' in, *A Theory of Justice* will also be analysed. Such an analysis is important as Saul,[11] has argued that globalism has collapsed and hence the world needs to be reinvented specifically as the digital revolution is perhaps the cause for a reinvention of our social engagement.

We will reach back to the 19th century and look at the principal historical events and ideas which shaped social changes. Specifically, Marx and Hegel are of importance as their ideas have shaped the thinking of contemporary thinkers like Heidegger, Berger and Luckmann and Rawls. The 19th century indeed was a time when the world was experiencing wars, revolutions, social unrest, and the important emergence of philosophical ideas which further developed the ideas originally proposed by the Greek philosophers. It will lay the foundation in the discussion of how our current society is shaped by the events of

10 See Turchin, 2023.

11 See John Raston Saul. 2005. *The collapse of globalism: And the rebirth of nationalism. Harry N. Abrams.*

the digital revolution and analyse the driving forces of instability and arguably look for a way forward.

It is a valid question to ask why are Marx, Hegel and other thinkers of any relevance today to look for a way forward? The fact is that great thinkers are always influenced by the newer generation, for example Marx was influenced by Hegel. Marx as an example is still relevant today. Considering the *Communist Manifesto* a political pamphlet written by Marx influenced the Russian revolution, and the consequences of that are still shaping today's world. By analogy to build a house requires many bricks and all are equally important to the finished product. Each individual brick is equally important as without each of these single bricks the house could not have been built. Great thinkers throughout the ages are like bricks – put together – they influenced and shaped society as we know it. Just like a house, a society cannot be built or renovated instantly. It takes time and a conscious effort from institutions and thinkers to reconstruct the social reality.

The changes are due to one important fact namely our communication via machines instead on a personal level. An understanding of the changes in our socialisation processes is also dependent on a basic understanding of the data economy.

We have so far only touched on issues of concern to this book which will be fully explored in detail. The next part will lay the foundation of how we understand the digital environment.

5 The Digital Environment

Society functions not in a vacuum but within an economic and social network. While coal fueled the British industrial revolution, data now fuels the digital revolution. The dominant feature shaping and influencing individuals currently is the collection of data by the technology giants. The fact of collecting data is not a new phenomenon but what is new is an all-embracing net which has been thrown out by the internet catching everything in its path. The problem is that the collection of data is just the beginning, the technology giants also want our heartbeats and our souls that is our feelings and the way we interact and what we think. This is orchestrated by creating the social platforms where people interact and communicate via the machines. These platforms have been developed as all-consuming attention seekers. One fact has not changed data and that is information is still an important commodity in determining economic decision making.

What has changed is that machines have now an increased ability to determine and forecast what the consumer wants and hence the data has become a predictive tool. It is the collection of data which is the starting point of a new way to influence and guide society. After all data is the lifeblood – the very purpose – of the operation of some of the technology giants.[12] Arguably they have the ability to engage in arbitrary social de-construction. There is also a possibility of misconception of a number rather than a person when counting data-by-data consumers. Newport correctly argues that "[increasingly data points of access] dictate how we behave and how we feel, and somehow coerce us to use them more than we think it is healthy, often at the expense of other activities we find more valuable."[13] It is therefore not surprising that Zuboff defines "surveillance capitalism" as the prolific progression of a new economic order that claims human experiences as a free raw material for hidden commercial practices of extraction, prediction, and sale.[14] These new powerhouses assert their dominance over a data society and make a challenge to democracy itself.[15]

The point is that technology companies have progressed from providing generic data to data which is granulated down to each person's interest within the information economy. Being liked or followed has become important information Facebook (Meta) users are craving for. It promises all users a chance of being at least fleetingly noticed by millions. Simply put it does not take much imagination to conclude that Facebook (Meta) is not a charity nor a benevolent world citizen as they are simply driven by profit motives. The point is that a few people at technology companies such as Elon Musk through their choice are able to steer what people will be thinking today. They are said to be "thought leaders". This fact is still present, but the question is, have we already forgotten how it feels like to have conversations and relationships we want not what we are told we want?

Ward – in a study – discovered that checking social media and texting has an effect on people, especially the young as "the mere presence of these devices [smartphones] reduces available cognitive capacity and includes 'brain drain' by occupying limited capacity cognitive resources for purposes of attentional control."[16] Also the problem is that smartphones do not develop the capacity

---

12 See Shoshana Zuboff. 2019. "The Age of Surveillance Capitalism. The Fight for a Human Future at the New Frontier of Power" *PublicAffairs*, 8.

13 See Cal Newport. 2019. *Digital Materialism*, 8.

14 See Zuboff, 8.

15 See Zuboff, 1.

16 Adrian F. Ward, Kristen Duke, Ayelet Gneezy and Maarten W. Bos. 2017. "Brain drain: The mere presence of one's own smartphone reduces available cognitive capacity." *Journal of the association for consumer research* 2, no. 2: 140–154.

for empathy and the art to listen. Observing people, it appears that mobile phones are a permanent attachment. This is not by accident as the fixation with smartphones is a carefully engineered design feature.[17] However there is a positive side, devices like smartphones allow instant exchanges, varying from accessing informative data on the internet to "chatting" with special people.[18] If smartphones are used as a tool and not a replacement for personal contact there is no problem. To be a positive addition to an individual's life, technology must be used for benefit and to enrich an already existing pattern of behaviour but not as a replacement of a social connection.

6 The Attention Economy

It is undeniable that the digital revolution has spawned new patterns of activities and of interrelationships among people. Previously, as an example, young people went to the monthly dance in the community hall now they surf the dating apps like eHarmony and Tinder. Goldhaber understood that there is a tension between information and attention which are at the forefront of the internet. He observed:

> ours is not truly an information economy. By definition, economics is the study of how a society uses its scarce resources. And information is not scarce – especially on the Net, where it is not only abundant, but overflowing. We are drowning in information, yet constantly increasing our generation of it.[19]

He also noted that [many] names for the new era have been invoked: the information age, the third wave, the move towards cyberspace, all of which point, vaguely at least to the fact that the new patterns of activity and of interrelationships among people are now emerging. He also noted that "[t]here is something else that moves through the Net, flowing in the opposite direction from information, namely attention." [20]

---

17 Newport, 2019, 16–17.

18 Ward *et al.*, 2017, 140.

19 Michael Goldhaber. 1997. "*Attention Shoppers*", *Wired*, https://www.wired.com/1997/12/es-attention/.

20 Michael Goldhaber. 1997. "*The Attention Economy and the Net*", *Firsy Monday*, https://firstmonday.org/ojs/index.php/fm/article/view/519.

It is somewhat troublesome that despite the constant reminder that technology impacts the cognitive skills which includes intellectual curiosity, ability in problem solving, critical thinking and communication. The fact that especially the education system moves even closer to rely on the online technology and just like the technology giants want it to save money hence increases the bottom-line. One possible reason is that data providers offer data users with instant access to information which is an irresistible inducement for users to access the IoT.

The social reality is that many IoT users are not terribly concerned with either the business model of the technology giants or the data they generate as long as their instant access to the social network is functioning. This the way – users think – to keep in contact with the world at large which results in "instagramification" which also reduces the attention span of the users making them data objects. The internet is has become essential to their social participation.[21] Simply put two factors are interconnected, firstly the desire for attention and secondly the vehicle used for that attention the IoT. Data obvious can only be generated if the IoT gains the attention of the users by capitalising on their desire to be noticed that is the "attention syndrome". The problem is not so much the attention seeking which is a human trait but that it takes place in the virtual world and not in the real world. The issue for the system owners is that either parties must not lose their interest or attention for the cycle to be successful. The IoT is also faced with exactly this problem namely how to keep the attention of the users. Facebook (Meta) as an example holds the attention by not only linking to one individual but to many other realities in a given society. An important tool is that the machine reality is removed from actual humans and hence the machine delivers "likes" and "followers" metrics. The point is that those who likes or follows do not understand the person as they have not experienced a real-life interaction, hence the other person is not a real personal connection. The metrics are measuring information whether it is fake or real. The disturbing fact is that machines are forming patterns of behaviour and "educating" users to come back and hence generate more data.

7 What Next?

If technology giants have managed to "infiltrate" the way in which our social activities take place. This leads to the question have we lost our ability to

21 Zuboff, 2019, 10–11.

socialise? Has distance communication through the internet disavowed the value society once placed on face-to-face communications and personal connections? Alternatively, even if the dark side of the IoT is acknowledged, is there a way of encouraging the development of its positive social attributes? Also, will we be able to recognise it if and when it happens?[22] These are the questions this book will discuss in the following chapters.

Chapter 1 will introduce the topics covered in the book and include an explanation of how the selected legal theories and philosophies can be of assistance in the elaboration of why and how our society is changing. Chapter 2 explains the lessons from history, views of society and justice including well-being, social status and wealth. Chapter 3 will discuss the conflict and the drivers of instability as well as the role of the social world before the digital revolution. Chapter 4 is devoted to a discussion of the new world order and an acknowledgment of the end of globalisation. Chapter 5 will outline Berger and Luckmann's social construction of reality and will include an analysis of institutionalisation. Chapter 6 will highlight the theory of justice as noted by John Rawls. It will allow a comparative view as to possible changes in the construction and functioning of society. The importance of such a discussion lies in the fact that it offers the starting point when arguably society was still in equilibrium. Before the digital revolution there was no enigma of certainty, knowledge and understanding within society but these were identifiable and did exist. There was social cooperation between individuals without interference. This chapter is complete with a critical analysis of Rawls. Chapter 7 will discuss how the social world is viewed to assist in the formulation and understanding of the effect of the digital revolution including the changes brought about by the IoT. The online social world has now diversified into social networks, online tribes and online communities. Chapter 8 analyses the effects of specifically Artificial Intelligence (AI) on social structures. It will also examine the effects the European Union (EU) AI proposal will have on the development of AI. Chapter 9 will analyse how power is used to shape relationships and sets the stage for the delineation of class and functioning of society hence how it affects social life. This chapter will also include a discussion of the importance of reshaping education. Chapter 10 will draw together the threads in this book in order to propose a solution or at least highlight issues which need to be taken into consideration in the formulation of the social construction of a digitally dominated reality. The algorithmic culture

22 See generally Bruno Zeller. 2021. "The Internet of Things – A Machiavellian plot or the Dawn of a New Reality?" *Houston Journal of International Law*, Vol 44, No 1, 12.

is a growing phenomenon with significant implications because it is everywhere. Transhumanists are predicting that humans are in an early phase of their evolution and legal definitions are changing. Chapter 11 concludes with a question about our relationship with technology and whether technology's influence is out of our control.

CHAPTER 2

Lessons from History

1 Introduction

This book argues that the way a society 'digests' change and deals with progress requires sociological and philosophical dialogue which filters from the intellectual elite into the mainstream of thinking. The reason is that literature, education, and academics build on what is already within the consciousness of thoughts. Simply put this chapter will demonstrate that the same issues are still occupying thinkers of today but the environment in which social issues – specifically the notion of justice – are discussed is always changing. That said it is also clear that the historical knowledge and learning of the 19th century are still influencing the thinkers of the 20th and 21st century. This chapter therefore will lay out the background knowledge in order to understand current developments. This chapter therefore is not intended to be "complete" or scholarly but rather a sketch of past analysis on societal behaviour. It is in effect a "genealogical tree" of ideological thinking.

We specifically look at how critical analysis is driven by legal thinkers such as Berger and Luckmann and Rawls who were responding to and assisting in creating the environment where changes were assimilated into societies at large. Of great importance is the notion that any changes need to be and are perceived to be just, hence the fact that justice needs to be recognised is pivotal in bringing about change.

The point is that justice has many stakeholders, and the problem is that the principles of justice can never be truly understood without having at least an understanding of the socioeconomic environment and a perception how justice is applied. Rawls himself grappled with setting the principles of justice within an economic framework as did Marx. Wellbeing and hence justice is dependent on economic activities especially in an increasing complicated world order. The importance of such a consideration is founded in the fact that the mid-twentieth century saw a transformation from public finance to the finance of public economies.[1]

1 See Maxime Desmarais- Tremblay, Marianne Johnson and Richard Sturn. 2023. "Mapping the history of public economics in the twentieth century: an introduction to the special issue." *The European Journal of the History of Economic Thought*, 30, no. 5, 689–712.

 | DOI:10.1163/9789004702691_003

One fact history tells us is that the rise and fall of economic cycles have affected all societies irrespective whether they are farming, trading, or any other combination as the economy is a repetition of mathematically precise cycles.[2] In most cases the cycles of change are triggered by famines, epidemics, revolutions, ideas or any other events such as currently inflation causing discontent. These triggering events also appear to be contagious affecting sometimes more than just one country. The Arab Spring is an example that started in Tunesia and spread to Algeria in 2010. In 2011 it spread to Jordan, Oman, Saudi Arabia, Syria and Yemen. By the end of February 2011, it spread to the rest of the Arab world with different effects and intensities. The same contagious changes are well documented in history. As an example Turchin noted social events in 1848 starting in Italy, spread to France then Germany, Denmark and Sweden and eventually to Ireland.[3]

Turmoil was and always will be a fertile ground where thinkers develop new ideas regarding the social construction of a functioning society. Historically this has been documented for many centuries specifically in Europe but also in many other places across the globe.

2 Historical Developments of Societal Theories

This book argues that in each significant historical period the perception of what is real changes. Our idea of absolute objectivity – a social notion – is changing. Two of the main thinkers this book analyses to understand reality and the function of justice are Berger and Luckmann who wrote *The Social Construction of Reality* 1967 and John Rawls who wrote *A Theory of Justice* 1971.

Importantly though many innovative ideas which are persisting today had their origins in the 19th century in Europe during great social upheavals. Rawls for example attempted to provide an alternative to utilitarianism and refocussed moral and political thought. In doing so he broadened the modern liberal thought and justified democratic use of coercive power. He accepted pluralism and now pluralism is spoken of both as a fact and as a theory. When expressed in modern times the idea of pluralism refers to the awareness that the modern world is simply faced with a wide range of competing religious and secular ethical standpoints.[4] Thus it is important to bear in mind that most

2 See generally Turchin, 2023, 44.

3 Turchin, 2023, 32.

4 Peter Lassman. 2004. "Political Theory in an Age of Disenchantment: The Problem of Value Pluralism: Weber, Berlin, Rawls." *Max Weber Studies* 4, no. 2, 254.

modern societies today are pluralistic. "This means that they have a shared core universe taken for granted as such, and different partial universes coexisting in a state of mutual accommodation."[5]

Berger and Luckmann's work in sociology defined social interactions, cultures and habits and has been influential to several different fields of study. Rawls introduced the ideas of equality and an overlapping consensus among reasonable comprehensive doctrines on justice as fairness as a freestanding political conception of justice, which in turn provided 'content' to 'public reason' in a democratic society.[6] Before analysing the works further we step back in time to capture the context of the influences on Rawls and Berger and Luckmann.

Turning to the early 19th century the German philosopher Hegel wrote the *Elements of the Philosophy of Right* which was published in 1821. His main interest was to understand how the free will wills the free will, and not mere arbitrariness.[7] It is an important point that Hegel lived in a time of wars and social unrest, in a sense he was reflecting the current time. The French Revolution in 1848 heralded a new awakening and the end of an old regime. The revolution spread throughout Europe where arguments for social reform were fuelled by Descartes, de Spinoza and Locke.

The early decades of the nineteenth century were a time when French biology and medicine had dominated the world. The revolution heralded a new spiritual awakening for natural science as Darwin was attempting to explain evolution and natural selection which showed that populations do become adapted over time to their new environment. The French intellectuals in 1859 in contrast were living in the same world as they did in 1830.

> there had been no change in their outlook. The same facts led them irrevocably to the same conclusions … this is probably the major reason why so many Frenchmen remained completely indifferent to Darwin and why he never achieved the support of a single important French biologist.[8]

5 Berger and Luckmann, 1967, 142.

6 Samuel Freeman. 2023. "Ideal theory, political liberalism, and the well-ordered society." *Journal of Social Philosophy,* 6.

7 See Stanford Encyclopedia of Philosophy, 2024. https://plato.stanford.edu/entries/hegel-social-political/.

8 John Farley. 1974. "The Initial Reactions of French Biologists to Darwin's 'Origin of Species." *Journal of the History of Biology*, vol. 7, no. 2, 279.

Arguably the new outlook or view on society was Materialism. It arguably was a product of Darwinism which maintained that consciousness was dependent on matter. Simply put it is a belief that nothing exists except matter and its movements and modifications. The effect was that spiritual values were not any more important and poets like Schiller and Goethe lost influence. A byproduct of these developments was that Germany expanded its commercial capacity.

However the decline in "thinking" and poetry in favour of materialism came to an end with the recognition of Arthur Schopenhauer and his work *The World as Will and Representation* 1818. He was deeply influenced by Kant and he was also influenced by Idealism noting that there is no object without a subject. He believed that there was no clear delineation between the experience of a dream and reality.[9] His conclusion being that the world simply is an imagination. "At the same time, the inner being of this world, what is outside of our cognitive apparatus or what Kant calls the thing-in-itself, is the will; the original force manifested in every representation."[10]

But Schopenhauer contrary to Kant argued that as the will has no purpose or goal the will can never be satisfied. He thought that every force of nature and every organic form of nature participates in a struggle to seize matter from other forces or organisms. Thus, existence is marked by conflict, struggle and dissatisfaction. The attainment of a goal or desire, Schopenhauer continued, results in satisfaction, whereas the frustration of such attainment results in suffering. Since existence is marked by want or deficiency, and since satisfaction of this want is unsustainable, existence is characterised by suffering.[11]

The influence of the philosophy of Schopenhauer was felt as long as into the 1870's punctuated by wars in Italy and in Germany as well as the German-French conflict which eventually saw the rise of Prussia under Bismarck. The rise of the political awareness of the population was the forerunner of socialism and social democracy which influenced the social thinking of among others Marx. It needs to be noted that the French Revolution in 1798 as well as the German Revolution in 1848 were led by the bourgeoisie. Given the increased

9 See Theobald Ziegler. 1911. *Die Geistigen und Sozialen Stromungen des XIX Jahrhunderts*, Georg Bondi, 335.

10 See Internet Encyclopedia of Philosophy, 2024. https://iep.utm.edu/schopenh/#:~:text=Arthur%20Schopenhauer%20has%20been%20dubbed,challenges%20the%20value%20of%20existence.

11 See Internet Encyclopedia of Philosophy, 2024. https://iep.utm.edu/schopenh/#:~:text=Arthur%20Schopenhauer%20has%20been%20dubbed,challenges%20the%20value%20of%20existence.

interest and involvement of the people in political affairs. Socialism and communism were not a mainstream idea.

Germany was at that time basically an agrarian state and hence not as like England which was open and unaffected by the labour issues created by the industrial revolution. It took the development of building and towns in Germany where villas of the industrialists could be compared by the poor living in ghettos and a class divide could be identified. It was Ferdinand Lasalle, the founder of the labour movement, a disciple of Marx, who was the first man in Germany, and the first in Europe, who succeeded in organising a party of socialist action. After Lasalle's death Marx and his theories gained in importance though they were not as radical as Lassalle's.

Of importance to this book – and hence understanding society in the digital age – are in essence two of Marx's theories namely the fetishism of commodities and reification. We later in the book will analyse how they are viewed through the lens of the 21st century. It is argued that to analyse the total work of Marx goes beyond the aim of this book. However, some comments and observations about Marx are necessary to understand the theories of Berger and Luckmann and Rawls. In order to understand and appreciate Marx and hence Rawls and others, the influence of Hegel needs to be understood.

3 Hegel and the Social Order

Hegel was instrumental in explaining and also shaping social changes through his ideas about free will. Modern German philosophy was dominated by Kant and Hegel. Hegel covered a vast range of topics including many of the most important subject-matters of human reflection, such as metaphysics, epistemology, law, ethics, politics, theology, arts, and history.[12] His most relevant works were the *Phenomenology of Spirit* 1807, the Encyclopedia, the *Grundlinien der Philosophie des Rechts* 1820, and the *Über die wissenschaftlichen Behandlungsarten des Naturrechts.*[13] Hegel described the imagery of 'World-Spirit' but it is unknown what he actually saw. Arguably these ideas of spirits may have come from the Greek deities. What is known is that Hegel witnessed the emperor Napoleon riding through Jena. He wrote to his friend Friedrich Neithammer in 1806 and told him that he has seen Napoleon, mounted on

12 Gianfrancesco Zanetti. 2023. *Handbook of the History of the Philosophy of Law and Social Philosophy.* Edited by Mortimer NS Sellers and Stephan Kirste. Springer International Publishing AG. 129.

13 Zanetti, 2023, 130.

the back of a horse, surveying the territory. Hegel supposedly experienced the spirit connected at a single point with the world.[14] Hegel thought that "abstract Right isolated from other forms of normativity would lead to society's self-annihilation".[15]

The philosophical stream of thought from Fries to Kant criticised the natural philosophy of Feichte, Hegel and Shelling for distancing itself from the actual natural sciences.[16] Putting this criticism aside the value in Hegel's philosophy are his ideas about social order:

> In a social order ruled by norms conceived of merely as normative relations between private individuals, social relations are converted into commercial transactions and are threatened by potential clash of rights that menaces to dissolve society. At the same time, here the State is thought of as the principal proprietor among other proprietors. Accordingly, the *res publica* becomes the private property of an extremely powerful proprietor that ends up being the only actual rightsholder under whose will and power all other rights are submitted to. The princeps becomes the lord of the world.[17]

The fact is that not much has changed as the state is still – at least in theory – "the lord of the world". The digital revolution has however advanced another powerful "Lord" namely the technology giants. What has not changed since Hegel's time and before that is that the state in whatever form has always been subject to the influences of the powerful and the elite. What has changed and needs to be defined anew by a society – as it always has – is the question of justice as well as the question of what is ethical?

Hegel noted that an ethical life is the element in which abstract right, and morality are integrated into what Hegel calls an ethical substance. An actual community that includes elements such as family, civil society, market, corporations, and the state. In this context, norms are not conceived of only as contractual relations (abstract Right) or as subjective-based moral laws (morality). Norms include complex actual social practices in charge of achieving the integration of individuals and society seen as a whole. Conflicts are thought to be solved by profit making entities and the state. This concept of Hegel's

---

14 Martyn Hudson. 2023. *Social Ghosts and the Dead of World History: Ghost Theory,* Routledge, 4.

15 Zanetti, 2023, 133.

16 Tadahiro Oota. 2023. *Confronting the German Idealist Tradition,* Routledge, 59.

17 Oota, 2023, 133.

philosophy: the state, Hegel distinguishes between (1) the state within the system of civil society, external state or state of necessity and understanding (Not- und Verstandesstaat) and (2) the ethical state.[18]

Hegel's concept of recognition implies a relation between self-conscious subjects who exist in a society. In this relation, each subject realises that in order to be autonomous, he or she must be recognised as such by another autonomous subject. Accordingly, one's freedom implies and requires the freedom of others. The legal, political, and moral recognition of a plurality of individuals is a condition for there to be a society at all.[19] Hegel's understanding of the individual in society shaped social changes follows and was recognised by others such as Marx.

The observation that the plurality of individuals as a condition for the existence of a society is correct. But equally correct is the fact that the state plays an important role. Society is less and less speaking as one voice hence it is the state and now the powerful and elite of society which makes the ultimate choice in regard to question of how society is structured and what is perceived to be real but also what is to be just.

As Rawls and Berger and Luckman today drew inspiration from the thinking and hence conclusions of Hegel so did Marx. His views on fetishism and justice are still of importance to understand the functioning of a viable society.

4 Marx, Fetishism and the Notion of Justice

Lassalle was another German philosopher who was influenced by Hegel and corresponded regularly with Marx. Lassalle referred to his exposure to Hegel as his "second birth."[20] He consumed Hegel's works, as well as those of young Hegelians like Strauss and Feuerbach. Marx however responded to Hegelian philosophy in his own way.

It is useful to note a brief background to Marx who was the editor of the *Rheinischer Zeitung* and expressed an interest in trade. Marx as well as his colleagues belonged to the radical Hegelian left movement.[21] His interest in social problems resulted in his termination as editor. He moved via France to England where he met up with his friend Engels and together published the *Communist Manifesto* 1948. Marx died in England with much of his work not completed.

18 Oota, 2023, 134.

19 Oota, 2023, 135.

20 See Edward Hallett Carr. 2022. *Studies in revolution*. Routledge, Vol. 30.

21 See Ziegler, 1911, 468.

Two issues are of relevance for this book which are that both Berger and Luckmann and Rawls discussed these issues as well and were affected and influenced by Marx. Of specific importance first is Marx's treatment of materials and hence fetishisms. Secondly Marx also discusses the notion of justice which was further developed by Rawls.

5 Fetishism of Commodities

Marx writing about the subjectivity in capitalist societies noted "[T]he commodity reflects the social [that is, interdependent] characteristics of men's own labour as objective characteristics of the products of labour themselves."[22]

Marx specifically detailed his definition of fetishism of commodities:

> A commodity appears at first sight an extremely obvious, trivial thing. But its analysis brings out that it is a very strange thing, abounding in metaphysical subtleties and theological niceties ... The mysterious character of the commodity-form consists simply in the fact that the commodity reflects the social characteristics of men's own labour as objective characteristics of the products of labour themselves, as the socio-natural properties of these things. [The commodity-form] is nothing but the definite social relation between men themselves which assumes here, for them, the fantastic form of a relation between things. ... I call this the fetishism which attaches itself to the products of labour as soon as they are produced as commodities.[23]

Mulhern argued that commodities in Marx's view "have value because of the amount of work they entail – or, to speak precisely, their value, their exchange-value, is determined by the amount of socially necessary labor-power expended in their production."[24] The irrational devotion to commodities – the fetishism – is after all still the deciding factor in achieving a change in one's social class. It can be expressed as a subtle comment such as where do you live or what do you do. The answer then is translated into the social class the

---

22 Karl Marx and Ben Fowkes. 1976. *Capital. Introduced by Ernest-Mandel. V1*. Penguin Books, 164–65.

23 Marx and Fowkes, 1976, 163–65.

24 Francis Mulhern. 2007. "Critical considerations on the fetishism of commodities." ELH 74, no. 2, 479–492, 484.

person belongs to. The 'commodity' of suburbs or 'work' is the determinative factor of one's standing.

Marx also notes that there are two forms of value these are the relative and the equivalent.[25] Mulhern explains the difference between them in the following way. Value of commodity A is to be exchanged for commodity B. The exchange value is that A is worth two of B. "In this instance, B appears in the aspect of the equivalent form of value, as the measure by which the relative value of A is determined. Each in turn illustrates the role of a particular equivalent."[26]

Marx also addressed the issue where goods can be used as a means of exchange which he coined the reserved commodity. An example of this is when cigarettes are used as exchange in wars. He notes "[T]he simple commodity-form is ... the germ of the money-form,"[27] This is where Marx notes fetishism which can attach itself to any commodity as soon as it is used as means of exchange. Mulhern points to the problematic issue of fetishisms as "it is only as the embodied equivalent that the commodity may turn fetish, and we should not forget that every exchange requires two commodities, and that the other one cannot also, at the same time, take that role."[28] As Marx turns his attention to the money form of exchange he writes:

> "The money-form is ... the reflection thrown upon a single commodity by the relations between all other commodities."[29] Marx in the end states that interest bearing capital in this mode attains "its pure form, self-valorizing value, money breeding money [and] 'fetishized form'".[30]

Mulhern explains that "fetishism is a disposition inhering in the structure of commodity exchange; yes, the potential for it is everywhere in the ensemble of exchanges; and it may be that the system as a whole promotes the fetishism of money."[31]

That said Marx arguably rejected the thinking of his time that "under capitalism, decisions about what to produce and how to distribute it are determined "naturally" by the "values" of the commodities to be produced and

25 See Marx and Fowkes, 1976, 139–54.
26 Mulhern, 2007, 485 also see Marx and Fowkes, 1976, 152–54.
27 Marx and Fowkes, 1976, 163.
28 Mulhern, 2007, 485.
29 Marx and Fowkes, 1976, 184.
30 Marx and Fowkes, 1976, 515–517.
31 Mulhern, 2007, 486.

distributed."[32] Marx on the other hand believed that it is people that is individuals who make decisions on production and distribution. The question who owns the productive resources? This has not been answered in Marx's view on fetichism. What Marx in understanding capital has advocated is a model "of how people actually exercise powers they don't know they have, of how that unconscious exercise of powers can lead eventually to the discovery of the powers, and of how the discovery of powers can make it obvious that we should exercise them consciously to achieve the goals we have."[33]

The short version of the fetishism of commodities is something like this: There is a "commodity mode of production" that has both a technical and a legal/conceptual element (people understand one another to be "owners"). Producers in this mode develop a form of consciousness, or understanding of their productive and distributive activities, that is appropriate to their situation. At first, they see the world governed by the value of commodities but experience the fluctuations of value as arbitrary deviations from custom. Then they grasp value as congealed labor, and understand the fluctuations as reflecting changes in necessary labor time (or in "social needs").[34] Of importance to the discussion of power and fetishism is the fact that data has now taken on the mantle of commodity and the power of holding data and influence is wielded by the technology giants. The unique fact is that the supplier of data and the consumption of data is the same person namely the user of online technology.

Marx in a sense attempted to understand what reality is and arguably linked it to what is social. The mechanism or process of seeing something as being objective can be found in Marx's discussion of fetishism of commodities.

The importance of Marx's view on fetishism lies in the fact that today commodities specifically the new commodity namely data generated by digital systems is extending its position and social reach. Data now can contribute to class consciousness and in Marxism this is the set of beliefs that a person holds in relation to their social class.

It is the wealth pump, the movement and ownership or commodities which influences not only political participation but features as well in the production of elites. In this context it is important to note the comments of Slavoj Žižek:

> [T]he fetishist illusion resides in our real social life, not in our perception of it – a bourgeois subject knows very well that there is nothing magic

32 Duncan Kennedy. 1984. "The role of law in economic thought: essays on the fetishism of commodities." 34 AM. U. L. Rev., 969.

33 Duncan Kennedy. 1984, 972.

34 Duncan Kennedy. 1984, 991.

> about money, that money is just an object which stands for a set of social relations, but he nevertheless acts in real life as if he believed that money is a magical thing.[35]

Of interest to this book is that Berger and Luckmann fleshed out what Marx began in fetishism with the process of analysing essentialism. This is a helpful tool in the construction of an objective reality which in the context of the 21st century is in the process of being re-structured. Social construction of reality will be discussed later in the book. We will now turn to another important aspect in constructing and understanding society namely the idea of justice.

6 The Concept of Justice

Justice was a topic noted by Marx in his *Critique of Hegel's Philosophy of Right* 1843 where he stated, "Already as the resolute opponent of the previous form of German political consciousness the criticism of speculative philosophy of right strays, not into itself, but into problems which there is only one means of solving – practice."[36] The question of course is what did Marx mean with the term 'practice'? Yanli explains it in the following way "When we think about justice in this sense, we see that it is necessarily rooted in practice; it embodies the justice principle of certain class interests and unifies both the realistic and idealistic logic of *de jure* reality."[37] Arguably what Marx has indicated is that rights must be contained in how we practice and hence how we react in daily life, he did not directly define 'justice' but referred to the justice of law. In other words, the law of the land is the just way to resolve injustices.

In his critique of Hegel a shift in Marx's views can be detected in his writing. He said that: "a sphere ... claims no particular right because no particular wrong, but wrong generally, is perpetuated against it; which can invoke no historical, but only human, title; which does not stand in any one-sided antithesis to the consequences but in all-round antithesis to the premises of German statehood."[38] The term 'sphere' is arguably the political system which he was

35 Slavoj Žižek. 2006. *The Universal Exception*, edited by Rex Butler and Scott Stephens" New York: Continuum, 254–55.

36 Karl Marx and Friedrich Engels, 1973. *Karl Marx on society and social change: With selections by Friedrich Engels*. University of Chicago Press, 9.

37 Feng Yanli. 2020. "The Marxian Concept of Justice Based on Historical Materialism." Social Sciences in China 41, no. 1, 9.

38 Marx and Engels, 1973, 15.

attacked as editor of the *Rheinische Zeitung*. His clearest indication can be seen in his publication of '*The German Ideology*' where he argued that:

> The production of ideas, of concepts, of consciousness, is at first directly interwoven with the material activity and the material intercourse of men, the language of real life. Conceiving, thinking, the mental intercourse of men, appears at this stage as the direct efflux of their material behavior. The same applies to mental production as expressed in the language of politics, laws, morality, religion, metaphysics, etc., of a people.[39]

It needs to be noted that when Marx wrote *The German Ideology* he also grappled with the idea on materialism and fetishisms which is detectable in his writing,

> to expound the real process of production, starting out from the material production of life itself, and to comprehend the form of intercourse connected with this and created by this mode of production (i.e., civil society in its various stages), as the basis of all history; and to show it in its action as state, to explain all the different theoretical products and forms of consciousness, religion, philosophy, ethics, etc. and trace their origins and growth from that basis.[40]

What then is Marx notion of justice? Yanli put it in the following way,

> In Marx's view, justice is not some kind of a priori value that exists prior to practice; instead, it is a product of the social mode of production, a product of practice. Marx believes that there is not and cannot be any permanent justice; justice is merely a product of certain historical conditions. In general, the concept of justice is subject to self-consciousness, scarcity of resources, material production, social and economic mechanisms and other factors.[41]

In essence and in brief Marx started and developed his theory of justice based on the economic process of materialism that is productive and distributive justice. If Marx is correct, then – as far as justice is concerned – it needs to be redefined. As the historical conditions have changed with the influence of

---

39 Marx and Engels, 1973, 151.
40 Marx and Engels, 1973, 171.
41 Yanli, 2020, 11.

the digital revolution Rawls' conclusions as discussed later in this book will be significant.

7 Conclusion

Engels's *Ludwig Feuerbach and the End of Classical German Philosophy* 1886 remains a classic statement on the philosophies of Marx and Hegel. Following his work, Engel suggested that the great fundamental question of all, especially that of modern philosophy, is about the relationship of thought and being.[42] Perhaps Hegel was trapped by his own historical period as Lukács thought, Hegel "could only choose between utopian illusions and resigned acceptance of the miserable reality of Germany as it then was".[43] Hegel's *Philosophy of History*, were lectures in which he traces the growth of freedom from the ancient Eastern civilisations, the Greek and Roman worlds and feudalism, to the Western European nations where individual freedom finally begins to take formal shape and demonstrates just how important historical knowledge can be.[44] While Marxian philosophy has been described as the successor of Hegelian dialectic almost all the ideas that Hegel formulated in this context went in one way or another into Marxian philosophy. The commonality of the fate of Hegelian and Marxist philosophy at the hands of the social-democratic intellectuals concludes that Hegelian and Marxian philosophies are either going to be defeated altogether or they are going to win altogether.[45]

The important lesson is that the reforms, democratic gains and establishment of freedoms for individuals that came from the division, fragmentation and shifts in monarchies and political parties in the French, English and American revolutions have been incorporated into the Constitutions of many modern countries. Incorporating these gains has benefitted both individuals and societies. Similarly, the digital revolution may lead to the incorporation of many positive outcomes. There is no doubt that the new revolution has brought about what is said to be increased access to information, productivity and the demand for new jobs. While these gains will be of benefit to individuals and

42 David MacGregor. 2014. *Hegel and Marx: after the fall of communism*. University of Wales Press, 1.

43 MacGregor, 2014, 8.

44 MacGregor, 2014, 16.

45 See Dogan Gocmen. 2007. "Rosa Luxemburg, the legacy of classical German philosophy and the fundamental methodological questions of social and political theory." Critique 35, no. 3: 375–390.

societies the negative effects of addiction, compromised security, manipulation and overload have never been chartered before. The speed of these new changes is a challenge in itself and all we have to guide us is a look back in time. Legal theories have always been available to us and give us the context we need to navigate these new challenges.

CHAPTER 3

The Drivers of Instability

1 Introduction

As we have seen, changes in perceptions of the functioning of a society are arguably driven by factors of instability either wars or economic disparities. We have again entered a period of instability and hence this chapter will attempt to explain and highlight some of the factors driving instability.

The obvious fact is that wellbeing and contentment with one's own life are key indicators of individual welfarein a stable society. In this book we highlight that social connections are also an important factor in wellbeing. Wellbeing is substantively driven by geography and economics as well as biological indicators such as health. Komlos and Baur for example – building on existing research – argued that the most sensitive indicator of health is the average height of a given society.[1] Their proposition is that:

> in the absence of offsetting forces, height generally increases in good times and contracts in adversity. It is affected by the state of medical technology, the access to health care, the cost of medical services, the quality of perinatal care, the attitude toward preventive medicine, the virulence of the disease environment, and the degree of pollution.[2]

Arguably therefore social status is an important determinant for an individual as is income,better educated parents generally have better knowledge in choosing healthy meals and affording medical services. It would seem obvious that well-off nations are taller than the poorer ones. However, Komlos and Baur discovered that:

> the average physical stature of Americans has been lagging well behind West-European levels [and in addition] within half a century a veritable metamorphosis in the shape of the American population took place without notice: from being the tallest in the world still around World War II,

1 See John Komlos and Marieluise Baur. 2004. "From the tallest to (one of) the fattest: the enigmatic fate of the American population in the 20th century." *Economics & Human Biology* 2, no. 1 (2004): 57–74.

2 Komlos and Baur, 2004, 1.

 | DOI:10.1163/9789004702691_004

> Americans have become one of the most obese at the onset of the 21st century.[3]

Considering that the United States is one of the wealthiest countries, perhaps it has not translated into biological wellbeing relative to other advanced countries like Europe. This is remarkable despite significant scientific progress, extraordinary technical changes, and economic growth. According to the data, the well-being in the United States must have declined which arguably could explain the increasingly social fragmentation not only in economic but also in political terms and the spikes in violent crimes.

The fact is that five major differences between the United States and Europe have been discovered by Komlos and Baur and these support their claim. First social inequality in the United States is greater than in Europe and secondly the focus on health care for citizens is different "Health care systems in Europe provide a much more comprehensive coverage than in the United States."[4] Health delivery is complicated and is bogged down in overlapping jurisdictions in the United States and in addition, "The West-European welfare states, in which a subsistence income is more-or-less guaranteed, provide a more comprehensive social safety net in other respects as well, including unemployment insurance."[5]

Importantly the fifth factor is that "Spatial inequality is much greater in the US than in Europe, as characterised by the suburb-inner city dichotomy that does not have a Western-European analogue."[6] The hypothesis that Komlos and Baur put forward is that:

> … the West-European welfare states have some advantages in providing a higher biological standard of living to their populations than the American more market-oriented one. The patterns elucidated here imply also that per-capita income is not an exhaustive indicator of the quality-of-life. Instead, other welfare measures, such as those pertaining to the health and biological indicators of the population are relevant in providing a broader perspective on well-being.[7]

3 Komlos and Baur, 2004, 3.
4 Komlos and Baur, 2004, 18.
5 Komlos and Baur, 2004, 18.
6 Komlos and Baur, 2004, 19.
7 Komlos and Baur, 2004, 19.

Extrapolating from Komlos and Baur's work, the conclusion is that specifically in the United States, well-being has been eroded and hence society is not in balance. From the indicators that are used it seems that a reconstruction of society and the services we rely on is needed. What has been learned is that social factors such as class determination, wage structure and politics culminate in welfare versus growth and all of these factors play an important role. The question is whether all these factors are just indicators or symptoms of a greater problem. Europe features less inequality as does Australia, but this does not necessarily correlate with content populations. It is arguable that the digital revolution has played an important part in destabilising society whether there is inequality, or a content population and hence social wellbeing is important. This issue will be further elaborated on as the book progresses.

2 Social Well-Being

A casual observation indicates that there is a decline in economic conditions of the less educated members of our society. In addition, social services such as housing assistance, the importance of family, free education and the influence of institutions such as the church have declined. Simply put, too many people lack social connection and this results in loneliness and hence a lack of social connectedness. Blanchflower and Oswald have discovered that in the United States extreme distress in the population rose from 3.6% in 1993 to 6.4% in 2019 and "(1) at the personal level, the strongest statistical predictor of extreme distress was 'I am unable to work,' and (2) at the state level, a decline in the share of manufacturing jobs was a predictor of greater distress."[8] Likewise the number of young Australians in psychological distress continues to rise sharply. The annual 2024 Hilda survey of 17,000 Australians shows "a clear trend of younger people becoming lonelier and feeling more isolated".[9]

These observations are a strong indicator that the digital revolution has affected the social fabric through labour saving devices rendering unskilled jobs redundant and this has shifted the wealth unequally away from the working class to the upper class. In other words, the wealthy have given rise to a

8 See David G. Blanchflower and Andrew J. Oswald. 2020. "Trends in extreme distress in the United States, 1993–2019." *American Journal of Public Health* 110, no. 10, 1538–1544. https://ajph.aphapublications.org/doi/full/10.2105/AJPH.2020.305811.

9 See the Melbourne Institute: Applied Economic and Social Research, "*Household, Income and Labour Dynamics in Australia* (HILDA) *Survey*", https://melbourneinstitute.unimelb.edu.au/hilda.

phenomenon of meritocracy of others. Michael Sandel put it in the following way:

> Winners are encouraged to consider their success their own doing a measure of their virtue – and to look down upon those less fortunate than themselves. Those who lose out may complain that the system is rigged, that the winners have cheated and manipulated their way to the top. Or they may harbor the demoralising thought that their failure is their own doing, that they simply lack the talent and drive to succeed.[10]

The problems continue to grow with the digital revolution – and one can only guess what the effects of new developments will be. One factor is clear, namely that many manual skilled jobs have become obsolete. For example, the skilled job of a tool maker has disappeared as automated machines can do the same work quicker and hence cheaper. The changes to the job market are not new as we have seen in times gone by a coach maker became the car maker and now there is a highly automated process to produce a highly sophisticated vehicle. The difference today is that the tool maker has nowhere else to go and does not have skills transferable to other jobs. Marx's class distinction defined by the relation to the means of production has disappeared. As Turchin notes we now have the educated and the "immiserated".[11] These are not classes as defined by Marx but modern observations which may have the same meaning. In addition, unlike past times where education, including university education, was free and the class divide did not affect education because it was based on a level of competence. The divide between the classes now is harder to traverse. As noted earlier, wage dynamics or simply getting a secure job is an important driver of well-being which has acted as a resilient factor cushioning external as well as internal shocks to the economy and to society. Simply put, in past times, when one door closed another one opened. Today though, the same applies but only to a limited class and not to the whole population. The fact is the rich are getting richer while the poor are trapped in welfare or in job insecurity.

10 Quoted in Angus Deaton and Anne Case. 2021. *Deaths of Despair and the Future of Capitalism*. Princeton University Press, 54–55.

11 Valentin Fedorovich Turchin and V. F. Turčin. 1977. *The phenomenon of science*. Vol. 1. New York: Columbia University Press, 78.

3 The Wealth Pump

The problem with a decline in relative wages in general and well-being in particular is that it causes issues of fairness and justice and as a result it undermines the stability of society. As a consequence, the legitimacy of institutions is questioned. This includes scrutiny of the state. Looking back in history similar such events led to the peasant revolt in England and the bourgeoise who were the driving force in the French revolution. The question is who will be the driving force in the next revolution? This disharmony does not appear to be a fantasy as Hanauer noted:

> If we don't do something to fix the glaring inequities in this economy, the pitchforks are going to come for us. No society can sustain this kind of rising inequality. In fact, there is no example in human history where wealth accumulated like this, and the pitchforks didn't eventually come out.[12]

The 'pitchforks' have not yet come out but not all is well on the 'western front' either. Politicians cannot agree on a way forward and we have witnessed this through the media specifically in the United States. Politicians squabble among themselves, they investigate each other's personal lives and as a result they have lost sight of the 'end game'. What is undeniable – and perhaps what is a driving force – is that the wealth pump is turned on to direct funds unequally. The fruits of the economy obviously must go somewhere. Unequal policies seem to drive one sector more than others such as "ultra-low interest rates proved the greatest wealth pump ever devised, loading the dice in favour of the financial elite".[13]

What is observable is that people without college and university degrees have seen their real wages decline, on average since 1980, and even workers with a college degree but no postgraduate education have only seen limited gains.[14] Demand for tasks and demand for different types of workers does not necessarily grow at the same rate so inequality may increase because of

12 Nick Hanauer. 2014. "*The Pitchforks are coming for US Plutocrats*", Politico Magazine, https://www.politico.com/magazine/story/2014/06/the-pitchforks-are-coming-for-us-plutocrats-108014/.

13 Edward Chancellor. 2023. "*Interest rates have broken the global wealth pump*", Reuters. https://www.reuters.com/breakingviews/interest-rates-have-broken-global-wealth-pump-2023-06-23/.

14 Simon Johnson and Daron Acemoglu. 2023. *Power and Progress: Our Thousand-Year Struggle Over Technology and Prosperity*. Hachette, 13.

innovation.[15] Automation and "offshoring" have raised productivity and multiplied corporate profits but no shared prosperity to the United States and other developed countries has occurred.[16] How we use knowledge and science depends on vision. The bad news is that even at the best of times, visions of powerful people have had a disproportionate effect on what we do with our existing tools and the direction of innovation. The good news is that choices and vision can change.[17]

A further problem is that the desire to be university educated and the completion of educational degrees is not a solution as it creates new members of an aspiring class – that is – some succeed and hence it creates an elite overproduction which arguable makes the situation worse.

4 Overproduction of Degrees

It is true to say that education is an essential part of the well-being of a nation. But with most things overproduction or oversupply has a negative effect. In America by the 1990's more than 50% of the 18- to 24-year-olds had college degrees. An undergraduate degree proved not to be the ticket to a prosperous job. However, now we can see the same end effect is visible for those with PhD's and post graduate degrees. The elite over production is in full swing. The problem now is that supply of degrees has outstripped demand.

One of the answers for the upwardly mobile working-class people was to study and gain professional degrees like those of doctors and lawyers. As a result, the enrolment in other educational areas such as the humanities suffered. The teaching of history, geography, philosophy and the like is declining. Individuals in modern society give little time to these arts. The effect is that young people have lost the ability to understand social issues and put simply, general knowledge and hence a broad understanding of why the world is the way it is has suffered. Historical events and lessons learned in the past are not known and the saying that "we perfect the mistakes made in past years" is true. The upshot is that the losers in the overproduction game are the ones who will drive social upheaval and perhaps conflicts.

Turchin argues that the most dangerous occupation and sector today is the graduates from the law schools. Just as a reminder, Robespierre, Lenin, Gandhi and Castro were all highly skilled lawyers and revolutionaries. The most

15 Johnson and Acemoglu, 2023, 14.
16 Johnson and Acemoglu, 2023, 17.
17 Johnson and Acemoglu, 2023, 24.

problematic issue is that the shortcut into politics runs via the law schools. The question must be asked whether law graduates devoid of any significant social science education and lacking significant life experience are the perfect fit to be an advisor to a minister, let alone a politician?

That said Callahan wrote:

> As the ranks of the affluent have swelled over the past two decades, so have the number of kids who receive every advantage in their education. The growing competition, in turn, has compelled more parents to spend more money and cut more corners in an effort to give their children an extra edge. Nothing less than an academic arms race is unfolding within the upper tiers of U.S. society. Yet even the most heroic – or sleazy – efforts don't guarantee a superior edge.[18]

The failed aspirants to the elitist banquet convert to become counter elites which results in a fragmentation of ideologies and hence discontent, the root cause of all the revolutions in history. The election of Former President Trump and the current fractions in the Republican party are a case in point. We ought to take care of what Bannon the ideologist and former chief strategist to Trump said namely "I want to bring everything crashing down and destroy all of today's establishments."[19] Political leaders such as Trump advance ideologies that create inequality and lead to a real risk to fragmentation of our institutions.

A well-made observation by Turchin is that "as of 2002, we are clearly in transition from the pre-crisis phase, when the state is still struggling to maintain control of the ideological landscape in the face of a multitude of counter-elite challenges, to the next phase, when numerous contenders struggle among themselves for primacy."[20] The Republican party in the United States as noted before is a case at hand. We are seeing these challenges from some quarters of the elite class, and this brings us to the next question, namely who is the real ruling class?

18 David Callahan. 2007. *The cheating culture: Why more Americans are doing wrong to get ahead.* Houghton Mifflin Harcourt, 211.

19 Gwynn Guilford and Nikhil Sonnad. 2017. "*What Steve Bannon really wants*", Quartz. https://qz.com/898134/what-steve-bannon-really-wants/.

20 Turchin, 1977, 106.

5 The Ruling Class

The undeniable general principle is that every institution including states have a ruling class. It is a small proportion of the population which has a disproportionate share of social power. There is nothing wrong with such a situation as long as the social power is exercised to the benefit of all. The question is how and from where are the elites chosen?

Historically early states were governed by force, that is wars were the method to settle disputes or expand by conquests. In addition, early rulers also had the economic power that is they owned land on which food was grown. As states grew bigger it gave rise to another class namely the bureaucrats and officials who also held power. The issue then was that the military ruler the King or Queen also needed to control bureaucracy. The problem now is that in many states the bureaucracy is a ruling class by themselves as they decide what information needs to be given to the politicians. Unfortunately, the TV show "Yes Minister" is far too real. A well known episode shows Sir Humphry, the Minister's advisor nearly having a heart attack when he was informed that the minister had left his office and was talking to people.

Turning to the present, the United States is dominated by the economic elite rather than a monarch.

> "The top of the power pyramid is the corporate community: the owners and managers of large income-producing assets, such as corporations, especially today with the global warming debate we are witnessing the power of mining companies, banks, and law firms. According to this 'class domination' theory, the corporate community rules America indirectly."[21]

This phenomenon is not only relevant to America as in Australia the government relies heavily on consulting firms for advice in areas where the public service does not possess the relevant expertise. As noted above – the public service in itself has become a ruling class as they are heavily politicised and capture excessive media attention. Not surprisingly the advice given to the government via the public service by consulting firms is indirectly used to expand revenues as these advisors are now in a privileged position to be able to give advice to their own clients.[22] Another feature of an economy dominated by elites is

---

21 Turchin, 1977, 125.

22 Kate Ainsworth. 2023. "*PWC tax advice scandal*", ABC News, https://www.abc.net.au/news/2023-06-05/pwc-pricewaterhousecoopers-government-tax-leak-scandal-explained/102409528.

that the reward of corporates is often related to lucrative positions in political offices. Thus there is control of the ideological basis of power. The 'backwash' of asking for corporate advice is that retiring public servants and politicians are given the lucrative positions such as board members and trade commissioners in foreign countries due to their connectiveness to the economic elite. After all, as Burnham has noted the real power, that is, the determination what will be done and how, lies with managers as they occupy the key directing positions.[23] The reality is that despite a domination of the political system by the elites, some states do well and others fail. Hence the question is what are the indicators or reasons for states to succeed or fail?

6 State Breakdowns

As we have seen in recent years some states have either collapsed or are in a long-term turmoil such as Cuba, the Dominican Republic, Chile to note a few. Afghanistan is the most recent example of a country where top officials simply ran away, and the Taliban filled the vacuum. Simply put, one elite was replaced with the elite of the winners of the conflict. The interesting point Turchin is making is that Ashraf Ghani the former president of Afghanistan was an academic and studied state collapse and nation building. He wrote a book in 2008 on this subject. It did not appear to have helped him, but he became very wealthy in the process of trying.[24] Arguably it is also not completely out of the question that a state collapse cannot happen in the United States or Western Europe. There is however no doubt that the quality of leadership matters. It is the skill of working with the constraints, the social structure of a state which is imposed upon leaders. This is one of the reasons why this book concentrates on how social reality is constructed in order to see the fault lines in enough time to implement remedial actions.

"The best predictor of whether a country will be experiencing a violent internal conflict next year is whether it is already in conflict this year."[25] Walter described several factors which are causes of a breakdown.[26] First a move away from democracy, secondly factionalism based on religious or ethnic factors, the third factor, and also a matter this book discusses, is the internet. Walter

23 See generally James Burnham. 1941. "*The Managerial Revolution*".

24 Turchin, 1977, 163.

25 Turchin, 1977, 168.

26 See Barbara F. Walter. 2022. *How Civil Wars Start, and How to Stop them*, New York Crown, 127–128.

recognised concerns about the use of smart phones and the rise of social media spreading fake news, conspiracy theories and now the yet unregulated AI affecting social structure. Walter specifically notes: "It is at this point that violence breaks out: when citizens become convinced that there is no hope of fixing their problems through conventional means."[27] One only needs to remember that when Trump suggested that he lost the election through fraud the result was the violent riots and storming of Capitol Hill. The question is how can such events be predicted? Cederman and Weidman are of the sobering opinion that:

> Ultimately, the hope that big data will somehow yield valid forecasts through theory free 'brute force' is misplaced in the area of political violence. Automated data extraction algorithms, such as web scraping and signal detection based on social media, may be able to pick up heightened political tension, but this does not mean that these algorithms are able to forecast low-probability conflict events with high temporal and spatial accuracy.[28]

The point is that the power structure of a country needs to be understood from the knowledge of which is the influential interest group. Any "uprising" is only successful if the revolutionary group is organised, and such a group could be the armed forces like in Sudan or those in power by elite overproduction. Any disturbances like those seen frequently in France will always fail because the "rebellion" is not organised.

Turchin correctly argues that the elite overproduction in association with the wealth pump "is one of the most destabilizing social mechanisms known to humanity."[29] The real danger in destabilisation is that the political class is preoccupied in "naval gazing" and lost in their political games which are far removed from reality.

7 Conclusion

It is well-known that social well-being is linked to stability and social equality. The promotion of wealth and the activation of the wealth pump disturbs the

---

27 Walters, 2022, 127–128.

28 Lars-Erik Cederman and Nils B. Weidmann. 2017. "Predicting armed conflict: Time to adjust our expectations?" *Science* 355, no. 6324, 476.

29 Turchin, 1977, 189.

balance in a society and creates greater inequality. Inequality can trigger conflict as we have seen so many times before in history. Vigilance to counter conflict is important and so is political leadership. As Turchin noted it falls to all of us "to demand that our rulers act in a way that advance our common interests. Complex human societies need elites – rulers, administrators and importantly thought leaders to function well."[30]

It is the thought leaders such as Berger and Luckmann and Rawls are needed to understand how societies construct their own realities. A drift away from democracy can have powerful implications on societies. Likewise factionalism and cleavage into groups within a population can be very destructive to overall wellbeing if these groups have slightly different ideals from the main group. While we can see diversification of ideas developing online the challenge is managing these. Knowledge gained from history has shown that any deviation from democratic principles can potentially be detected and remedied. This book therefore needs to be understood to contribute an understanding to how the digital revolution shapes our society and how the many excesses or problems which are identified can be remedied. Hence the next chapter will attempt to sketch out a new world order.

30 Turchin, 1977, 241.

CHAPTER 4

The New World Order

1 Introduction

As this book investigates societal rather than individual problems, we need to gain a basic understanding of the economic sector and our social system. This is so as the world is experiencing a growing complexity in the digital ecosystem which combined with increased global risks has put a sharp focus on an examination of the infrastructures of the Big Data Society, the current driver of the economy. It appears that societal issues are a priority focus for governments if these affect the economic wellbeing of individuals, an example is the cost of living. The focus is on a well-run economy while at the same time there are attempts to regulate digital systems.

There is no debate that asymmetrical power exists in relation to the usage and control of the internet and the question has been asked as to "who has the power to raise issues, define problems, or propose and create the solutions to the problems created?"[1] The issue is that the new world order believes that through the digital technology all societal problems are solved but in fact the problems have been exacerbated and are being laid bare.[2] Saul noted that the difficulty in adapting to change is not to be found in internationalism or international commerce, "It is in Globalisation's construct of how the two come about."[3] The problem however is as Saul has argued: globalisation has collapsed, and the world has been reinvented.[4] He argues that unfortunately:

> The sign of mediocre leaders is that they believe things will continue as they have. Why do they insist on believing this? Because they compensate for their lack of talent or ethical centre or intelligence or courage with a conviction that the forces of inevitability are at work.[5]

1 Gry Hasselbalch. 2021. *Data ethics of power: a human approach in the big data and AI era.* Edward Elgar Publishing, 15.

2 Frankfurter Hefte. 2021. "*Aktuelle Ausgabe: Red-Green-Yellow*", https://www.frankfurter-hefte.de/aktuelle-ausgabe/ 63.

3 John Ralston Saul. 2018. *The collapse of globalism.* Atlantic Books Ltd., 35.

4 Saul, 2018, 35.

5 Saul, 2018, 217.

 | DOI:10.1163/9789004702691_005

Importantly history has shown that every change – currently the advancements in cyberspace – are associated with changes in the structure of society. The structure of a society is never static as changes in the environment may it be man-made or environmentally influenced and these will demand a response from not only individuals but society at large. There is evidence to suffice that the world is in the process of such a change and as a result the structure of society and the priority of needs has changed as a consequence of the digital revolution. Change however is not new – it is inevitable – in each of the fundamental changes in society. As an example, the invention of the printing press heralded the beginning of the Renaissance period and the explosion of scientific inventions due to the increased availability of books and hence dissemination of knowledge was accelerated. The commercial world in the Industrial Revolution in England saw a similar change in not only economic terms but also in intellectual and social changes through the writings of Marx, Hegel and Kant to note a few.

2 The Economic Background

It would be trite to argue that the economy does not shape a society's well-being. Globalism and internationalisation were key words to describe the economic driver in the 1970's and 80'. Looking back, the results of changes in economic balance can be analysed. Saul notes:

> [The results] include some remarkable successes, some disturbing failures and a collection of what might be best called running sores. In other words, the outcome has had nothing to do with truth and inevitability and a great deal to do with an experimental economic theory presented as Darwinian fact. It was an experiment that attempted simultaneously to reshape economic, political and social landscapes.[6]

One of the issues was that there was a belief that commerce needed to be free from the shackles of government. Economic events would as a byproduct or arguably even as a direct result shape social policy. As with the digital revolution, globalism heralded a period of uncertainty which for some was also a

6 John Ralston Saul. 2005. *The Collapse of Globalism and the Reinvention of the World.* New York: Viking, 3.

period of opportunity. The problem was that the opportunities were concentrated on big business and even more on international big business.

The openness of the world was the opportunity for big business to relocate into states with the lowest costs in labour and taxes. It was a period "where we [had or believed to have] the power to choose in the hope of altering society for the greater good."[7] The effect in many cases like in Australia was a declining industrial sector and hence a declining market for an unskilled or even skilled labour force.

However there is and always will be an interim unsettled time when changes take place, but equilibrium should be achieved once the changes are 'bedded down'. Currently however we live in a vacuum due to the yet unexplored effects of the digital revolution and specifically where AI is competing for our attention. Rawls explains the vacuum in the following way:

> Most of these vacuums become filled with a swirl of concerns, not just militarily or economic or religious. They reflect the complexity of real-life. Some of them have been used intelligently, some disastrously. And in some cases, people are so convinced that the reigning ideology is inevitable that they never realise they are in a vacuum. So, they are amazed to find themselves abruptly heading in another direction.[8]

It is interesting to look back what Maynard Keynes said after the First World War in 1919 as the same argument is still valid today:

> The power to become habituated to his surroundings is a marked characteristic of mankind. Very few of us realise with conviction the intensely unusual, unstable, complicated, unreliable, temporary nature of the economic organisation by which Western Europe has lived for the half century. We assume some of the most peculiar and temporary of our late advantages as natural, permanent and to be depended on, and we lay our plans accordingly.[9]

This fact is as an example in 1939 when European trading partners despite the close economic ties went to war with each other. Today it is the digital revolution that is the technology that binds us inevitably one to the other via gadgets such as the mobile phones and watches which we must have – not need – to

---

7 Ralston Saul, 2005, 5.

8 Ralston Saul, 2005, 7.

9 John Maynard Keynes. 2017. *The economic consequences of the peace*. Routledge, 1.

function in life. Are we abruptly heading into another new direction due to the technology?

Furthermore, globalisation was thought of as the innate force of commerce and not the people being the leading force in shaping our civilisation. In the meantime, we have found out that this is not true. Earlier Polanyi in 1944 pointedly said: "the idea of a self-adjusting market implied a stark utopia."[10] The problem was that in open trade the relationship between trade and growth in wealth was never seriously discussed. Trade has always been transitionary and it follows the places where the highest value and least costs are incurred and moves abruptly again if the situation changes. Historical examples are the Silk Road and the spice trade. More recently the clothing trade moved to China then to Bangladesh and it is moving again once a higher value and a cheaper place is found. The same applies to the modern phenomenon of call centres as a customer of a business in Australia does not call the business but a person takes the call perhaps in Manilla or anywhere else for that matter.

The problem which appears to be repeating itself is the fact that much of a society's instability is of economic origin. Growth in wealth is either not distributed equitably or it is only paper wealth. In addition, the obsession with consumption that is materialism has also assisted in the sharpening of the gulf between the haves and have nots. Saul observed that during globalisation a myriad of international binding agreements on a global level have been forged but no agreements in the area of human interaction such as work conditions, health and taxation to note a few.[11] Wealth moves with the corporations and will not stay in countries where it has been earned. There are many imaginary market activities such as money markets, commodity exchanges and the stock exchange which do not produce any goods. The same applies to mergers and acquisitions; they produce and build intangible paper wealth.

An important issue which has come to the fore is the transformation from public finance to public economics. It was during the second World War which forced an outcome called the "radical transformation of national fiscal systems"[12] due to the financing of the war effort. Before the war Keynesianism was driving the economic theories as the contribution of public finance directed to employment policy was being well understood and practiced. "The presumption that national governments could engineer macroeconomic stability

10 Karl Polanyi. 2002. "The great transformation." *Readings in economic sociology*, 41.

11 Saul, 2018, 25.

12 Maxime Desmarais-Tremblay, Marianne Johnson and Richard Sturn. 2023. "Mapping the history of public economics in the twentieth century: an introduction to the special issue." *The European Journal of the History of Economic Thought* 30, no. 5, 693.

led to increased scrutiny of the role of taxation to this end. Inspired by the state-centred monetary theory of Knapp, Lerner's "functional finance" went so far as to argue that the systemic purpose of taxation was to adjust consumer expenditures to control inflation."[13] The question also arose of how should welfare be structured to avoid "individuals to free-ride in an attempt to avoid paying their share for a public good?"[14]

Vickrey in 1960 recognised that progress might only come from a collaboration with "ethics, political science, sociology and psychology."[15] The end of the 1960's after post war growth the "the post-war enthusiasm for growth as a cure for poverty receded, economists came back to the study of poverty and the inequality of the distribution of income."[16] By the end of the 1970's welfare issues penetrated most of the thinking of economists. It was mainly directed to find a solution to the cost-benefit dilemma. It is interesting to note a change in thinking namely:

> Many economists no longer believed that markets would spontaneously bring about high employment and price-level stability. Instead, economic output and standards-of-living needed to be engineered through fiscal policies that were continuously fine-tuned to the state of the economy. Instead of a necessary evil to be minimised, taxes were re-envisioned as a tool to manipulate private consumption and moderate inflation.[17]

It is argued that the realisation in the 1970's that the market is not able to maximise justice for all is significant and according to Rawls this has not yet been resolved. This dilemma has arguably caused the collapse of globalisation as it was originally envisaged.

3 The End of Globalisation

Ralston suggested that 1999 was not only the highpoint of globalisation with the creation of World Trade Organization (WTO) and the inclusion of intellectual property via Trade-Related Aspects of Intellectual Property Rights

13 Desmarais-Tremblay, Johnson and Sturn, 2023, 693.
14 Desmarais-Tremblay, Johnson and Sturn, 2023, 695.
15 William Vickrey. 1960. "Utility, strategy, and social decision rules." *The Quarterly Journal of Economics* 74, no. 4, 535.
16 Desmarais-Tremblay, Johnson and Sturn, 2023, 704.
17 Desmarais-Tremblay, Johnson and Sturn, 2023, 706.

(TRIPS) into the WTO. Around the same time the Organisation for Economic Co-operation and Development (OECD) started the negotiations in the creation of Multilateral Agreement on Investments (MAI). At about the same time commodity prices dropped and foreign development aid shrunk as well. In addition, it took until 1995 to put an end to the war in the Balkans with the Dayton Peace Agreement.[18] Tellingly the leader of Georgia went to London with a warning. The London Times wrote: "enormous sums of money were spent in ending the cold war; no similar amounts are being put towards helping to build democracy ... We do not have a triumph of Western democracy ... Regimes with markedly Fascist tendencies [have come to power, Rampant nationalism poses] threats to nuclear Armageddon."[19]

The problem was well known, and this was namely that the wealth was not spread across the classes. Annan then the UN Secretary General at the 1999 Davos meeting stated that: "History teaches us that such an imbalance between the economic, social and political realms can never be sustained for very long." The imbalance is exhibited by unacceptable level of unemployment, job insecurity and exploitive work conditions.[20] The rhetorical question is whether history taught us anything?

By 2000 and 2001 it should have been clear that a big change was afoot. Stiglitz who later was given the Nobel price resigned from the World Bank. He addressed the American Economic Association attacking some of the assumptions of globalisation. He said: "Capital market liberalisation has not only not brought people the prosperity they were promised, but it has also brought these crises, with wages falling between 20 to 30 percent and unemployment growing by a factor of two, three, four or ten."[21] In 2001 Argentina collapsed (and perhaps it will go the same way again). September 11 of 2001 saw a massive terrorist attack on New York city. These are arguably all symptoms of a deep malaise, and conditions of the times.

What are some of the destabilising issues which are still a running sore? Privatisation and deregulation of markets would be one issue as this has allowed for an ever-increasing corporate size and has ending up in vertical integration. As an example, Fonterra in New Zealand controls about 50 percent of the dairy market and is also active in Australia. Privatisation by the Federal Government in Australia began in the 1990s and received bipartisan support. Now a subtle form of corruption is evident in the form of lobbyists and consultants. The

18 See generally Ralston Saul, 2005, Chapter 15.

19 The London Times, February 17, 1995, 12.

20 Ralston Saul, 2005, 146.

21 The Boston Globe, January 9, 2000.

public service "buys" in a lot of expertise by engaging big consulting firms like PricewaterhouseCoopers. Likewise in Australia in 2019 the report of the Royal Commission into Misconduct in the Banking, Superannuation and Financial Services Industry exposed misconduct by the big four banks and made 76 separate recommendations. In contrast, there was an explosion of share options for executives, and this included enormous salaries and bonuses. How just is a 20 million dollars departure package when most working people will not reach that sum in a lifetime of work?

Already in 2000 it was reported that the majority of the thirty largest revenues in the world belonged to corporations not countries.[22] There has not been much of a significant change since then. In addition, the political system is not assisting as all debates are bogged down by technical details. Simply put: "the bureaucratisation of both the leadership and the creative process makes thought seem irresponsible and clear action seems to be unprofessional. This provides a sensation of activity while creating a broader sense of powerlessness. This is what used to be called being *nibbled to death by ducks*".[23] The question is what happened to justice for all?

4 The Economy and the Principle of Justice

There is a fundamental difference between the reality perceived by individuals and societal changes. To understand and digest the changes through time can be difficult as the changes are different for individuals or society. "If we do not lose ourselves in anger or despair or the ideology of certainty, society allows us to call upon the strength of community. That is the strength of the *other* whose reality confirms our own."[24]

Of importance is the theory and also the perception of justice. The fact that at "the end of the 1960s, as the post-war enthusiasm for growth as a cure for poverty receded, economists came back to the study of poverty and the inequality of the distribution of income."[25] However the problem of fiscal challenges faced by governments did not diminish. The political problem of creating and maintaining stability poses problems, specifically as the expectations of the business sector and the consumers as well as the welfare sector were and still are at odds with each other. One of the current problems is that

22 Ralston Saul, 2005, 190.
23 Ralston Saul, 2005, 230.
24 Ralston Saul, 2005, 14.
25 Desmarais-Tremblay, Johnson and Sturn, 2023, 704.

economically driven migration of the scale never seen before exasperated the problem of how public expenditures are allocated in a just manner. In addition the question what is just is not always recognised by all but as Desmarais-Tremblay *et al* argued:

> The new analytical political philosophy established in the wake of Rawls made possible a renewal of ethical discussion in economics, even if economists conceived of ethical issues mostly in an abstract economic style. The institutional implications of Rawls' ideas could lead to a level of redistribution far beyond what democratic governments ever achieved. Yet, his politics seemed moderate and so his ideas appealed to economists' concern for social justice while staying clear of the radical politics of the late 1960s and 1970s.[26]

In the past, conceptions of justice have been embedded in social welfare functions and as time has gone by economists have understood that markets were not geared to bring about high employment and stability of prices as the desire to maximise profits was a more appealing outcome. Interestingly Hansen's views in 1945 are still ringing true namely that the economy and hence standards-of-living need to be engineered through fiscal policies and taxes are a tool to manipulate private consumption and moderate inflation.[27]

Besides the economists' observations, Rawls also observed economic influence in his writing and a gradual shift in self-interest is noticeable. In 1958 Rawls noticed that society is a cooperative venture but still a game played by the rational. There was an element of control exerted by self-interested individuals "designing a practice in which [their] enemy were to assign [them their] place."[28] It is clear that Rawls saw the economy as a system in which individuals despite being self-interested but rational saw the benefit for all by cooperating. Rawls noted voluntarily paying taxes instead of acting as free riders.[29] Arguably Rawls had a view that self-interest takes a "backseat" when the principle of justice for all is endangered. Arguably this is not consistent with the facts as taxes are paid because not paying would result in the levying of penalties by the state. He considered that the welfare economics only considered "justice as a kind of efficiency."[30] It can be assumed that Rawls believed

26 Desmarais-Tremblay, Johnson and Sturn, 2023, 705.

27 See Alvin H. Hansen. 1945. "Three methods of expansion through fiscal policy." *The American Economic Review* 35, no. 3: 382–387.

28 John Rawls. 1958. *Justice as fairness*. 172.

29 Rawls, 1958, 180–183.

30 Rawls, 1958, 184.

that in the end individuals perceive the benefits of cooperation will outweigh self-interest. He noted two principles which supported his analysis namely first that everyone should have "an equal right to the most extensive liberty compatible with a like liberty for all" second that "inequalities are arbitrary unless it is reasonable to expect that they will work out for everyone's advantage."[31]

The point is that economists and Rawls agreed on one principle namely that control of the market that is economic life is necessary "since even a perfectly efficient price system has no tendency to determine just distributive shares when left to itself."[32] In effect Rawls' view of a guiding hand in economic affairs must be based on justice which is based on rational choices. Walraevens arguably put Rawls' views in perspective by stating that they are a social welfare function of choice to arbitrate a trade-off between efficiency and equality.[33] It can be argued that the digital revolution has influenced the way the economy as directed by the state is viewed due to the instant access of information which unfortunately is not always a verified view based on facts. In addition, it is argued that the state has to contend like never before with more powerful global businesses like the technology giants. The outcome is that to achieve a balance between economic growth and an equal just distribution of wealth is more difficult to achieve if at all. It is of value to have a preliminary look at the effects of the digital revolution considering its all-pervasive influence.

5 The Digital Revolution

Within the operation of the courts digital systems already exist in case management, e-filing and in the exchange of data and documents. Traditional digital technology has assisted access, equal treatment, efficiency and effectiveness of procedures. More recently the development of AI for example has promised a new wave of changes to not only affect procedures but decisions as well. This includes legal analysis, advice, prediction of decisions and autonomous decision-making by "robot judges".[34] It is trite to argue that the digital technology and the current developments of AI within the current economic

31 Rawls, 1958, 165.

32 John Rawls. 1967. "Distributive Justice." In *Philosophy, Politics and Society: Third Series*, edited by Peter Laslett and Walter Garrison Runciman, 58–82. Oxford: Basil Blackwell, 79.

33 Benoit Walraevens. 2023. "Rawls's Maximin and Optimal Taxation Theory." *The European Journal of the History of Economic Thought*, 30, no.5: 860–882.

34 Francesco Contini. 2020. "Artificial intelligence and the transformation of humans, law and technology interactions in judicial proceedings." *Law, Technology and Humans*, 2, 6.

framework has fundamentally changed the way we work and live in society. For the purpose of this book a discussion on the ability of AI in the context of change is of importance as an AI trained engine called Generative Pre-Trained Transformer 3 (GPT-3) was asked to describe AI. The result was:

> AI stands for artificial intelligence. AI is the result of applying cognitive science techniques to artificially create something that performs tasks that only humans can perform, like reasoning, natural communication, and problem solving. AI is important because it has the potential to help humans become better at completing cognitive tasks, and to automate tasks that are currently difficult or impossible for humans to do.[35]

As a change or disruption this in itself is not new as already discussed above. This is so as 'all socially constructed universes change, and this change is brought about by the concrete actions of human beings.'[36] The question is how far can AI be developed before it changes the structure of society as we know it now? The digital revolution is distinctive from other revolutions as it has taken place remarkably quickly. Machines competing against humans has been a staple of science fiction since Shelley's *Frankenstein* in 1818.[37] Undoubtedly technology has added value at least to the way we do business but at the same time it has disrupted our social fabric. Aunt Lydia's observation in the Handmaid's tale is important, 'It started before ordinary citizens were paying attention. We lived as usual by ignoring. Ignoring isn't the same as ignorance, you have to work at it.'[38]

Newport also noted that '[W]e added new technologies to the periphery of our experience for minor reasons, then woke up one morning to discover that they had colonised the core of our life.'[39] It is not primarily the data collection of technology giants, but the systems used to collect data which have affected societal values and how society functions. The fundamental question is whether the law can control the powers of those who control us? The real issue this book discusses is the effect the machine age has on society and

35 See generally the Impact of Artificial Intelligence on the Future of Workforces in the European Union and the United States of America, US and European Commission, https://www.ospi.es/export/sites/ospi/documents/documentos/TTC_ECCEA_study_on_impact_of_AI_on_workforce_EKMvplHkRRLSBESRdR7PhQSd1U_92124.pdf

36 Berger and Luckmann, 1966, 134.

37 Johnson and Acemoglu, 2023, 11.

38 Margaret Atwood. 1986. *The Handmaid's Tale*, 63–71.

39 Newport, 2019, 6–7.

specifically the devices controlling our daily lives. Newport observed that 'the urge to check Twitter or refresh Reddit becomes a nervous twitch that shatters uninterrupted time into small shards too small to support the presence necessary for an intentional life.'[40]

The definitions of consciousness and awareness are changing in the new digital age and AI is "showing signs of artificial general intelligence".[41] The question is whether teaching or transferring knowledge in the digital world is effective in imparting necessary historical knowledge not only to grasp technology but also to understand fundamental societal values. The teaching of contract law at universities is an excellent example. Some universities have taught contract law in an intensive week, or a six-week course or online and still claim that students understand contract law. It is perhaps fitting to remember the words of Klass Hendrik Eller who observed:

> Contract is arguably the most chatoyant legal institution – appearing in changing light when seen from a wide array of legal perspectives, but also the centre of an unmatched set of other disciplinary inroads, including political philosophy, ethics, economics, sociology, anthropology, psychology, and gender studies.[42]

The same comment is also applicable to the construction of social reality, one of the topics of this book.

That said the point is that "we should treat with great care any new technology that threatens to destroy the way in which we connect and communicate with each other. If you mess with something so central to the success of our species, it's easy to create problems."[43] Implanting a sufficient stock of knowledge in individuals would equip a society to lead an intentional life and not a life dictated by technology.

Given the fact that we are entering a reshaping of culture any changes must be based on some fundamental principles. One of the principles of a functioning society – as noted earlier -is the maintenance of justice. Indeed Rawls notes that justice is the first virtue of social institutions,[44] and he states that 'the aim

---

40 Newport, 2019, xii.

41 Matthew Sparks. 2023. *"Is GPT-4 already showing signs of artificial general intelligence?" The New Scientist,* https://www.newscientist.com/article/2365864-is-gpt-4-already-showing-signs-of-artificial-general-intelligence/.

42 Klaas Hendrik Eller. 2020. "Comparative Genealogies of "Contract and Society." *German Law Journal* 21, no. 7, 1393.

43 Newport, 2019, 130.

44 John Rawls. 2001. *Justice as fairness: A restatement.* Harvard University Press, 3.

of justice as fairness is to provide an acceptable and moral basis for democratic institutions and thus to address the question of how the claims of liberty and equality are to be understood.'[45] This is not a new phenomenon, already as early as Aristotle and later Kant and recently Rawls, attempt have been made to explain the function and necessity of justice in a workable society. The new problem which needs to be confronted is that modern technology and generative AI for example are in effect the equivalence of an Industrial Revolution at ten or more times the speed.

As an example GPT-4 has shown the ability to clearly distinguish and extract data, information, knowledge, wisdom, and purpose when natural language is used as an expression method.[46] The crucial point is that radical changes in the social structure "may result in concomitant changes in the psychological reality."[47] Arguably the increasing mental distress among young people is an effect of the rapid changes and increased exposure to negative content.

The key element in subjective reality is that identity which changes with social change in effect needs to be reshaped. The point is that specific identities appear over a span of time with different identities. Berger and Luckmann suggest that different individual identities exist in examples such as between an executive, a worker, or an unemployed person.[48] It is argued that technology is reshaping identities at such a rate that the relevant identity of an individual is not reshaped in a timely manner. The point is whether justice for all has been changed as it forces classes of people such as the middle class into the lower class. It is in effect a revisit of the English Industrial Revolution where initially the middle class disappeared. At the same time technology has also created new opportunities hence new identities but to the detriment of a whole class of people.

It should be remembered that Marx argued that automation is an expression of the integral dynamics of capital replacing human labour with machines. Marx in brief always considered history as the starting point in developing a materialistic view of historical events.[49] He observed and explained the continuing class struggle during the French Revolution as driven by natural law and logical dialectic processes and it was the bourgeoisie which were first to

---

45 Rawls, 2001, 5.

46 See Yingbo Li and Yucong Duan. 2023. "*The Wisdom of Artificial General Intelligence: Experiments with GPT-4 for DIKWP.*" arXiv preprint.

47 Berger and Luckmann, 1966, 200.

48 Berger and Luckmann, 1966, 194.

49 Ziegler, 1911, 465.

abolish the feudalistic system of government. Historically and very quickly thereafter the weapons of oppression were directed against the proletariat.

It is true to argue that due to economic crisis and the lack of effective planning, overproduction and hence unemployment was the outcome. Marx as well as the proletariat viewed private ownership in the same way as feudalism which according to Marx would inevitably give rise to a conflict in which the proletariat would hand the private property and the means of production over to society at large. Marx never intended to merely explain the class struggle to the proletariat. He considered his views to be academic socialism and intended to see a practical application of his theory of socialism in order to radically change the world order of the time. Marx also believed that the changes would come as a natural process, that is as an evolution.[50]

We see the same phenomenon today again where digital technology in general and the yet untested invention of AI are replacing human labour like in the Industrial Revolution.[51] However the machinery of capital has not replaced the commodities produced by machines indeed 'the work [that] takes place within capitalist firms – the modern feudalism – and the product they produce remains a commodity.'[52] The new commodity is the data that the technology giants produce and the technology giants are the new feudalistic system. What has changed in the new age and is therefore determinative is the loss of some traditional trades and importantly the loss of privacy. There has also been the social impact of surveillance capitalism upon consumers. Goldhaber in 1997 noted we've turned the corner towards an economy where an increasing number of workers are no longer involved directly in the production, transportation and distribution of material goods but instead earn their living managing or dealing with information in some form. Most call this an "information economy."[53]

The determination of identity can arguably be institutionally programmed in the operation of control as in the institution of law.[54] The issue is not so much how the law protects the individual but how much the technological revolution has changed society, and specifically has justice changed or is justice

50 Ziegler, 1911, 465–466.

51 See Peter Lee, Sebastien Bubeck and Joseph Petro. 2023. "Benefits, limits, and risks of GPT-4 as an AI chatbot for medicine." *New England Journal of Medicine* 388.13: 1233–1239.

52 James Steinhoff. 2019. Canadian Communication Association Annual Conference, University of British Columbia,) on file with authors.

53 Michael Goldhaber. 1997. "*Attention Shoppers*", *Wired*, https://www.wired.com/1997/12/es-attention/.

54 Berger and Luckmann. 1967, 202. The term institution is used to denote a group of people meeting or working together to achieve a particular goal.

not so much a factor in the structure of society as it was. While technological innovation has brought vast sources of information it has also brought uncertainty. The point is that individuals can only prosper within a society, that is, a society is the basic structure in which individuals gain their identity and this is necessary to be an individual human being. Once we understand what justice means, institutions such as the law can design and implement rules which are based on basic principles informed by justice. Brownsword is correct when he notes:

> In small groups operating in a stable context, once the basic code of conduct has been agreed, governance should largely run itself. However, in larger groups and particularly in groups where the context is more dynamic – where the group has to adjust to new technologies, new applications, and new circumstances, to new challenges and new opportunities, or where the group regularly contemplates a change of direction – then governance will be more challenging. Indeed, in many contexts, finding the right regulatory balance between stability and change will always be work in progress.[55]

To that end Professor John Rawls also makes an important point that:

> … justice is the first virtue of social institutions, [and for that reason] justice denies that the loss of freedom for some is made right by a greater good shared by others. It does not allow that the sacrifices imposed on a few are outweighed by the larger sum of advantages enjoyed by many.[56]

The problem with such an aspirational goal is the fact that "there is no society known to us that does not have some divisions of labour and concomitantly, some social distribution knowledge; and as soon as this is the case, secondary socialisation becomes necessary [which] is the internalisation of institutional or institution based 'sub-worlds'".[57] Arguably the class distinction that is upper, middle and lower class is the outcome of the secondary socialisation process which takes place within each economically based class. In addition, each of the sub-groups would also exhibit a variation in language based on their view of reality. Therefore it would be inconceivable that in each sub-world, justice

55 Roger Brownsword. 2023. 11. *Technology, Humans, and Discontent with Law: The Quest for Better Governance*. Taylor & Francis.

56 John Rawls. 1971. "*A theory of justice.*" Cambridge, 3.

57 Berger and Luckmann, 1966, 158.

would be viewed and understood as an overarching nationally inspired goal. The above observation has also occupied Rawls as he acknowledges a class difference. He notes that "there is no injustice in the greater benefits earned by a few provided that the situation of persons not so fortunate is thereby improved."[58] He went on to argue that "justice as fairness, like other contract views, consists of two parts: (1) an interpretation of the initial situation and of the problem of choice posed there, and (2) a set of principles which, it is argued, would be agreed to."[59]

One fact is immediately clear namely that the digital revolution has changed the social fabric of society by not only by distributing more wealth to the leading class but also the slow disappearance of the middle class and the shift in the class structure. Another aspect of changing social behaviour is noted by the shift in the class structure but also the perception what is important. One group is busy making money whereas the other group is busy attempting to change institutional rules. Others are busy changing history by attempting to change geographical names and some just enjoy their lives in the process money spent on this progression could have been better used to assist those who struggle financially. Simply put personal ideas and aspiration are put first.

To maintain social cohesion three groups or systems require specific attention. First it is the individual who requires legislation to protect privacy. Secondly linked with the individual is the accountability of collectors of data in the case that there are breaches of data protection legislation. Thirdly and most importantly society needs to be protected from misinformation and disinformation that circulates online. Information, especially in the form of news and media needs to be fettered and corrected.

6 Conclusion

Each court and judge will continue to define and establish specific practices within the legal boundaries of the rules.[60] However the problem is that at times of rapid economic, social, and technological disruption, the concern for doctrinal coherence can inhibit major development of the law. While critics will say that the law should move with the times, judges will tend to exercise

58 Rawls, 1971, 13.
59 Rawls, 1971, 14.
60 Contini, 2020, 256–259.

restraint and be mindful of being accused of assuming an unauthorised legislative role.[61]

The progress of technology and innovation is inevitable and there will always be new and improved methods of producing goods and services to keep up with consumer needs and demands. The market for technology is driven by businesses, cultures and marketplaces but ultimately by people. Many speculations and predictions have exaggerated the effects of the digital revolution and while it is multifaceted and complex in nature it still relies on people to participate and supply data. A significant weakness in the technology we are witnessing is that the cost of machines that complement human work means that if there is an economic downturn in one sector, new technology is not attractive to organisations who are cutting costs.[62] For example, the plummeting flows of trade, capital, and people at the beginning of the Covid-19 pandemic prompted a wave of speculation about the end of globalisation and the resumption of state autonomy. The Russia's invasion of Ukraine has brought even more predictions of a retreat toward national self-sufficiency.[63]

The bottom line is that there will be global adjustments and fluctuations and the calculation of risks will ultimately determine strategies and positions taken by large entities in the future. Diversification and new ideas are a feature of modern progress and the challenge for the legal systems around the world will be to manage these types of variations across populations. The law, politics and systems of government are institutions that will need to keep up with progress. Democracies such as our own will need to balance individual freedoms and choices on the one hand with restrictions of technology on the other hand.

61 Brownsword, 2023, 22.

62 Johnson and Acemoglu, 2023, 332.

63 Steven Altman and Caroline Bastian. 2023. *"The State of Globalization in 2023" Harvard Business Review*, https://hbr.org/2023/07/the-state-of-globalization-in-2023.

PART 2

Transformation of Society

CHAPTER 5

The Social Construction of Reality

1 Introduction

The question could be asked why do we need to acknowledge or simply why do we discuss the writings of Berger and Luckmann? The answer is two-fold, first *The Social Construction of Reality* is one of the rare and extraordinary publications of the human and social sciences that has been receiving a far reaching and perennial acknowledgement since it came out in 1966.[1] Admittedly there were diverging views about Berger and Luckmann's ideas, but they emerged much later such as Knoblauch in 2012,[2] and Hjelm in 2014.[3]

Secondly as already noted in this book, we cannot understand the present unless we understand the past. To that end an introduction of the social theories of Hegel, Kant and Marx have been included and discussed as far as necessary above. Why are Berger and Luckmann also chosen? The answer again is based on history and namely the compelling fact that the book was written "in the eve of the cultural revolution in the Western World in the late 1960's."[4] Berger himself described the 1960's as an enormous rock concert but their book as classical music, "it is not possible to play classical music at a rock concert."[5] The reason for that comment was that the appreciation of the book came much later after the cultural upheaval. Now, instead of an enormous rock concert we in society are experiencing the digital revolution. Arguably the important difference to be noted is that in the late 1960's we did have a cultural revolution but in the 2020's we have the impersonal and isolating digital revolution. It should be absolutely clear that there is a vast difference in these two moments in time, namely one was culturally driven, and the latter driven by data and machines, that is by technology. This fact alone poses the question

1 Jochen Dreher. 2023. *Peter L. Berger's The Social Construction of Reality*, Cambridge University Press, 108.

2 See Hubert Knoblauch. 2018. "Conclusion: The Social Construction of Reality as a paradigm? 1." In *Social Constructivism as Paradigm?* Routledge, 325–338.

3 See Titus Hjelm. 2014. *Social constructionisms: Approaches to the study of the human world.* Bloomsbury Publishing.

4 Dreher, 2023, 102.

5 Peter L. Berger. 2011. *Adventures of an accidental sociologist: How to explain the world without becoming a bore.* Prometheus Books, 92.

 | DOI:10.1163/9789004702691_006

of what happened to culture and what can be learned from the previous social reality?

2 Social Construction

It is of value to briefly note what the social construction of reality means. Howard Becker put it succinctly stating:

> simply that people talk to each other, in person or otherwise, and decide what to call things around them and how to understand those things. Other people might decide those questions differently and that's why the notion of social construction has some traction, because it makes you see that what you think is real, isn't necessarily real for some other people, and that that creates a very fruitful area for research and understanding.[6]

That said this chapter relies heavily on Berger and Luckmann's theory of the social construction of reality which needs to be understood within the context of the environment experienced by both authors. Only then can we fully understand and appreciate the legacy of the social construction of reality. This book argues that Berger and Luckmann are eminently relevant today as they were at the time their book was written. This is so as the similar social tensions, unrests and upheavals then, are happening today and can be observed. Berger himself noted:

> In 1966, when the book came out, there was a broad dissatisfaction with what had been the long hegemony of structural functionalism theory and a narrow positivism in the day-to-day practice of most sociologists. Especially younger people in the discipline were looking for something new, something that would transcend the aridity of both Parsonian scholasticism and the endless refinements of quantitative techniques. Something new was indeed about to engulf sociology, but it was not the marriage of Weber and Schutz celebrated in *The Social Construction of Reality*. It was, of course, the orgy of ideology and utopianism that erupted all over the academic scene in the late 1960s, almost immediately after the publication of our book. Neither Luckmann nor I had any

6 Miloš Jovanović. 2021. "Bourdieu's Theory and the Social Constructivism of Berger and Luckmann", *Philosophy and Society* 32 (4), 521.

> sympathy with this Zeitgeist, but even if we had been more sympathetic, our sort of sociology was not what all these putative revolutionaries were clamouring for. It is not possible to play chamber music at a rock festival.[7]

Both Berger and Luckmann came from Europe. Berger escaped the Nazis. He settled down in America whereas Luckmann returned to Europe. Both migrated and hence changed from one culture to another one. Interestingly Parks in 1928 published a paper about migration where he argued:

> … the 'cake of custom' is broken and the individual is freed for new enterprises and for new associations. One of the consequences of migration is to create a situation in which the same individual … finds himself striving to live in two diverse cultural groups. … This is the "marginal man".[8]

Both Berger and Luckmann experienced life on the threshold between two cultures. Parks commented further on the effect of migration which is relevant to them.

> … this release [from one society] is followed in the course of time by the reintegration of the individuals so released into a new social order. In the meantime, however, certain changes take place … in the character of the individuals themselves. They become, in the process, not merely emancipated, but enlightened. The emancipated individual invariably becomes in a certain sense and to a certain degree a cosmopolitan. He learns to look upon the world in which he was born and bred with something of the detachment of a stranger. He acquires, in short, an intellectual bias.[9]

Living in two worlds has the effect of sitting on two chairs at the same time and hence a reflexive perspective on the world is the result. An example can be seen in migrants who enter a new country and always speak more than one language. Hence they are able to access diverse views. In other words, the old is brought into the new world and forms a different "product". These observations are historically fitting where migration was needed. In the past migration was looked upon differently when filling work shortages in Australia. Migrants

---

7 Peter L. Berger. 2017. "Reflections on the twenty-fifth anniversary of The Social Construction of Reality." In *The New Sociology of Knowledge*, Routledge, 11–16.

8 Robert E. Park. 1928. "Human migration and the marginal man." *American journal of sociology*, 33, no. 6: 881.

9 Park, 1928, 888.

were needed in programs to build huge infrastructure like the Snowy Mountain Hydro Scheme and also to work in emerging factories such as the automotive industry. Today migration is not driven principally by a necessity of filling gaps in the host country but rather the desire to leave poverty behind and seek a better life. These days the problem is that at the end of the rainbow there is no pot of gold.

It is appropriate to commence this chapter by noting one of the effects of the digital revolution on society before fully engaging with the social construction of reality.

The first observation is that without stable communication resources, people on the socio-economic margins are especially vulnerable to losing access to resources that are distributed remotely, for example job applications.[10] In the United States, looking for work requires technologies that presuppose a home, a mobile phone that can be charged easily as well as relatively long stretches of access to a computer with internet.[11] It is no longer the case that an individual can present themselves at a workplace and begin working. Technology has intercepted every task that we do as individuals operating in a functioning society. The same argument is also true when suggestions emerge that cash as a means of exchange will be abolished. Here lies the problem. Technology has no doubt provided many improvements and advantages for society, but it has also contributed to a class divide, namely what is known as the digital divide. Arguably therefore changes in our social structure are inevitable but have they improved societies' wellbeing, that is, are societies in equilibrium?

The first observation is that the stable communication method since the beginning of time has been face to face communication. This means that communication has been socially based. The social re-structuring of society due to the digital revolution has been driven by a change in the important vehicle of reality maintenance namely conversation, that is people speaking and communicating with one another by gestures.[12] The important fact – which is lost in the habit of texting and messaging on messenger and messaging platforms – is that face-to-face conversations and the important multidimensional non-verbal communication has been diluted. Berger and Luckmann made this important point by stating that conversation "takes place against

10 Ilana Gershon and Amy Gonzales. 2021. "You got a hole in your belly and a phone in your hand: How US government phone subsidies shape the search for employment." *New Media & Society* 23, no. 4, 855.

11 Gershon and Gonzales, 2021, 868.

12 Berger and Luckmann, 1966, 172.

the background of a world that is silently taken for granted [and] the exchange confirms the subjective reality of this world."[13] The importance of this view is that:

> Its massivity is achieved by the accumulation and consistency of casual conversation – conversation that can afford to be casual precisely because it refers to the routines of a taken-for-granted world.[14]

In other words, humans exist in everyday life by continually interacting and communicating with others. The problem with digital communication is that there is no background and no taken-for-granted world. The view of the world by looking at an influencer or reading a Facebook (Meta) posting is a different world or aspects of different worlds and in isolation without the benefit of a routine afforded by casual conversations. The problem is that online society is moving in a virtual but not an objective or real world.

A virtual world is not real as it is generated by machines and reinforced by the input of accumulated data. Of importance is that "Berger and Luckmann [have shown] that this shared objective reality is socially constructed. According to them, this process arises out of a dialectic and ongoing interaction among the aspects of 'externalization', 'objectivation' and 'internalization' of meaning."[15] The reality of everyday life and other realities is in a transitional stage as increased uncertainties are observable. Berger and Luckmann use the theatre to illustrate this point.

> As the curtain rises, the spectator is transported into another world with its own meaning and an order that may or may not have much to do with the order of everyday life. As the curtain falls, the spectator returns to realist that is to the paramount reality of everyday life by comparison with which the reality presented on the stage now appears tenuous and ephemeral, however vivid the presentation may have been a few moments previously.[16]

This holds especially true as devices such as the mobile phone represent a new form of theatre where some people are watched such as influencers,

---

13 Berger and Luckmann, 1966, 172.

14 Berger and Luckmann, 1966, 172.

15 Silke Steets. 2016. "Taking Berger and Luckmann to the realm of materiality: Architecture as a social construction." *Cultural Sociology* 10, no. 1: 100.

16 Berger and Luckmann, 1966, 39.

recognisable figures and connections and others in the online population just watch. The problem is that the real and illusionary world is not distinguishable by many spectators. The spectators merge the illusionary world with the real world. The spectator feels the emotions, the thrill and satisfaction as if they had done the act but they have done nothing at all.

The problem is that the virtual world though it appears to be real is not an ongoing interaction and hence not socially constructed. The process of a socially constructed reality arises out of an interaction of "externalisation", "objectivation" and "internalisation" of meaning. Steets has argued that through "acts of externalisation, human beings establish a relationship with their physical and social environments. They develop languages and concepts ..., to make themselves 'at home' in the world. This does not happen in [isolation or in the virtual world] but always in concrete and predominantly contested contexts. 'Objectivation' is then the transfer of material and immaterial human products into a 'reality that confronts its original producers as a facticity external to and other than themselves'".[17]

There is no doubt that our attention span is changing and while our short-term and long-term memory is also changing, questions about digital consciousness are becoming ever more pressing. Consciousness has many different dimensions, the sensory experience of perception, the affective experience of feelings and emotions, the cognitive experience of thought and reasoning, the agentive experience linked to action and the self-consciousness, awareness of oneself.[18] An important distinction needs to be drawn here as one might be conscious of the existence of the object – in this case digital systems – but one may not be conscious of its effect on everyday life.

The problem is that only subjective experiences are internalised in individual consciousness. Facebook (Meta) – is an example of digital consciousness – it is not a subjective experience and an internalisation process is not possible as just knowing of it is not an experience in the conscious sense as individual consciousness is socially determined.[19] AI in many cases is not a subjective experience, only fragments of it such as an AI generated picture of oneself. The digital revolution has in effect narrowed subjective experiences in such a way that they might be subjective, but they lack the social context such as face to face conversation to be truly a social experience which can be internalised. Consciousness in any form must be derived and is anchored in an institutional

17 Steets, 2016, 100.

18 See David Chalmers. 2023. *"Could a large language model be conscious?" arXiv preprint arXiv:2303.07103.*

19 Berger and Luckmann, 1966, 96.

order which arguably has been disturbed and hence needs to be reconstructed. This book argues that the digital world in general has not been objectified hence it is not truly socially real or institutionalised. The issue is that digital technology has created a "segmentation of the institutional order, with only certain types of individuals performing certain actions, and following that, a social distribution of knowledge with the role-specific knowledge coming to be reserved to certain types."[20] The result is that consciously acquired knowledge is a new configuration of socially constructed reality and needs to be objectified.

It follows that one of the issues with the digital world is the fact that our subjective reality is being radically reshaped and only a small part of the digital effects is retained in consciousness. As the digital world changes and moves quickly, reactivation of the past becomes important by refreshing "the memories which is to converse with those who share their relevance."[21] The point is that humans are wired "to be dependent upon specific plausibility structures, that is, the specific social base and social processes required for its maintenance. One can maintain one's self-identification as a man of importance only in a milieu that confirms this identity [by retaining] one's significant relationships."[22]

The problem of the digital age is that we have changed our structure of everyday life both spatially as well as temporally. The spatial structure used to be peripheral but in today's world it has taken on an increased meaning. It has a social dimension as it intersects with the temporal everyday world via the internet, but it lacks the intrinsic property of consciousness namely it must be ongoingly correlated.[23] The problem is that this is not the case now, the spatially dominated part of our consciousness interferes with the temporal world. This cannot be reversed as it is part of our everyday experiences and of our life cycle. Simply put it is the temporal world which is the reality of life and our very essence of being human as it is shared with others. The virtual world, that is the spatial world, is not shared with others.

Once social media is closed and the lights turn off it can be a lonely and isolating experience for some. Loneliness and isolation can be harmful in many ways to people. Where once there were significant relationships with others, for some there is now an empty space. Where once there were sounds of voices of reason giving direction, there is now an overwhelming amount of noise.

20 Berger and Luckmann, 1966, 100.
21 Berger and Luckmann, 1966, 175.
22 Berger and Luckmann, 1966, 174.
23 Berger and Luckmann, 1966, 40.

The point is that only the face-to-face situation in the fullest sense is real. A text or Facebook (Meta) posting is not real as it is spatial and not flexible. It is the pattern that texts convey which are not flexible and open to immediate scrutiny as well as they can simply be ignored. Face to face confrontations however need to be interpreted and need to be modified by such means as expressiveness and acts. As Berger and Luckmann put it 'the reality of everyday life contains typificatory schemes in terms of which others are apprehended and dealt with in face-to-face encounters, unless challenged though, the typification will hold until further notice and will determine my actions in the situation.'[24] It follows that face-to-face encounters in contrast to texting or online messaging and social platforms are not anonymous as they are constantly changing and adapting to real and not perceived situations.

As we have created social organisations within our world, we will always be subject to changes. It is obvious that it takes individuals or groups of people to define reality. Now we are seeing a new specialisation of knowledge that is emerging as new knowledge and is becoming more specialised and competitive among its members. Also, specialisation means that there is a distinct division of labour. The digital revolution has produced new experts laying claim to a novel status, "They are not only experts in a specific sector of the societal stock of knowledge they claim ultimate jurisdiction over that stock of knowledge its totality."[25] We can see this with the entities who monopolise data, store data, use, administer and obviously sell that data. Data protection in reality only attempts to protect privacy, but privacy is not scrutinised if all of the data of a particular group of people is bundled together and sold. When accumulated data becomes unidentifiable, unrecognisable, and unanimous, and that data is therefore not private information anymore. The result which is not surprising is that rivalries will emerge among the various groups or institutions, and this leads to social conflict.

If we consider that justice as noted above is an interpretation of a situation where choices are possible it is difficult to imagine how this is achieved as the digital systems have made the users simply as spectators without the opportunity engage. The problem is that if you feel injustice and you want to restore balance, that might make you behave differently from how you usually would behave. Not surprisingly the social reality of society has changed, and it is abundantly clear that society as described by Berger and Luckmann is vanishing and needs to be redefined. Considering that "the fundamental

24 Berger and Luckmann, 1966, 45.

25 Berger and Luckmann, 1966, 135.

reality-maintaining fact is the continuing use of the same language to objectify unfolding biographical experience. In the widest sense all who employ this same language are really maintaining others."[26]

The point is that a newly constructed social reality needs to be put in place as the two-way lived experience has given way to an experience akin to a bystander or somebody watching activities without having the opportunity to participate. The increased occurrence of mental illnesses and loneliness appears to be a product of a changing reality and the stark isolation of the offline digital environment. Another point is that the digital revolution is moving at a very fast pace and perhaps society has not yet developed a sound mechanism to manage change. The old order of Amish traditionalists for example had a unique way to adapt to change. They start with the things they value most, then work backwards to ask whether a given new technology performs more harm than good in respect to those values. The Amish are clear about what they value, and new technologies are evaluated by their impact on those values. The key is building a good life – not fretting about missing out on some minor short-term pleasure or interesting diversion.[27] Arguably therefore the Amish can be characterised as having achieved a world openness dominated by social cohesiveness. Interestingly, the Amish evolved from the Anabaptist movement around the time of Huldrych Zwingli (1484–1531) who led the Protestant reformation in Switzerland.

The next point to discuss is how each individual self combines into a cohesive social structure. This is achieved by the process of institutionalisation.

3 Institutionalisation

To start with, a society is ultimately controlled by institutions whether it be small like the institution of the family or larger like the institutions of the law, the government or the church. Each of the institutions and its members are controlled by patterns of conduct, that is conduct is predefined by members of the institution. As an example if one would like to be a member of the institution of the church they must believe in God. It follows that conduct within an institution needs to be controlled. The individual group members need to rely on and accept what the institution demands from them. It is argued that the internet with its multitude of platforms has now taken over as an institution

26 Berger and Luckmann, 1966, 173.

27 Cal Newport. 2017. *"Approach Technology Like the Hamish",* https://calnewport.com/approach-technology-like-the-amish/.

with the power to control information and the followers. The devotee, that is the member of a platform craves for recognition by people who have possibly never met nor are otherwise connected to. The power of the virtual world controls the behaviour of the users but how can the users understand themselves and their place?

Berger and Luckmann argue that we, ourselves can only be understood "from the particular social context in which they were shaped."[28] It follows that once the social context changes so will we and our social context is shaped through the institutionalisation process and the roles we play within that process. Simply put, the institutionalisation process is always subject to socially determined interferences. One of the very influential interferences is evolutions and on a smaller scale revolutions. It can therefore be argued that the digital revolution has interfered with the social reality as it was known in the 1970's and to a lesser degree the 80's. Berger and Luckmann did argue that all interferences are socially determined.[29] It follows that the self is a social product and cannot be properly understood unless the social context in which it is shaped is understood. It follows that if evolutions or revolutions occur in quick succession and the social equilibrium may not find a balance before the next change hence a coherent and self-maintaining social world may not be possible. Such a state will be manifested through constant upheavals and a lack of social coherence. A good example is the changes and polarisation of discontent in the United States during and after the recent election of the president. As Berger and Luckmann observed "social order exists only as a product of human activity."[30]

It is obvious that not all sectors of a society are institutionalised as some will be left un-institutionalised. It depends on factors such as the relevance of the activity.[31] If structures are shared by many, institutionalisation is wide. However, this does not mean that the institutional order is total that is all members of the society adhere to the relevance of the particular activity that is the relevance of the problem which needs a resolution. As an example if all in a society such as the Amish are members of the institution of the church, all members share and adhere to the relevance of that institution. In this case all problems are common and "all solutions are socially objectivated and all social actions are institutionalised."[32] However if the institution of the church

28 Berger and Luckmann, 1966, 68.
29 Berger and Luckmann, 1966, 67.
30 Berger and Luckmann, 1966, 70.
31 Berger and Luckmann, 1966, 97.
32 Berger and Luckmann, 1966, 97.

is highly fragmented where the Catholics belong to one and the Protestants to another institutional order, institutionalisation is narrow and solutions to problems brought about by change may not be solved. The importance of institutionalisation lies in the fact that a common stock of knowledge is applied, and this results in consistent action. As an example, driving a car is highly institutionalised as we all drive on the left had side of the road and not on the right one as other societies do. If there is no common problem institutionalisation is not necessary as knowledge is role specific.[33] The inherent instability brought about by changes in patterns require that specialisation is needed, and this will direct the drivers of institutionalised habits.

The division of labour that is specialisation results in a differentiation of institutions and hence segmentation specialisation in the common stock of knowledge. Berger and Luckmann have also pointed to an issue namely that segmentation "makes possible knowledge subjectively detached from any social relevance that is pure theory."[34] In a hunting society some individuals are freed from hunting not only to forge weapons but to fabricate myths.

> Thus we have the 'theoretical' life with the luxurious proliferation of specialised bodies of knowledge, administered by specialists whose social prestige may actually depend upon their inability to do anything except theorize.[35]

Arguably today an example would be the education department and their ministers advising teachers how to teach but they have never been in a classroom themselves hence they are acting from a level of unfamiliarity instead from a level of first-hand knowledge.

As society changes so does the process of institutionalisation change. Berger and Luckmann note that "the private sphere that emerged in the modern industrial society is considerably de-institutionalised as compared to the public sphere"[36] this is a result of institutional segmentation. Segmentation produces sub-universes of meaning and can be a result of role specialisation. Where specialisation occurs, it can result in progressive division of labour and economic progress and results in social conflict between groups. An example is the party system in politics where each group is seeking to establish itself by discrediting the other groups. The result is often that the system is paralysed,

33 Berger and Luckmann, 1966, 98.
34 Berger and Luckmann, 1966, 99.
35 Berger and Luckmann, 1966, 99.
36 Berger and Luckmann, 1966, 99.

like in the United States where the effect of the Trump administration is still playing out among the hardcore Republicans. As Berger and Luckmann put it:

> The important principle for our general consideration is that the relationship between knowledge and its social base is a dialectical one, that is, knowledge is a social product and knowledge is a factor in social change.[37]

One of the problems with the accumulated or general knowledge is the effect of the vast flow of information which is readily available on any digital system like the mobile phone. The "quick short grab" syndrome has resulted in the reduction of our attention spans and the reduction of the ability to put together reasoned arguments. If it cannot be put into a text, it is not worth saying appears to be rule of an unwritten system. This pattern of behaviour has the members of this new institution esoterically enslaved.

The problem in the rapidly changing institutional order and the proliferation of subgroups puts the legitimation processes of particular institutions at risk. If legitimation is lagging a society is not in equilibrium and hence vulnerable to unrest, revolutions or simply exhibiting dissatisfaction as noted in the current climate brought about by the digital revolution.

Berger and Luckmann also realised that changes in the institutional order are essential hence reification or changing a thought into something that is real is necessary.

3.1 *Reification*

Turning briefly to Zarubavel who explains reification as follows: "Reification presupposes a process of making the merely conventional seem inevitable, which, of course, is also a process of making the merely intersubjective seem objective."[38] Five pillars or attributes are said to be necessary for reification and these are namely, religion, science, reason, universalism and eternalism. These elements were discussed by and influenced the writing of Marx. These elements are outlined here.

It is recognised that religion and hence the idea of God is the prototype of legitimation. Preachers and people in general account for events that happen and that are also inevitable, such as God punishing you for your sinful actions. This perspective explains events and these events can be taken as fact – that

37 Berger and Luckmann, 1966, 104.

38 Eviatar Zerubavel. 2016. "The five pillars of essentialism: Reification and the social construction of an objective reality." *Cultural Sociology*, 10, no. 1, 70.

is – if an event cannot be denied, and this is an unassailable position because it cannot be proven otherwise.

Nature did not replace God, but it created a new objectivity in explaining reality. It is scientific evidence which is the new logic. "Nature" operates just like "God," only with a scientific rather than a religious aura. This is exemplified by the way evolutionary biologists have effectively replaced the biblical narrative of the creation with Charles Darwin's notion of "monophyly".[39]

Nature with scientific knowledge as a weapon spawned the third pillar. Logic was the response of the 18th-century enlightenment that followed in its footsteps. It is rarely logic alone that determines what we consider relevant and/or irrelevant, but logic cannot be ignored as a way to construct reality.

The fourth pillar is everybody. It is:

> … effectively implied in the first three, it is universalism, as manifested in our notion of 'Everybody' (or 'Everywhere'), which involves the epistemic fallacy of mistaking the merely collective for the truly universal. Tacitly implying some absolute notion of normality, it thus presents merely conventional views of the world as objective and therefore inevitable.[40]

Essentialism in essence is a view that all objects have a set of attributes that are necessary to their identity.

> The fifth pillar of essentialism, effectively also implied in the first three, is eternalism, as manifested in the notion of 'Always', which, as the historicized form of 'Everybody,' involves the epistemic fallacy of mistaking the historically specific for the truly eternal. As such, it reminds us that not only do essentialism and reification imply ignoring cultural variability, but they are also blind to change.[41]

Berger and Luckmann indeed have adopted the five pillars in a general sense and explained that the world we take for granted is assumed without realising that these decisions are made. They note that reification "implies that man is capable of forgetting his own authorship of the world, and further state the dialectic between man, the producer, and his products is lost to consciousness."[42]

---

39 Eviatar Zerubavel. 2012. *Ancestors and relatives: Genealogy, identity, and community*. Oxford University Press, 39.

40 Zerubavel, 2012, 73.

41 Zerubavel, 2012, 73.

42 Berger and Luckmann, 1966, 106.

It is obvious – and as history also taught us – as soon as an objective world is established it will never take long for reification to commence. The problem is how deep the changes will be and how long it will last. This book argues that our society is going through a phase of reification with all the problems of social discord, wars, declining wages and the wealth pump continuing to operate. Berger and Luckmann argue that reification can be described as "an extreme step in the process of objectivation, whereby the objectivated world loses its comprehensibility as a human enterprise … and becomes an inert facticity. That is man is capable paradoxically of producing a reality that denies him."[43] Arguably the digital revolution and specifically AI are the vehicles in this transition and have confirmed the process of reification.

It is not only institutions which can be reified but also the roles played in societies. As an example one might say "I have no choice in the matter as I have to act in this way because of my position". This sentence sounds more and more familiar whether in business or in government as decision making has been elevated to the higher levels of the bureaucracy hence making the ones who do the work powerless and hence disinterested and even non-caring as long as the rules are followed. Simply put the individuals are apprehended as decisions are taken in a vacuum that is the effect on individuals does not really appear as a deciding factor in the bureaucratic decision making. It appears that reification of roles is more pronounced in advanced industrial societies as the economic surplus can afford to refine the typification past a level of usefulness. Hence the issue is how do institutions and therefore how does institutionalisation affect societal realities.

3.2 *Origin of Institutionalisation*

Human activity repeats itself as it is subject to habitualization that is repeating what we are doing so that a pattern emerges. As an example "I draw, I experience the movements of my hand as a bodily feeling, which I – at the same time – can observe visually as 'movements of my hand'. As soon as forms of movement gain relevancy for our everyday life, they are subject to 'habitualization'".[44] Naturally habits are diverse and new patterns emerge such as mobile phone use where texting is more prevalent than face to face discourse. Of importance to habitualization is that in order to stabilise a pattern of use, they are institutionalised.

---

43 Berger and Luckmann, 1966, 106 and 107.

44 Steets, 2016, 100.

It is obvious that in every institution activity will take place which is based on the common patterns of knowledge held by its members. Rawls arguably used the veil of ignorance as the starting point to describe a common knowledge among the members of an institution. Berger and Luckmann defined knowledge within an institution as "referring to what is socially defined as reality and not some extra-social criteria of cognitive validity."[45] Simply put institutional order is defined by the typification of performances of the members of a society. As an example, a hunting society would have different defined realities when compared to an agrarian society as their activities are functionally different. As such roles are defined and as an example in some societies a father will arrange a marriage of his daughter whereas in others this is not the case. The point is that if members of a group behind a veil of ignorance are joining into an institution the question must be asked what is their stock of knowledge and how do they arrive at just and fair conclusions? The answer perhaps lies in the fact that humans have an inherent sense of justice and fairness and hence over time this will exhibit itself as the culture or reality of that particular group or institution. In other words, the roles each member plays constitutes the institutional order and legitimises the institution itself. Hence it can be argued that the digital revolution has not altered the underpinning reasons of institutional order but as the roles have changed the fundamental face to face discussions have given way to virtual communications via the internet. If this is correct individuals are required to trust that the institutions are the cornerstones of society and cannot be corrupted.

Berger and Luckmann explain why in Rawls' theory of justice he notes "once discovered is perpetuated". This is so as actions by an individual as well as others are objective actions which are repeated at appropriate times as an identification of the self.[46] Here we can see that Rawls and Berger and Luckmann point to the same important self-experience.

> After the action has taken place, the actor reflects about his action. Now a part of the self is objectified, as the performer of this action, with the whole self again becomes [at least] partially involved in the action ... and the socially constructed world is internalized in individual consciousness.[47]

45 Berger and Luckmann, 1966, 88.
46 Berger and Luckmann, 1966, 90.
47 Berger and Luckmann, 1966, 90–91.

By internalising roles individuals participate in the social world but it must also be noted that roles can only be played within a social setting. It is doubtful whether the digital world and specifically the virtual world on the internet can be classed as a social settings as long as social means direct not virtual interaction. It follows that a world must be in existence but is it a social world or a world broken up into class systems with no cohesive institutions? Hence what are the roles played by individuals?

Roles commonly occur in the institutions, and they represent an order namely an institutional order. Berger and Luckmann describe as an example the institution of law in the following way:

> The institution of law also represents the legal language, codes of law, theories of jurisprudence and, finally, by the ultimate legitimisation of the institution and its norms in ethical, religious or mythological systems of thought. Such man-made phenomena as the awesome paraphernalia that frequently accompany the administration of law, and such natural ones as the clap of thunder that may be taken as the divine verdict in a trial by ordeal and may eventually even become a symbol of ultimate justice, further represent the institution. All these representations, however, derive their continuing significance and even intelligibility from their utilization in human conduct, which here, of course, is conduct typified in the institutional roles of law.[48]

Given the fact that it is more and more apparent that there is an increased division of labour and specifically into highly complex professional skills such as the AI specialists. Highly complex skills narrow accessibility to others who may not be in those specific institution of developing AI knowledge. However, on the other side of the coin is the fact that the specialists such as the technology giants represented by their labour force become the administrator and in fact the sole guardian of the particular stock of knowledge. The point is that specialisation has reached the point where only the people whose role is defined by the institution can understand the true stock of knowledge. On the other hand specialisation and increased digital knowledge has resulted in the abolition of what were once traditional manual jobs such as blacksmiths, carpenters, toolmakers to note a few. Even unskilled jobs are lost to industrialisation. The effect is that new roles need to be constructed that is a division in the institution has emerged. Those that follow and assist on the small scale for

48 Berger and Luckmann, 1966, 93.

little return can be caught in a non-escapable cycle of poverty or discontent. As noted previously the traditional middle class is slowly disappearing either moving into the upper class or being relegated to the lower class. What we once knew as a structure of society is vanishing and simply put a new reality has emerged.

The question therefore will be how will two institutions with different social goals meeting together within a society react? That is, how is social order maintained? Are we in the process of a transition to digital institutions or is this a passing phase?

4 Constructivism

It is not a coincidence that Berger and Luckmann chose the word "construction" in the title of the book. Vera argued that nearly 50 years after the publication of their book that "Comparable to other distinguished concepts in the social sciences and humanities, such as 'paradigm' and 'deconstruction', the formula of 'social construction' has been appropriated and used – or misused – in extensive and diverse social circles."[49] Arguably the function and use of "construction" has been overlooked at times. The 1960's and 70's have been described as the golden years, that is, when the economy was going well, we had near full employment and the hippy years fostered social debates and relatively few disputes as we experience actively today.

What can be said in hindsight is that this time was arguably the start of the Constructivism movement which is defined in the following way:

> Constructivism is the theory that says learners construct knowledge rather than just passively take in information. As people experience the world and reflect upon those experiences, they build their own representations and incorporate new information into their pre-existing knowledge (or schemas).[50]

Within their work, Berger and Luckmann attempted to draw our attention to what is perceived as real, and they compared this to what we take for granted

49 Hector Vera. 2016. "Rebuilding a classic: The social construction of reality at 50." *Cultural Sociology,* 10, no. 1, 4.

50 University at Buffalo. 2024. *Office of Curriculum, Assessment and Teaching Transformation, Division of Academic Affairs,* https://www.buffalo.edu/catt/develop/theory/constructivism.html.

in everyday life. The question is whether the social construction as perceived by Berger and Luckmann is still real and hence applicable? It is important to note at the beginning that *The Social Construction of Reality* "stressed the ideas of the sociality of reality and the social processes of its construction. It is in this sense, that the book was a beginning of the paradigm of social construction."[51]

In this book we recognise and argue that Berger and Luckmann's ideas are as valid today as they were "yesterday" because they looked at principles which are part of humanity namely the values, logics, and stocks of information.

Vera alludes to a most important point which seems to be forgotten in the digital age namely that "reality to be firm and enduring, it must be a shared reality."[52] The problem today is that the mobile phone and social apps are shared as instruments but importantly they are not shared physically as they are merely a façade of pictures people look at without a social connection. As an example, if an influencer on the internet points out that red should be the new and prominent colour, mimicking such a statement is not sharing the statement, it is more like a command for following, like sheep follow without understanding the purpose and utility of their journey. Following is not a shared conscious activity, without a social purpose that is built on logic, it is merely a copy and hence not truly internalised.

4.1 *The Social Construction of Reality*

It is also important to look at the word 'construction' in the title of Berger and Luckmann's book, *The Social Construction of Reality*. Like the word 'social' it hints at the most important issues in a world that is made by humans. First it has to be 'social' that is humans interact with each other to make experiences real and meaningful. In other words, it has to be a shared reality. Is a social world a world where people are at a dinner table or at home each engrossed in their mobile phone without engaging in social interaction? It is questionable that the digital world is social and meaningful. However, the digital world is meaningful to the technology giants as it is the tool of their profitmaking machine. It is also interesting to note that resilience the word used to explain robustness and adaptability is used by companies stating that "organizations must identify their most critical functions and assets, define dependencies that enable the continuity of these functions, and consider the full range of

51 Hubert Knoblauch and René Wilke. 2016. "The common denominator: The reception and impact of Berger and Luckmann's The Social Construction of Reality." *Human Studies* 39, 52.

52 Vera, 2016, 6.

threats that could undermine functional continuity,"[53] but in a social world the resilience to change and adaption to change has not yet been seriously discussed. Cybersecurity is not only needed to protect business assets but also the culture of a society.

Construction therefore implies "that the social world is built and maintained by the transformative activity of individuals who construct society as their second nature."[54] The resulting institutions are not a generically or digitally constructed but by social interactions. Berger and Pullberg elaborate on this idea in the following way:

> Every human society can [...] be understood as a world-building enterprise, that is, as world-building human activity. The reality of such a world is given neither in itself nor once and for all. It must be constructed and reconstructed over and over again.[55]

Admittedly what is real is a product of the world we live in therefore the digital revolution is also real and hence a construct of society. Arguably though it lacks the important component of "social" which is based on socialisation. It is argued that socialisation is not the solitary activity of staring at mobile phones but the face-to-face interaction with others in society and sharing and learning from each other's real experiences. This leads to the question of what is real?

4.2 *Reality*

It is best for Berger to explain the inspiration of looking at reality in the context of construction. Berger took inspiration from Thomas, and he noted:

> Thomas' well-known dictum on the 'real consequences' of social definition was presumably intended, and has been generally understood as intending, to say that once 'reality' has been defined, people will act as if it were indeed so. To this important proposition must be added an understanding of the realizing (that is, reality-producing) potency of social definition. This social-psychological import of Thomas' 'basic theorem'

53 Paul Kurtz. 2023. *"Harnessing Emerging Technologies to Transform Cyber Resilience"*, Cyber Talks, https://cybertalks.upgather.com/2023/.

54 Vera, 2016, 7.

55 Peter Berger and Stanley Pullberg. 1965. "Reification and the sociological critique of consciousness." *History and theory*, 4, no. 2, 201.

> was developed by Merton. The sociology of knowledge [...] would extend this notion of the social construction of 'reality' even further.[56]

A clear link to constructivism was seen but what then was the main contribution of Berger and Luckmann and is it still valid today is a real question?

5 The Contribution

Berger and Luckmann have attempt to shift the academic debate of what is real to the practical activities of people as they noted:

> To exaggerate the importance of theoretical thought in society and history is a natural failing of theorizers ... The sociology of knowledge must first of all concern itself with what people 'know' as 'reality' in their everyday, non- or pre-theoretical lives.[57]

They also recognised that the world is consisting of multiple realities.[58] It is a taken for granted world where acute threats need to be internalised as well. They note that "the marginal situations constitute a 'night side' that keeps lurking ominously on the periphery of everyday consciousness."[59] Arguably the night side or dark side existing today is the digital where real experience is confused with a virtual one. Developing the idea even further there is the dark web. Hence the question of what is real is sometimes difficult to ascertain. Arguably what used to be a marginal reality such as texting has turned out to be a paramount reality displacing the face-to-face interaction that used to exist in the past. However it has not been sufficiently recognised that the key shortcoming of many virtual stimulations has been the challenge of reproducing an appropriate real experience. The problem is whether the line between other realities such as interactive fantasy games using avatars and real realities has been blurred.

Hoffman commented on this topic:

56 Peter L. Berger. 2017. "Identity as a problem in the sociology of knowledge." In *The New Sociology of Knowledge*, pp. 115–126. Routledge, 84.

57 Berger and Luckmann, 1966, 15.

58 Berger and Luckmann, 1966, 21.

59 Berger and Luckmann, 1966, 98.

> One can look at a street scene using a phone or eyewear and see both the street (filtered by the onboard camera), along with layered directions to the nearest subway, reviews of nearby restaurants, details about real estate for sale or rent, Flickr or Instagram images recently taken in the area, alerts that people on your Twitter account are nearby.[60]

The above demonstrates that reality is compressed into a virtual representation of the current moment without having the lived experience of the viewer. Simply put it is like a spectator in a theatre watching a virtual but not real experience. The problem as we have already noticed is that these "technologies become more widespread, their quality as an 'other reality' bracketed from the paramount reality of everyday interaction will likely become less and less recognized."[61] The interesting point is that this development has already been recognised as far back as 1985 as Haraway noted "we are all already cyborgs" (cyber altered organisms).[62]

What this discussion clearly demonstrates is that there are other realities which can affect everyday life. The question is whether the virtual reality we are able to experience has deviated sufficiently from the reality as described by Berger and Luckmann? Perhaps the last word belongs to Berger and Luckmann who noted:

> All social reality is precarious. All societies are constructions in the face of chaos. The constant possibility of anomic terror is actualized whenever the legitimations that obscure the precariousness are threatened or collapse.[63]

The issue is that we understand that the social reality under the influence of the digital revolution and specifically the yet not fully developed new technology such as artificial intelligence systems will create a new reality. However,

60 Steve G. Hoffman. 2016. "The practical use of other realities: Taking Berger and Luckmann into the wild." *Cultural Sociology*, 10, no. 1, 120. Donna J. Haraway, 1985. *"A Manifesto for Cyborgs: Science, Technology, and Socialist Feminism in the 1980s"*, https://archive.org/details/anarchy_Cyborg_Manifesto_Harroway.

61 Steve G. Hoffman. 2016. "The practical use of other realities: Taking Berger and Luckmann into the wild." *Cultural Sociology*, 10, no. 1, 120.

62 Donna J. Haraway. 1985. *"A Manifesto for Cyborgs: Science, Technology, and Socialist Feminism in the 1980s"*, https://archive.org/details/anarchy_Cyborg_Manifesto_Harroway.

63 Berger and Luckmann, 1966, 103.

we still need to question change and we cannot get "analytically lazy when we treat these processes as if they are inevitable or simply an expression of false consciousness."[64]

6 Conclusion

The impact of *The Social Construction of Reality* needs some further comments. It appears to have left a puzzling legacy "first, scholars keep classifying this book as one of the most important sociology books of the twentieth century, secondly it is a serious struggle to trace direct theoretical follow-ups emerging from the book or scholars who explicitly position themselves in the tradition of the 'new sociology of knowledge', not to mention a 'sociological school' in its name."[65]

> Berger [30 years later] delineates the ground-breaking idea in aiming at a synthesis of several strands of theory that often have been understood as contradictory. On the one hand, he mentions the voluntaristic approach of Weber, which emphasizes that society is created by meaningful acts of individuals. On the other hand, he sees the approach of the French school of Durkheimian sociology that emphasizes social institutions as facts that resist the individuals.[66]

A point of importance in the book is that it is "the investigation of the social construction of the world within the dialectical relationship of objective and subjective reality."[67] The idea was to take the institutional world as a pivotal fact. It followed that as we live in an institutional world it is the experience with objectification and habitualization which forms the subjective reality of the self. The typification relevant for the institutions are shared by the members of the social group, and at the same time, the individuals as members of the group are typified by the institution. Legal marriage under the law and incest taboo are rules in institutions for members of specific groups. The individual group members need to rely on and accept what the institution demands from

64 Steve G. Hoffman. 2016. "The practical use of other realities: Taking Berger and Luckmann into the wild." *Cultural Sociology* 10, no. 1, 122.

65 Silke Steets. 2016. "Playing chamber music at a rock festival? The social construction of reality in US sociology." *Human Studies* 39, 72.

66 Dreher, 2023, 101.

67 Dreher, 2023, 102.

them.[68] Simply put institutions are part of a shared history and group members accept what the institution demands from them. It follows that any changes can only be rectified or understood by looking back, in other words, we need a starting point, and this book argues that Berger and Luckmann are the current historical starting point of understanding the reality of our social world.

Importantly and still eminently relevant today is what Luckmann himself stated namely, "What Berger and I set out in the book that seems to be partly forgotten, is the weight – and occasionally heavy weight – of tradition, of history, of past constructions, if you wish."[69] Simply put the social construction of reality as described by Berger and Luckmann are gaining in relevance and importance as we are again in a changing pattern requiring a definition and recognition of what is real and not virtual.

As we leave past social constructions behind us, the next chapter will look at the important aspect of justice and hence the writings of Rawls' and how justice affects institutions and importantly the social fabric of society as we know it.

---

68 Berger and Luckmann, 1966, 54.

69 See Jochen Dreher and Hector Vera. 2016. "The social construction of reality, a four-headed, two-fingered book: An interview with Thomas Luckmann." *Cultural Sociology* 10, no. 1, 30–36.

CHAPTER 6

Rawls' Liberal Political Theory

1 Introduction

Before moving onto Rawls' *A Theory of Justice* it is instructive and important to look again back in history, namely how the world was depicted by the fresco of Ambrogio Lorenzetti in the Palazzo Pubblico in Siena. The fresco dates back to 1338 and represents the Allegory of Good and Bad Government. Lorenzetti in the central panel depicts how civilisation works. A woman called Wisdom is set above another woman called Justice. From the head of Justice the two arms of a scale emerge, and Wisdom assists in balancing the scales. In one of the panels a small figure dispenses justice. The other panel dispenses justice to merchants. From the two panels ropes hang down to be grasped by another woman – Concorde. Concorde winds the two ropes together to pass them on to the 24 magistrates who govern the city. They in turn pass the cord to a bigger figure Ben Comun, the common good. On either side of the male figure are six large women – Peace, Fortitude, Prudence, Magnanimity, Temperance and, again Justice. These are the essential elements of the common good supporting society. What is most surprising is that a simple fresco can hold all the secrets and elements representing a society in balance.

It is one thing to recognise that justice is an important element in one's life, but it is equally important to recognise that society will enforce justice. This is left to the institution of law, but the law must also be guided by justice in its decision making. It is therefore useful to commence the discussion of justice by analysing how the law views the issue of justice. The important point is that a strong ethical or political consensus has to be formed for any institution to avoid the dispensation of justice based on personal values. Hence whether it is the law or philosophy, an overarching principle of justice and hence morality needs to be in place to govern legal obligations. Justice is also not a new concept as it is based on the make-up of humanity. In effect there are four principles of justice which are recognised in law namely corrective, retributive, procedural and distributive justice. Two of these principles will be mentioned briefly, these are corrective and retributive justice as they are only of peripheral interest to this book.

As Posner put it:

 | DOI:10.1163/9789004702691_007

> The idea of corrective justice comes down to us from Aristotle, and it has seemed to many legal scholars an attractive principle for orienting legal inquiries, particularly in such common law fields as tort and contract ... distributive justice – justice in the distribution by the state of money honours, and other things of value – requires distribution according to merit. Corrective justice is different. The corrective principle applies not to awards but to transactions both voluntary and involuntary, the distinction corresponding roughly to our law between contract and torts.[1]

As far as procedural and distributive justice are concerned Posner was influenced by philosophers such as Aristotle, Kant, Ackermann and Rawls and judged the usefulness of philosophy as wanting and not of high value as far as the law was concerned. It is sufficient to note that "Ackermann in the end modified his egalitarian concept of distributive justice to allow for compensating inequalities – affirmative action in a broad, and also in its conventional narrow sense."[2] Arguably in Posner's view distributive as well as procedural justice is grounded in either a constitution or branches of law and hence left to courts to apply the principle of justice within the legal framework. In effect the law in its interpretive endeavours will and has shaped the law to include justice as a feature of a judgement relying of statutory or common law.

There is no doubt that justice is at risk, and this was noted by Hilderbrandt,

> What we should face, however, is the possibility that due to the assumptions and trade- offs inherent in their design, specific data- driven technologies determine our choice architecture in ways that diminish our agency. This is not merely a technological question as the relevant design, operations and uptake of legal technologies will often depend upon the political economy that informs them. If the market is organized such that companies compete by way of algorithmic optimization of advertising revenue in ways that prioritize extreme content and fake news, it may be very difficult to solve that problem at the level of the technology. The relevant technological solutions will probably require various types of algorithmic censure and moderation, which has radical drawbacks for the freedom of information.[3]

1 Richard A. Posner. 1993. *The problems of jurisprudence*. Harvard University Press, 313–314.

2 Posner, 1993, 339.

3 Mireille Hildebrandt. 2023. "Boundary Work between Computational 'Law' and 'Law-as-We-Know-it.'" *Data at the Boundaries of European Law*, 62.

What justice actually is, and how is it defined has been left to philosophers like Rawls which will be discussed now.

1.1 *Rawls' Theory of Justice*

It is interesting to see how Rawls explains one of the supporting institutional systems of society namely justice. For Rawls as an observer, society was structured unfairly giving many people reason to fear injustice and allowed a privileged group to profit from it. He broadened modern liberals' "fear of poverty" into a quest for equality, to be achieved by redistributing wealth and opportunities so as to make them fair. Rawls' second fear was of political and social instability. It is interesting to speculate whether Rawls had a new revolution in mind when he wrote and theorised on the topic of justice.

In Rawls' view there was a danger that a liberal society, even when based on justice, would nevertheless be illegitimate in many eyes and therefore unstable, ending in revolution or reaction.[4] Any socioeconomic difference between people, any deviation from equality, required justification to be considered fair. Equality was Rawls' benchmark,[5] and we test his theories here in a modern application.

We know that Rawls was influenced by liberal ideas. He was not the first thinker to look at and explain liberalism which was in similar times explained in the *The Good Society* which was published in 1937 by Lippmann. In his early career, Lippmann was mostly concerned with the relationship between liberalism and democracy. Lippmann concluded his book with a restatement of liberalism as the search for a society in which no one need to be afraid.[6] Rawls was an American political philosopher who also attempted to shape contemporary responses to democratic disagreement.[7] Rawlsian liberals moved further and further away from justifying the principles of justice to focusing on actual citizens. Instead, the principles he wrote about typically justified "reasonable persons" those willing to consider all sides of the argument, having knowledge of the question at hand, and able to exclude considerations irrelevant to the question at hand. As a result, it may be said that liberalism respects the persons 'better beliefs' those beliefs people may arrive at after fuller consideration

4 Alan S. Kahan. 2023. *Freedom from fear: an incomplete history of liberalism.* Princeton University Press, 386.

5 Kahan, 2023, 387–388.

6 Kahan, 2023, 333.

7 Andrius Gališanka. 2019. *John Rawls: The path to a theory of justice.* Harvard University Press, 1.

rather than their actual beliefs. One might even say that liberalism respects beliefs rather than persons who try to articulate them.[8]

Rawls' vision was conceived of political philosophy as having a task to offer a conception of justice that can solve disagreements and considered that task complete if citizens could agree on one such conception. If there were no objections, the philosophical conversation could stop, for the time being. Not only did he aim to show the possibility of agreement among reasonable persons, but he also thought that this agreement can be generated from the combination of many considerations that are incontestable and yet weak by themselves.[9]

Unlike Kant, Rawls aimed to remove us from the particularities of our persons and existence, but not from being human as such. Rawls presented human beings as living in the "circumstances of justice." According to him, human beings live in a world in which they coexist with others of roughly similar physical and mental powers. They do so in conditions of "moderate scarcity" which forces them to participate in cooperative schemes. Hence Rawls realised the need for virtues. Human beings have their own plans of life and different philosophical, political, religious, and other kinds of beliefs.[10]

2 Rawls' Theory of Justice

The social contract theory has many versions and includes those of Hobbes, Locke, Rousseau as well as Rawls. Hobbs believed that the fear of the present and future brings men together.[11] Locke regarded an individual as a free agent provided that they had their own property in a civil society. Locke also saw private property as a guarantee of individual freedoms against an absolute monarch.[12] Rousseau in his formulation of general will glorified the institution of private property for the sake of maintaining social order.[13] Rousseau criticised Hobbes and Locke but the relationship he made between production, freedom, order and its consequences are actually very similar to Hobbs and Locke.[14]

8 Gališanka, 2019, 2–3.

9 Gališanka, 2019, 5.

10 Gališanka, 2019, 179–80.

11 Mehmet Kanatli. 2021. *Private Property, Freedom, and Order: Social Contract Theories from Hobbes to Rawls*. Routledge India, 67.

12 Kanatli, 2021, 27.

13 Kanatli, 2021, 40.

14 Kanatli, 2021, 103.

The significance of Rawls' *A Theory of Justice* lies in the fact that "The social contract is an introduction to the answer to the question that if people were to set up a society, which principles of justice would they prefer."[15] He also noted that "[People] must develop a conception of the social world and of what is just and unjust if the sentiment of justice is to be acquired."[16]

These ideas in themselves are of importance as arguably the digital revolution will bring about a change in the structure of our society and the search for our definition of justice needs to be re-evaluated or re-defined. The crucial issue hence is what is a social contract within the confines of a social world and how is it achieved? Turning to the establishing of a social contract, Rawls explains that he carries the definition to a higher level of abstraction than previous traditional concepts.[17] The social contract was also represented and developed by Locke, Rousseau and Kant but further developed by Rawls. The starting point no doubt has to be that the members of a society must meet and the end product of such a meeting is the social contract. It is questionable whether a virtual meeting via digital instruments will lead to the same social contract as a face-to-face meeting. It can be argued that any meeting irrespective of the medium of the meeting is a social contract. The social contract therefore irrespective of its creation contains the 'principles that free and rational persons concerned to further their own interests would accept in an initial position of equality as defining the fundamental terms of their association.'[18]

The social contract therefore will contain steps or the way in which the major social institutions distribute fundamental rights and duties and determine the division of advantages from social cooperation.[19] The social contract then will be specifying the principles of justice which ought to guide politics and law to achieve the desired outcomes.[20] It is difficult to imagine but the essential and novel elements that the social contract according to Rawls is premised on, follows this assumption,

> Among the essential features of this situation is that no one knows his place in society, his class position or social status, nor does anyone know his fortune in the distribution of natural assets and abilities, his

15 Ulker Yukselbaba. 2022. "Can Rawls' Theory of Distributive Justice Become a Cure for Poverty?" In *Annales de la Faculté de Droit d'Istanbul*, no. 71, Istanbul University, 543.

16 Rawls, 1971, 433–434.

17 Rawls, 1971, 3.

18 Rawls, 1971, 10.

19 Rawls, 1971, 10–15.

20 Rawls, 1971, 75.

> intelligence, strength, and the like. ... The principles of justice are chosen behind a veil of ignorance.[21]

Rawls also maintained that it is important indeed crucial to his theory if "the imposition of disadvantages on a few can be outweighed by a greater sum of advantages enjoyed by others or whether the weight of justice requires an equal liberty for all and permits only those economic and social inequalities which are to each person's interests."[22] In addition, Rawls also looked at a well-ordered society where there is cooperation and individuals will only choose what is fair.[23] Rawls also argues that justice "applies to the basic structure of society as a whole because ... we raise the expectations of the more advantaged only in ways required to improve the situation of the worst off."[24]

Rawls described that the social contract needs to be one where free and rational individuals furthering their own interests would accept an initial position of equality defining the terms of their association. This would be fairness.[25] When Rawls turns his attention to the principles that applied to individuals, he specifically notes that fairness must play an important part.[26] He defines the principle as follows:

> This principle holds that a person is required to do his part as defined by the rules of an institution when two conditions are met: first, the institution is just (or fair), that is, it satisfies the two principles of justice; and second, one has voluntarily accepted the benefits of the arrangement or taken advantage of the opportunities it offers to further one's interests.[27]

However, Rawls does agree that nothing "guarantees that inequalities will not be significant, there is a persistent tendency for them to be levelled down by the increasing availability of educated talent and ever widening opportunities."[28] It is indeed true that education and widening opportunities in the digital age will affect the distribution of wealth. However, what it does is merely allow the educated and those taking the opportunities offered by the new age economy

21 Rawls, 1971, 11.
22 Rawls, 1971, 29.
23 Rawls, 1971, 29.
24 Rawls, 1971, 136.
25 Rawls, 1971, 10.
26 Rawls, 1971, 96.
27 Rawls, 1971, 96.
28 Rawls, 1971, 137.

to shift classes, that is, the move "up the social ladder" and those not capable or not favoured will stay behind. Rawls also recognised the possibility, at least theoretically, that by "giving up some of their fundamental liberties men are sufficiently compensated by the resulting social and economic gains."[29] It is unlikely that every individual operating in the new age economy is able to recognise when they are giving up their fundamental liberty in the form of privacy and whether in return they are compensated by social and economic gains. In many cases there is only a perceived social gain.

Reality tells us that the poorer classes, that is the low paid workers have no real bargaining strength and are not able to negotiate better conditions. Rawls did not anticipate or comprehend the enormity of changes that the digital revolution would bring and was not correct to argue that "in a competitive economy (with or without private ownership) with an open class system excessive inequality will not be the rule."[30] Rawls did realise that individuals need to restrict their own liberty for the good of all which is the basic tenet of a functioning society and therefore an obvious observation. But history has also taught us that a well-ordered democratic society will function if everybody can see a realistic pathway to a higher status, that is we have the upper-, middle- and lower-class structure. Unfortunately, in the digital age the middle class is disappearing as the internet and now increasingly AI has changed how we work. As an example, we need less draftsmen as drafting apps are quicker and cheaper. Also, businesses in their desire for increased profits are not relying on domestic workers as some online work does not know borders and the work can be executed at the point of the lowest cost that is in any country. This point alone has shifted our known definition of the economy and society.

Rawls preferred a structure of society that was egalitarian and favoured equality for all the people, "a society should try to avoid the region where the marginal contributions of those better off to the well-being of the less favoured are negative ... there is a natural sense in which the harmony of social interests is achieved; representative men do not gain at one another's expense since only reciprocal advantages are allowed."[31] This is a key point in the digital revolution because we are witnessing the power of technology giants and those who hold the knowledge of the digital technology over those who are less privileged with this knowledge and information. In addition, as noted above we live in a global economy and hence work shifts where the greatest profit can be

29 Rawls, 1971, 55.
30 Rawls, 1971, 137.
31 Rawls, 1971, 89.

achieved. As an example, the clothing industry shifted out of Europe to China and now – due to efficiency and cost – to Bangladesh.

Interestingly Rawls noted that it is "the two principles of justice [which] define what is a fair share in the case of institutions belonging to the basic structure. So, if these arrangements are just, each person receives a fair share when all (himself or herself included) do their part."[32] This might work in a small society where most people are aware of each other but in multicultural societies even what is a fair or just institution is disputed. Not surprisingly it is the government influenced by the big end of town and vocal pressure groups which in the end decides the path a nation will take. As an example, the prevalence of political correctness will silence or at least stifle real debate. The point is as Rawls also noted "the content of obligations is always defined by an institution or practice the rules of which specify what it is that one is required to do."[33] This leads us back to the contention that institutions are guided by the wishes of powerful groups and not by individuals who as Rawls himself noted are behind a veil of ignorance. "[O]nce the veil of ignorance is removed, the parties find that they have ties of sentiment and affection, and want to advance the interests of others and to see their ends attained."[34] The question though is whether the veil of ignorance is ever removed considering that technology giants are profit motivated and hence the question is how they conceive a social world to be?

Rawls also used an example in relation to institutional obligates namely:

> ... the political act of running for and (if successful) holding public office in a constitutional regime. This act gives rise to the obligation to fulfill the duties of office, and these duties determine the content of the obligation. Here I think of duties not as moral duties but as tasks and responsibilities assigned to certain institutional positions.[35]

Profit making has been scrutinised by many and Nussbaum analysed educational issues in *The Clash Within: Democracy Religious Violence, and India's Future.* Many of her arguments contrasted education and profit making. Where some focus on marketable skills, critical thinking and imagining are critical to promote human development as opposed to economic growth and economic enrichment. There is no objection to good scientific and technical education,

32 Rawls, 1971, 96.
33 Rawls, 1971, 97.
34 Rawls, 1971, 111.
35 Rawls, 1971, 97.

but other abilities are crucial to the health of democracy. Nussbaum recognised, "With the rush to profitability in the global market, values precious for the future of democracy, especially in an era of religious and economic anxiety, are in danger of getting lost." Rawls' *A Theory of Justice* is the clearest example of liberal tradition, and his views are shared with Nussbaum.[36]

One only has to think of the current issues in the United States in relation to the presidency in order to question Rawls' assertions. In Rawls' defence though one needs to say that he looked at an ordered, well function democratic society where the economy was well functioning. However, it is argued that today we see a change in values as the socially constructed society is breaking up without yet morphing into something else. Put differently, the digital age will change society, but the question is into what? If we follow Rawls' arguments, then "your worst enemy will decide what place you will obtain in society". This setup was arranged so that the principles of justice preferred by Rawls would be chosen. "The veil of ignorance is so thick that rational individuals cannot acquire information about facts that can affect their choices and thus will prefer the principles of justice as fairness."[37] Arguably Rawls thinks institutional actions are needed because individuals though rational are shrouded in a veil of ignorance. In essence the objectification of justice and fairness can only be achieved by the actors being acquainted with the meanings of justice and fairness which necessitates some form of educational process.[38]

Of interest is also the assumption made by Rawls, namely that people "cannot enter into agreements that may have consequences they cannot accept. They will avoid those that they can adhere to only with great difficulty. Since the original agreement is final and made in perpetuity, there is no second chance."[39] This assertion assumes that society is static, that reality as it exists once the agreement is forged does not change. However, society and specifically economic and political realities are always fluid. Specifically in our globally connected world it is not only issues within one country that determines outcomes but in other countries as well. It can easily be seen today as an example as the Chinese economy contracts it can and will affect other countries and hence agreements are never made in perpetuity, but agreements are drafted in such a way that they take care of changing circumstances. If for example a war breaks out in an oil rich country it will affect the petrol price across the globe.

---

36 Martha C. Nussbaum. 2016. *Not for profit: why democracy needs the humanities-Updated edition*. Princeton University Press, 1–192, 6.

37 Yukselbaba, 2022, 539.

38 Berger and Luckmann, 1966, 87.

39 Rawls, 1971, 155.

3 The Social Sphere

Rawls at the beginning of his theory puts justice into a social sphere that is it requires people to socially cooperate and chose jointly "the principles which are to assign basic rights and duties and to determine the division of social benefits."[40] In other words at first glance he follows the arguments of Berger and Luckmann that a conversation between people is necessary in order to work out basic rights that is to determine what is just or unjust. However, his proposition that justice is chosen behind a veil of ignorance has only merits as a starting point in a discussion of what is the perfect justice in a well-ordered society. The divergence between Rawls and Berger and Luckmann is obvious as Berger and Luckmann start with the observation that only face to face discussions are real. These discussions arguably also start behind a veil of ignorance that is ignorance of the other person's perception of reality. Stretching the point, one could argue that the differences between Rawls and Berger and Luckmann are only semantic in nature.

The changes brought about by the digital revolution do give weight to the presence of a veil of ignorance in a broad sense. Indeed, choices are made in ignorance of actual needs as a Facebook (Meta) post for example is a one-sided expression given in a social vacuum. It is hard to imagine that people will make the choices thinking of a response from a society together. Something has never changed in any society and that is namely that major decisions are made either by the ruling class such as the members of parliaments or a well organised pressure groups. In addition his assertion that no one knows his place in society is patently wrong in the current environment. It is reminiscent of the argument of a group of people in the education system wanting to abandon academic streaming of students because some might feel inferior and neglected to understand that each student in the class knew exactly where he or she stands. If a lower graded student did not compare his results with a top student but rather with his or her group, finding out who was the best in that group only would not be the full story. The result is that students are not taught according to their level of competence and hence justice for all is not achieved. In essence the class system is maintained, and it is not behind a veil of ignorance.

What is interesting to note is that Rawls alludes to the fact that justice begins "with the choice of the first principles of a conception of justice which is to regulate all subsequent criticism and reform of institutions."[41] It is arguable

40 Rawls, 1971, 10.

41 Rawls, 1971, 12.

that once the concept of justice has been formed in one way or another it will include the choice of a legislature which then will enact laws based on the principle of justice. In effect one could argue that we have a circular argument namely that the beginning and the end are indeterminate as they are dependent on a social contract. This means that Rawls addresses the issue directly rather than through "social welfare, as is the case in utilitarianism, and indeed he elevates justice – not maximum welfare as the first virtue of social institutions."[42] Arguably Rawls addresses the issue of justice though the lens of a capitalistic system of politics. Hamlin argued that contradiction which lies at the base of capitalism is that it can only maintain its existence through competition and inequality in the use of tangible resources whereas democratic societies are founded on citizens' demands for basic political equality.[43]

Despite the perceived shortcomings of any philosophical explanation of principles governing society, the importance lies in the fact that Rawls supplied a useful mechanism to explain distributive principles. The question is not so much whether Rawls' methodology will bear practical outcomes but rather how it can be applied to predict and more importantly guide the development of digital systems such as AI. Rawls arguably focused on people within society, but the real question is how will the integrated system respond to the veil of ignorance, as "the principles of justice are chosen behind a veil of ignorance."[44] After all there are many examples where the masses are subject to the government's will or ability to guide society in a meaningful way and in addition the digital age has produced the technology giants – the controllers of the digital systems – which are arguably out of reach of a meaningful control by governments. Rawls did argue that a well-ordered society should be stable and enduring, which is not the case anymore as the digital revolution has changed people's perception and how they interact with each other and society at large.

Rawls realised that "the more often individuals interact with one another, the more likely it is that friendly feelings develop between them".[45] This is an interesting point in the light of the digital revolution considering that digital contact between individuals is not conducive to develop friendly relations. The notion of a well-ordered society needs to be viewed in a different light which does not mean that Rawls' theory is either wrong or right, but the question is

---

42 Yukselbaba, 2022, 544.

43 See generally Peter Hamilton, 'Editor's Foreword' in Bryan Turner. 1986. *Types of equality*. Equality, Ellis Horwood Limited, USA, Tavistock Publications, 9–11.

44 Rawls, 1971, 11.

45 Rawls, 1971, 430.

whether the theory can still be maintained in a modern society that is well ordered?

4 Nussbaum Analysis of Rawls

Nussbaum recognised Rawls' depth and lasting implications. In *The Enduring Significance of John Rawls* Nussbaum spoke about Rawls as the most distinguished moral and political philosopher of our age. She went on to say that the influence of his ideas and his impact as a teacher made our age rich in arguments about justice, respect, and liberty.[46] Like Rawls, Nussbaum documented that people need norms to guide them and in the political life of a democracy we ought to deliberate together about the principles that guide us.[47] It is remarkable that Rawls did nothing to promote his ideas but they took hold through their own power, decisively shifting the climate of debate not only in philosophy but also in such fields as economics, law, and public policy.[48] "He has given new specificity and vigour to one of the most valuable legacies of the liberal political tradition: the idea that a person has a dignity worth that social structures should not be permitted to violate".[49]

While Nussbaum compares ethical implications of acting from emotional responses of compassion or empathy with the system advocated by Rawls. Rawls believed it was better to rationalise advantages and minimise the disadvantages of others. Nussbaum however, points to the fact that the original position is wholly hypothetical and that in fact people do know their actual circumstances in life. It would therefore seem more effective to generate emotional compassion for the least well-off than to rely on hypothetical situations to generate the kind of altruistic care for others that would make for ethical treatment of other people.[50]

Rawls' emphasis on respect plays a central role in many liberal theories. Nussbaum analyses and agrees with Rawls' idea of political liberalism and notes earlier liberals such as Mill and Raz viewed autonomy and freedom of choice are essential ingredients in valuable human lives. Nussbaum also

---

46 Martha Nussbaum. 2001. "The enduring significance of John Rawls." *The Chronicle of Higher Education* 47, no. 45, B7, 1.

47 Nussbaum, 2001, 2.

48 Nussbaum, 2001, 3.

49 Nussbaum, 2001, 4.

50 William Neher. 2020. *Communicating ethically: Character, duties, consequences, and relationships*. Routledge, 129.

argued with Sen that social equalities and inequalities should be formulated as capabilities rather than a list of things.[51] Nussbaum notes that Rawls omits the more extreme forms of need and dependency that human beings may experience, "for example, Rawls refuses to grant that we have any duties of justice to animals, on the grounds that they are not capable of reciprocity".[52] Nussbaum expanded on Rawlsian liberalism to the closing of cultural, political and social gaps. Nussbaum has been said to put Aristotle's concept together with Marx's emphasising the human society and the individual experience arise from social interaction. This approach shapes human life experience by adapting to diversity.[53]

It is also essential to at least briefly look at Friedman's concepts in relation to the views expressed by Rawls.

5 Friedman's Freedom

Friedman's views differed from Rawls in many ways, his "freedom" was substantively empty of moral content except for the necessity of free choice. "Freedom has nothing to say about what an individual does with his freedom; it is not an all-embracing ethic". He went even further than Rawls saying not only should liberalism not impose its comprehensive worldview on people, but it did also not have one. For Friedman, economic freedom was both an end in itself, that is a constituent part of freedom, and "an indispensable means toward the achievement of political freedom." His priority was economic and this was clear, "The direct importance of economic freedom is at least comparable in significance to the indirect importance of economic freedom as a means of political freedom." According to Friedman, liberalism was founded on this recognition. Competition protected people from coercion by giving them choices. Friedman recognised that the market was the source of cultural diversity (where people would buy diverse cultural products, given the opportunity to choose), while the government was the source of coercion and uniformity.[54]

51 Martha C. Nussbaum. 2007. "Capabilities as fundamental entitlements: Sen and social justice." In *Capabilities equality*, Routledge, 50–51.

52 Nussbaum, 2007, 52.

53 Wei Fei. 2023. "The influence of Karl Marx's notion of justice on Martha Nussbaum's capabilities approach." *Educational Philosophy and Theory* 55, no. 8, 978.

54 Alan S. Kahan. 2023. *Freedom from fear: an incomplete history of liberalism.* Princeton University Press, 404.

Friedman thought purely in terms of individuals, never in terms of groups. He was not a libertarian, that is, he did not wish to limit the functions of the state to those of a night watchman, or those of a rule-maker and umpire. Friedman supported two specific government policies that became significant subjects of political debate in the United States and elsewhere. The first was the "negative income tax" under which the government would guarantee a minimum income for all. This way, the poor were helped with the least cost – little bureaucracy was required to administer it – and given the most freedom – there were no strings attached to how the money was spent. Meanwhile, all other programs to assist the poor should be eliminated. Second, Friedman thought government had a duty to make sure that all children received an education. For a stable democratic society, literacy and a certain minimum amount of general knowledge were necessary, as was "widespread acceptance of some common set of values." This justified the government requiring and paying for non-vocational education, including elementary and high schools, and even liberal arts colleges, but not medical school or plumbing training – unless vocational students paid back any subsidy they received. But while the government had a duty to make sure all received an education; it did not provide education itself. Instead, "vouchers" should be given to every parent, worth a certain amount of money, to be given to the school of their choice, provided the school offered a minimum curriculum.[55]

6 Critical Analysis by Other Philosophers

Rawls, in an important contribution to political philosophy describes his own theory of an ideal society where individuals follow a set of principles of justice. The veil of ignorance ensures that there is equality and that the laws are just. Rawls describes inequality as permissible when it provides maximum benefit to the disadvantaged and reduces their burdens. In this sense Rawls means inequality such as differences in socio-economic benefits provided to some individuals. The social contract is the basis of Rawlsian justice and relies on the agreement and commitment to certain principles of justice. Critics point out that Rawls overlooks members in society who are not able to fully cooperate as a result of mental impairments, unsound mind, idiocy, and other severe disabilities. Nussbaum in particular sees a failure in adequately dealing with the needs of disabled people. Sen rejected the focus on primary goods and went

55 Kahan, 2023, 405.

on further to say that due to the diversity of human beings, even after providing the same set of liberties or rights, they may end up in different situations depending on factors such as health and body requirements, the longevity of life, etc.[56]

Mills argued that ideal theory is an ideology that rationalises the status quo, ignores social and political reality and a history of continuing racial and sexual oppression, and expresses the privilege of white male philosophers who dominate the profession. He later claimed, "Ideal theory represents an unobtainable target … it is an ideal with little or no practical worth." Mills claimed, it is not an ideal theory of perfect justice, but a non-ideal theory of racial justice that rectifies the long history of racial oppression in Western societies.[57] Sen intimates that the mere conception of what a just society looks like is not enough to settle a dispute. The main criticism is that Rawls overlooked people who are capable of achieving a greater well-being on the basis of their own capability.[58] Some critics agree that Rawls' principles of justice are appropriate standards for assessing injustice and its extent in our society but to show these principles do not apply to our society, one would have to show why the content of these principles is inappropriate to assess injustice and its extent in our society.[59] Sen contends that Rawls' "transcendent" ideals of perfect justice are redundant and irrelevant to determine what justice requires of us now.[60] Despite his critics, in the end Rawls contends that justice is compatible with human nature, and an essential part of human good.[61]

Critics also note that like Nozick, Rawls insists that a just society must guarantee secure principles of entitlement, extending at least as far as guarantees of personal property. In the original position, the choice of this guarantee reflects a fundamental interest in advancing the life goals and relationships that one values through one's own efforts. In *Justice as Fairness*, Rawls takes the ultimate goal of economic justice to be "to put all citizens in a position to manage their own affairs on a footing of a suitable degree of social and economic equality" and bases rights to personal property on "fundamental interests" including the interest in "a sufficient material basis for personal independence and a sense of self-respect". Interest in self-reliance gives priority to a system

56 Debangana Ray. 2021. "Critical Analysis of John Rawls ' Theory of Distributive Justice." *Jus Corpus Law Journal* 2, 10, 14.
57 Freeman, 2023, 4.
58 Ray, 2021, 15.
59 Freeman, 2023, 5.
60 Freeman, 2023, 4.
61 Freeman, 2023, 19.

of secure entitlement through which people are assured that their efforts to acquire material means to their own ends will not be deprived of point and value.[62]

Rawls' assertion on the freedom of association, effective engagement in valued relationships, and mutual caring among intimates is a highly important point. Within valued relationships, people committed to self-reliance willingly receive help, and are committed to reciprocity. Here effective concern for others in valued relationships is a fundamental interest. Critics highlight that to insist that laws and institutions thwart core interests in mutual caring among intimates in order to promote equal opportunity or material expectations for the worst off would be a violation of what people rightly want to protect to advance their interests. Rawls insists on protection of nurturance within families and beyond, despite the inevitable widening of inequality and opportunity.[63] Rawls' recognises the need to break up monopolies that interfere with "open and workably competitive markets," to eliminate unfair influence of "a wealthy few" in political elections, and to promote fair equality of opportunity.[64]

Critics rightfully highlight domination that exists where employers take unfair advantage of urgent needs of the desperately poor that weaken their bargaining power. On the larger scale the United States like any colonial powers in the past has, arguably, used developing countries' desperate needs for loans and markets to steer their course of development without equal regard for the interests affected by this domination. China arguably follows the footsteps of the United States on this point. People in developed countries, as an example the United States, continue to produce greenhouse gases, arguably evading their fair share of burdens of cooperation in reducing the global harm. Overall, there is still an unmet moral duty for those in developed countries to help people in developing countries.[65]

7 Conclusion

Like Scheffler, Forst zeroes in on Rawls' attempt to insulate political philosophy from other areas of philosophy.[66] Forst was a contemporary scholar of moral,

62 Richard W. Miller. 2011. "Rawls and Global Justice: A Dispute over a Legacy." *The Monist* 94, no. 4, 470.
63 Miller, 2011, 470–471.
64 Miller, 2011, 477.
65 Miller, 2011, 484.
66 See Rawls, 1971.

political and social thought. Forst called Rawls' theory "a liberal-egalitarian and constitutional Kantianism," whereas he names Habermas's discourse theory of democracy a "republican Kantianism". His argument is that while Rawls' conception of political autonomy falls short of what is required in a theory of political constructivism, "Habermas's conception of human rights does not adequately account for the moral constructivist content of the basic principles of justice."[67] One of the core ideas of Habermas's theory of communicative rationality is to make explicit the normative content implicit within the practice of argumentation. This normative content can be seen in the pragmatic presuppositions that participants in argumentation implicitly accept when they engage in arguments oriented toward justifying claims.[68] Rawls had and still does have many critics. For example, James in *Rawls, Lerner and the Tax-and-Spend Booby Trap: What Happened to Monitory Policy?* questions why Rawls neglects functional finance.

The next part is a natural extension of the discussions by Berger and Luckmann and Rawls who described the social world without the influence of the digital revolution. The next chapter will examine the influence of the internet on the creation and maintenance of the social world.

67 Seyla Benhabib, Jeffrey Flynn, Matthias Fritsch and Rainer Forst. 2015. "The Right to Justification by Rainer Forst." *Political Theory* 43, no. 6, 785.

68 Benhabib, Flynn and Fritsch, 2015, 795.

PART 3

Preserving Individual Identity

CHAPTER 7

The Digital Social World

1 Introduction

It should be abundantly clear that the fourth revolution and we refer to the digital one – has brought new challenges in defining our social world. One of the biggest challenges is building and adapting a structure behind the changes that are occurring due to increasingly sophisticated technology. Our society already has become two-tiered. On top there are the big tycoons, who firmly believe that they have earned their wealth because of their amazing genius. At the bottom we have regular people whom technology leaders view as dispensable and as a source of data to feed their profits. Despite concerns about the negative impact that the digital revolution and AI may bring, China decided to openly embrace the age of AI and accelerate its arrival. In 2017, the Chinese government openly spoke about its global ambition to become a leading AI power by 2030. Attracting considerable policy, academic and media attention, China's AI dream, led by its economic rise, heated up technology competition on the global stage.[1]

Goldhaber's conception of internet users is based on their interest in transmitting data in social discourse which is different to face to face encounters. Hence every digital conversation is a potential commodity for the technology giants. This conception does highlight the economic value associated with data use, particular to surveillance capitalists that are economically advantaged in harvesting personal data from data subjects. Zuboff, especially stresses that this economic value to data collectors is arising from the passing on of information. The demands of consumers to have "what I want, when, where, and how I want it"[2] is a demand which surveillance capitalists are pleased to satisfy. They are also able to trade that information to the highest bidder, with few ethical constraints applying to such data trading in general except in some discreet contexts.[3] Hence the question of what the social world is, needs to be asked again specifically in the digital context.

1 Jinghan Zeng. 2022. *Artificial intelligence with Chinese characteristics: National strategy, security and authoritarian governance*. London: Palgrave Macmillan, 1.

2 Zuboff, 2019, 30.

3 *See* Paul Lewis. *"Our Minds Can Be Hijacked': The Tech Insiders Who Fear a Smartphone Dystopia"*, Guardian, https://www.theguardian.com/technology/2017/oct/05/smartphone-addiction-silicon-valley-dystopia, describing how different companies pay for consumer data to help their specific agendas or marketing goals.

 | DOI:10.1163/9789004702691_008

2 The Social World

Zuboff describes the social world from the perspective of the data flow. Berger and Luckmann on the other hand have in detail discussed what constitutes a social world in a pre-digital world order, as seen in the previous chapters. Stewart analysed Rawls use of "social world" including the network of social relations. Stewart argues that Rawls uses "social world" preceded by the definite article, simply to refer to society or to the social as opposed to the natural part of the "actual world."[4] Stewart also notes that Rawls frequently refers to the specific social world that includes a well-ordered society operating in accordance with his conception of justice. Stewart cites Gaus (2016, 22–23) observing that social worlds are "crucial to Rawl's interpretation of Kant",[5] and also of Mill. There is also a plausible connection to historical figures such as Hegel who presented a vision of a rational social order based on the human need for deep and enduring communal attachments.[6] Stewart recognised that in Rawls later work he increasingly uses "social world" to refer to societies and basic structures.[7] While Hegel regarded three institutions essential to social order and hence the social world, these were the nuclear family, civil society and the modern constitutional state. Hegal also wrote about three conceptions of freedoms, these included personal freedom, the freedom of moral subjectivity and substantial freedom or social freedom.[8]

In this context it is important to understand that Marxist's theories are considered as relevant as they were formed during the Industrial Revolution. In concentrating on how capitalism has replaced human labour with machines, surveillance capitalism is grounded on machine learning that directs consumer behaviour. James Steinhoff, speaking at a conference in Canada, noted:

> Karl Marx showed that automation is an expression of the integral dynamics of capital, which is compelled to replace human labour with machines. His analysis was prescient as contemporary technologies such

4 Andrew Stewart. 2024. "Social Worlds and the Roles of Political Philosophy." *Political Theory* 52, no. 2, 3.

5 Stewart, 2023, 4.

6 Stewart, 2023, 6.

7 Stewart, 2023, 6.

8 Frederick C. Beiser. ed. 2008. *The Cambridge companion to Hegel and nineteenth-century philosophy*. Cambridge University Press, 205.

> as machine learning enable the automation of cognitive, as well as manual, labour processes.[9]

The Marxist machinery of capital is still applicable today as it was so historically. The same applies to the shift from the machinery of capitalism in the 19th century industrial revolution to today's 21st century digital revolution. However, the machinery of capital producers which Marx critiqued, did not displace the commodities produced by that machinery.[10] As Steinhoff stressed, the "work [that] takes place within capitalist firms and the products they produce remain commodities."[11] As far as society is concerned, labour and consumers do not become redundant but machines impact on the learning process and the structure of society. Centrally at work is the social re-construction of reality, including the social re-construction of privacy. What is determinative in individuals' lives now is the loss of privacy and in the context of online spaces this has the potential to have a significant impact on an individual's prospects. This determination and hence the understanding of these risks is grounded in social theory, in the social impact of surveillance capitalism and its effect upon consumers. What has changed over time has been that machines have determined and can determine and forecast what a consumer needs and wants, and hence machines have become a predictive tool in the production process for many outcomes.

Hegel specifically identified that individuals realise personal freedom when they recognise that a social world which is unhindered by others and when they can pursue whatever ends they choose.[12]

He wrote that:

> … if I live in a social world that supplies the conditions and resources I need in order to exist as a person and a moral subject – if my society educates me to value my freedom, enforces a system of individual rights, makes it possible for everyone to own property, and so forth – then there is a sense in which I am free "objectively" regardless of whether I affirm, reject, or I am indifferent to the institutions that in fact secure my freedom.[13]

---

9 Steinhoff, 2019.
10 Steinhoff, 2019.
11 Steinhoff, 2019.
12 Beiser, 2008, 206.
13 Beiser, 2008, 213.

Berger and Luckmann – influenced by Hegel – approached the creation of a social world by asking how a social world is legitimised that is how can it be explained and justified.[14] The important point is that a transmission of the social world from one generation to the next is crucial as it defines not only the social world, we live in, but it also legitimises the way "we do things".

Berger and Luckmann point to a very important issue namely that the transmission of a social world is based on historical events. Historically the creators of the first social world say A and B "can always reconstruct the circumstances under which their world and any part of it was established … and their recollection explains how their world and any part of it was established."[15] However once a new generation inherits the social world A and B have created, a different reasoning and approach is necessary. The new generation has no recollection of the original creation and hence it must be interpreted in legitimised forms – that is transmitted in order to carry conviction. In a perfect world the same story is told to all the children to legitimise the social world they will inherent. An example is the Indigenous people of Australia and their society. They will through their elders talk about dreamtime stories which explain not only the creation of their world but also the social context of their culture. The process of explaining the social world socialises the new generation into the institutional order. "The development of specific mechanisms of social controls also becomes necessary with the historization and objectivation of institutions [and] the more conduct is institutionalised, the more predictable and thus the more controlled it becomes."[16] Berger and Luckmann however make it clear that sets of institutionalisation processes take place concurrently without the need to "hang together" as long as sub members of a society share the common reason or belief. As an example, only judges are allowed to mediate disputes or only police are allowed to arrest people. But both subgroups understand and follow the rules of a common social world in the exercise of their duties.

Rawls on the other hand starts with the principle of justice which creates institutions and hence creates the social world. It appears that Rawls had not defined what exactly a social world is and also what leads to the creation of a simple institution. Arguably social structures must be based on the fact that humans only interact with a specific natural environment and hence this creates a social world with a specific cultural and social order mediated by

14 Berger and Luckmann, 1966, 79.
15 Berger and Luckmann, 1966, 79.
16 Berger and Luckmann, 1966, 79–80.

significant others.[17] Arguably therefore the social world is always subject to a continually determined interference by socio-cultural determinations.

The argument is that Rawls' approach is limited insofar as justice defined by various groups within a society will be a variance with a social world. Hence it will be the members of different social groupings with their varied notions of justice but with a combined aspect of mutual interest that will combine to create an institution.

This brings us back to the original question namely what did Rawls mean by social world? Stewart clearly noted that Rawls in his usage of social world has presented arguments pulling in different directions.[18] Rawls and Berger and Luckmann however do have thoughts in common arguably arriving at the same conclusion that a social world needs appropriate institutions. Rawls noted that "The principles of justice must lead to a scheme of basic institutions – a social world – congenial to [the] end [of developing citizens' moral powers]."[19] Stewart as a guide defined a social world as perhaps thought of by Rawls as "a logically possible closed network of social relations between two or more agents."[20]

The question which immediately emerges – considering the variations between Berger and Luckmann and Rawls – is the critical issue of communication. Berger and Luckmann note that only face to face communication is real. Stewart suggests that Rawls perhaps must be understood as meaning that "... the social relations condition requires that at least two of the agents who inhabit a social world relate to each other interpersonally – by way of communication, conflict, cooperation, and other social relations."[21] Arguably such a broad definition of the vehicles of communication does take into account face to face communication. This suggests that each community is self-contained depending on the means of communication. A community which exclusively uses texting as the means of communication will be self-contained but will have a different structure and comprehension of themselves compared to one which relies on face-to-face communication. Arguably therefore:

> It follows from this account that we actually live in a social world – perhaps more than one, depending on how we think about individuation and closure. Social worlds may be more or less realistic, feasible, historical,

17 Berger and Luckmann, 1966, 66.
18 Stewart, 2023, 7.
19 John Rawls. 1993. *Political Liberalism*. Columbia University Press, 162, 77.
20 Stewart, 2023, 9.
21 Stewart, 2023, 10.

> utopian, and/or dystopian. They may be characterized by scarcity or plenty, disagreement or consensus, peace or war. Their inhabitants may have various social technologies: democracy, bureaucracy, laws, market systems, and so on. Social worlds may contain formal and informal social hierarchies and various distributions of wealth, status, and power.[22]

If this definition refers to States or closed communities, there is logic in it as they are self-contained and follow their own interest. However, within a State or community, diversity if not managed correctly or effectively through communication will result in a destruction of the social fabric as we are currently witnessing in the developments in the United States. Self-interest is driven in many cases by fake news or even a lack of understanding is put before the needs of a society. The result is that alignments are based on families, race or class all results for at best in an evolution or at worst revolution if the society is not well ordered. The question of politics and the mode of communication between different interest groups or communities has also been addressed by Rawls.

Stewart narrows Rawls' views down to several roles one being a practical role using mechanisms such as an appeal to reason or tolerance of others. Maintaining social cooperation on a footing of mutual respect.[23] Orientation is the second role which helps to arrange and evaluate variations in a reasonable and rational way followed by reconciliation which again rests on rational decision making. Simply put Stewart proposes that "Rawls thinks that recognizing the possibility of an ideal social order can actually help to reconcile us to our own condition."[24]

Arguably each of the roles could be defended as being reasonable and real in a time of social "calm" meaning the social order is not stressed akin of being at peace and not at war. However, currently social cohesion and the way we communicate is in a flux that is subject to ongoing change. Like in any other revolutions in the last 100 or so years we are again in the middle of a digital revolution which fundamentally changes the way we interact, communicate and simply do business. The mere fact that influencers and quick grabs on Facebook (Meta) are used to form opinions is not contributing to rational decision making needed to promote order in a social world. The issue is according to Berger and Luckmann who argued that a society needs to explain the current reality to the next one as new generations inherit the social world. The

22 Stewart, 2023, 10.

23 John Rawls. 2001. *Justice as fairness: A restatement*. Harvard University Press, 2.

24 Stewart, 2023, 12.

problem arguably is that the pre digital world is different to the digital world, that is the new generation does not understand the old social order and the old generation does not understand the new order. Hence there is no passing on of the social world. It is simply the struggle of the old generation to understand the digital world and the new generation has no real building blocks to build upon. Arguably therefore the social world is in a complete reconstruction phase. The point, however, is that the reconstruction needs to learn how the world in the past reconstructed itself in order to adapt the old to the new. This is the purpose of this book, to rely on and explain historical thinking on issues affecting the construction and maintenance of society.

The current issue therefore is how is social cohesion maintained. Arguably it can be found in Rawls' view that any socioeconomic inequality is legitimate if the disparity is "beneficial to the least-advantaged individual in such a way as to be unanimously accepted by both the least advantaged and the most advantaged individual."[25] The problem is that it does not answer the question of "why the least-advantaged individual should be willing to be penalized by unequal sharing of the cake."[26]

There is no doubt and this needs to be stated frequently that "[A]ll socially constructed universes change, and the change is brought about by the concrete actions of human beings."[27] That fundamental concrete action in the context of this book is the creation of a mechanism to collect and analyse data – the new economic God. This new mechanism has changed the very way in which economic activities are conducted and it is controlled by only a few powerful actors. This does not infer that mega-corporations – the new elite – comprehend the full expanse of the constantly evolving world of digital and data technology. However, they do comprehend a great deal about the data revolution in which they are integral, and often founding, players.[28] After all, data is the lifeblood of their operations.[29] They orchestrate the mechanical process of collecting and distributing data.[30] They arguably also engage in arbitrary

25 Antonio Abatemarco and Francesca Stroffolini. 2023. "Optimal redistribution behind the veil of ignorance." *Economia Politica* 40, no. 3, 996.

26 Abatemarco and Stroffolini, 2023, 996.

27 See Berger and Luckmann, 1966. Klaus Schwab. 2017. *The fourth industrial revolution*. Crown Currency, 134.

28 Morgan Meaker. *"My Memories Are Just Meta 's Training Data Now"*, Wired, 2021. https://www.wired.com/story/my-memories-are-just-meta-training-data-now/.

29 *See* Zuboff. 2019. stating that human experience is the data exploited by corporations to turn profit.

30 Siobhan Lyons. 2017. *"Not Bothered Who Can See Your Digital Data? You Might Have 'Surveillance Apathy'"*, ABC *News*, https://www.abc.net.au/news/2017-11-08/surveillance-apathy-attitudes-to-privacy-and-monitoring/9129992, showing how corporations collect and use data.

social de-construction, and in some cases have a misconception of privacy and data relevance to individual consumers. The effect is that the way in which data is presented manipulates the impression of what is the social world. As an example, the body image presentation will influence what consumers are buying but it also creates a rift among those who do fit the image and those who do not.

3 Online Social Networks

It is an observable fact that elites either resist or foster and support societal wellbeing in times of change. The next question is how then is the influence of the new technology driven elite overcome or at least curtailed? Foucault advocated overcoming domination through resistance to the process of subject formation. From a sociological perspective, being a social subject is the only way for meaningful social interaction to take place with others, who are also social subjects. Being a social subject does entail accepting structural constraints and the successful performance of social life presupposes social subjects confronting and collaborating with other social subjects.[31]

Practices of surveillance, elicitation, and documentation constrain behaviour precisely by making it more thoroughly knowable or known. But these new forms of knowledge also presuppose new kinds of constraints, which make people's actions visible and restricts them to speak. It is in this sense primarily that Foucault spoke of "power/knowledge."[32] When surveillance is used, online knowledge is gained, and this knowledge can be used to inform many types of online activities and institutions.

Online social networks for example generate a wealth of digital trace data that provide evidence for the formations of new spaces or the redrawing of existing spaces.[33] The observation of Boyd then Conley demonstrated that online social networks do not necessarily mirror everyday social networks but constitute their own networks with distinctive rules and patterns of

31 Mark Haugaard. 2022. "Foucault and power: a critique and retheorization." *Critical review* 34, no. 3–4, 347.

32 Gary Gutting. ed. 2005. *The Cambridge Companion to Foucault*. Cambridge University Press, 99.

33 Mehmet Kanatli. 2021. *Private Property, Freedom, and Order: Social Contract Theories from Hobbes to Rawls*. Routledge India, 23.

interaction. Individual identities can move within and across online to offline social networks, so that online realities may inform the offline realm and vice versa. This reshaping of one's experiences across online and offline social contexts is well captured in the spatial paradox termed "augmented reality".[34]

Whereas face-to-face interactions and social "situations" would traditionally guide appropriate behaviour, media developments have evolved to allow the overlapping of many previously distinct social spheres that ultimately altered the "situational geography" of social life. "Media has supported the dynamic change of social situations and roles of affiliation or 'being' (group identity), which overlap with roles of transition or 'becoming' (socialization), which then overlap with roles of authority (hierarchy)."[35] Interestingly, Europe has the world's oldest traditions of independent public-service media, founded on the belief that wholly privatised broadcast media systems cannot serve the public interest even if they are well-regulated.[36] This is an important point and gives weight to the argument that privatised social media such as X cannot serve the public interest even if it aspires to. The question therefore which should be considered is how does an existing legal institution and hence the law grasp the changing social patterns and hence behaviour.

4 The Social World and Legislation

Regulators are only beginning to scrutinise in detail how legal control is exerted on a data society, including in redressing social harm arising from institutions that "predefine patterns of conduct".[37] The question, as posed by Graber, is how does the law learn in the digital society.[38] Karqvas unconvincingly argued that there is an "amalgamation of normative and digital expectations inside the digital medium."[39] The fact is that the only digital expectations emanates from the designers of the system that is the technology giants and certainly not the law. If Kanvas were correct, then machines would develop intentions which currently is not true.

34 Kanatli, 2021, 24.

35 Kanatli, 2021, 26.

36 Rachel Griffin. 2023. "Rethinking rights in social media governance: human rights, ideology and inequality." *European Law Open* 2, no. 1, 55.

37 See Berger and Luckmann, 1966. 72.

38 Christoph B. Graber. 2021. "How the law learns in the digital society." *Law, Technology and Humans* 3, no. 2, 12.

39 Vaios Karavas. 2009. "The Force of Code: Law 's Transformation under Information-Technological Conditions." *German Law Journal* 10, no. 4, 478.

> Rather than "digital expectations," normative expectations about the behaviour of technologies should be our focus [and] the behaviour of digital technologies emerge from society and under certain conditions-may become institutionalized as law.[40]

The introduction of privacy legislation has only touched the surface in defending the personal information of data subjects. Importantly, the regulation of such institutions has not truly addressed the social impact of those that set up "predefined patterns of conduct" in order to mine personal data. Nor have such regulations taken account of the macro effect of such data mining upon economies at large. Naturally effects can vary from local to regional and global commerce. This regulatory gap needs filling to respond to the changing nature of communication, its impact upon social ordering and in shielding data targets from data miners that engage in pre-planned manipulation of that social order. Also, the ever-increasing surveillance of society needs to be questioned, specifically the question of where the boundaries of surveillance are, and the scope of personal privacy needs to be discussed.

It goes without saying that an understanding of the legislation must be garnered, and remedial efforts must be guided by analytical realism. The point Waldron and others have made is that there is a widespread awareness about the structural limits of legislation.[41] It follows that the law alone is not capable of accomplishing every task as legal rules are not self-interpreting entities. The question always is what exactly has been intended or what has been willed by the legislature? "There must always be some interpreter to associate meaning to the otherwise dead letter of their words and phrases."[42] The very point this book has made is that the historical development of society has always been reconstructed and hence the law also needs to be reconstructed to disseminate digital information embedded in a society of networks.[43]

Judicial interpretation by selection can create laws and repair laws.[44] These functions are useful in assisting and in the maintenance of a stable society. But once the equilibrium has been disturbed, like at the current time, this task has been made difficult but not impossible. To be precise, current laws are not

---

40 Graber, 2021, 12.

41 Pierluigi Chiassoni. 2019. *Interpretation without truth.* Berlin: Springer International Publishing, 257.

42 Chiassoni, 2019, 2.

43 See generally Karl-Heinz Ladeur. 2010. "Die Netzwerke des Rechts." *Netzwerke in der funktional differenzierten Gesellschaft*, 143–171.

44 Chiassoni, 2019, 2.

totally obsolete, but attention must be directed to the other functions of the law namely the ability to repair loose ends or create laws by methodological innovations. To repair loose ends and gaps an investigation of the contradictions is important and hence a socio-philosophical understanding of the current societal changes is essential for any vehicle which drives these changes like as already noted, institutions like the law and other institution such as education.

The problem is that theories authoritative or otherwise are also not self-interpreting and are "methodologically ambiguous [and] creation by selection is a 'global' phenomenon."[45] The issue is that judges are part of the system and gatekeepers of the institution of law and hence also need to understand the social reality of the current social world. The interpretive process in other words must be guided by the values of the contemporary social world. Chiassoni argues that "legislation suffers from process product ambiguity."[46] Arguably the reason is that the digital revolution demands new and innovative statutory drafting and interpretations of current statutes. A problem as Posner noted is "that the modern judge particularly in constitutional matters has very little in common with the original draftsmen"[47] The fact is that the sender and the recipient have no social connection. After all the true meaning of words depends on what the writer of the text understood at the social time of writing.

We argue that a new distinction needs to be drawn between law making and applying the law. Law making is not an instant process and laws enacted in the past 100 years are still valid laws. This does not suggest that the underlying purpose of the law has changed but as the social world has changed the interpretation and hence application of the law needs to change. The question in other words is what precisely was the will of the legislator whenever it passed a statute? Chiassoni argues that "the idea of the legislature willing a given meaning-content for its statutes is sheer fiction."[48]

This is correct insofar as the drafting of the statute and then its interpretation is disconnected by social events that is the social structure and hence meaning of society has changed. More importantly members of parliament may vote for legislation which is drafted by public servants. They have no view of what it is all about as only the relevant minister and the inner circle is "on top" of the underlying issues. In the end it is possible that members of

45 Chiassoni, 2019, 7.

46 Chiassoni, 2019, 258.

47 Posner, 1993, 104.

48 Pierluigi Chiassoni, 2019, 261.

parliament voted along party lines even if they do not understand the purpose or agree with the sections in the statute.

That said it is clear that it is not only the text that is important but also the meaning conventionally embodied in it. In addition, it also depends on the audience that the particular text is directed to as a text takes on a different meaning depending on the audience. As an example, a statute may prohibit the importation of fruit but not vegetables. A botanist classifies tomatoes as fruit and similarly peas, but the ordinary citizen does not classify tomatoes or peas as fruit. Simply put the question is which is the relevant interpretive community for the new statute as words can be clear and straight forward but as we have seen many times the social context in which words are used can be overlooked.

This is where the problem sits. How do judges today elicit the meaning of a text which was drafted say 20 yes ago? The answer is they look at the text through the eye of their socially constructed reality. Chiassoni put it in the following way:

> From a strictly theoretical standpoint, statutory norms are the meaning-contents of statutory norm-formulations. Being meaning-contents, their identification depends on the interpretation of norm-formulations. Norm-formulations do not interpret themselves; they are not self-interpreting entities.[49]

Norm-formulations to be relevant need to be guided by what is understood to be the current expression of the cultural understanding of the particular norm. This is guided by the understanding of the social world we live currently in not where we were when the statute was drafted. The words obviously can be and mostly are the same whether the literal, contextual or purposive interpretation is used, however the meaning we apply to the words is culturally guided depending on the social world we live in. Judges, lawyers, jurists or people at large are always needed to interpret words as part of their job. Their view of their personal constructed social reality will determine what meaning is allocated to statutory words. The issue is that there is no correspondence between norms and formulation as norms depend on the social meaning given to them and the formulation depends on the social world in which the norm is interpreted. Simply put statutes do not have any meaning before they are interpreted. Posner puts it in the following way:

49 Chiassoni, 2019, 263.

> … it might be better to discard the word 'interpretation' altogether and speak instead in pragmatic fashion of the consequences of competing approaches to the judicial function in statutory and constitutional cases – the approach that stresses the judge's freedom versus the approach that stresses the judges responsibility as a subordinate official in the scheme of government.[50]

The conclusion is that statutes and the law in general depend not on the words used but on the social environment in which they are interpreted hence laws have the potential to be usefully applied in any social world. Put differently interpretations of words will not be the same in all social worlds. Words are unique only in the current applicable social environment. Hence an understanding of the social world is essential for the law to formulate socially meaningful outcomes. The fact is that "computer networks are the dominant media of the twenty-first century."[51] It is the new communication medium of this century relying on language like face-to-face communications, but it is not only a person-to-person activity but a person via machine to another person. Hence it is argued that the law needs to not only regulate the age old and tested person to person communication but must also look at the machines and their functions in the communication process, and the law needs to formulate regulatory responses beyond the privacy legislations. According to Vesting, "[t]he crucial change that must be accounted for is the transition from a hierarchical/centralized culture to a heterarchical/acentric one."[52] In effect the differences in the media from letter to digital machines needs to be taken into consideration in formulating relevant laws. Ladeur point to the inescapable fact which this book has noted, namely a societal development that is driven by media, leads from the "society of individuals" to the "society of organizations" [to] the "society of networks."[53] Ladeur confirms our view that social reality is changing due to computer networks which act as hybrid sociotechnical constructs and hence the law as part of social reality needs to change and take account of the new reality. Graber describes the transfer of knowledge from the social aspect to a legal system requires two steps namely:

> The first step involves an empiric observation and description of real legal problems and an analysis of their cause from the perspective of

50 Posner, 1993, 272.

51 Thomas Vesting. 2018. *Legal theory and the media of law*. Edward Elgar Publishing, Part IV.

52 Vesting, 2018, 446.

53 Ladeur, 2010.

> social science and social theory. The second step attempts to re-import the gained insights back into the legal system with the aim of furthering the law 's improvement. Importantly, the second step presupposes a change of perspective from describing social facts (external perspective) to prescribing normative ends (internal perspective).[54]

Graber's approach corresponds to Searle's "external realism," that is, the assumption that the natural environment "exists independently of our representations of it."[55] External realism unfortunately is sometimes overlooked or not fully understood by parts of society such as the democratic system which needs to be briefly discussed.

5 Democracy

A working definition or understanding of democracy has uses as defined by Graber. He argues that a democracy is constituted through institutions, practices, mentalities, and eventually, ideologies. Popular assemblies, a measure of free speech, a strong sense of community, and mentalities including egalitarianism, personal independence, self-worth, and a refusal to be cowed by the rich, powerful, or wellborn are reflected already in the earliest literary documents from archaic Greece.[56] Since a democracy promotes equality and arguably justice, once these cornerstones are removed the collapse of democracy follows which is an important political and historical phenomenon. Unlike democratic transition, or democratic consolidation, democratic breakdown lacks a systematic theoretical explanation. From a practical perspective, the third wave of democratisation, which started in 1974, has not ended yet.[57] It is known that if the issue of "political cleavage" arises among voters then a democracy can deteriorate and while polarisation of votes can be reduced by public policies, institutional arrangements and constitutional design are also critical to maintaining a democracy.[58]

Democracy and an unbiased collective vision are critical to our social status and our social wellbeing. Threats to democracy have in the past been the

54 Graber, 2021, 19.

55 John R. Searle. 1995. *The construction of social reality*. Simon and Schuster, 150.

56 Kurt A. Raaflaub. 2007. "The breakthrough of demokratia in mid-fifth-century Athens." *Origins of democracy in ancient Greece* 105–54, 22.

57 Gangsheng Bao. 2022. *Politics of democratic breakdown*. Taylor & Francis, 5.

58 Bao, 2022, 351.

subject of revolutions. Although we currently face a threat to democracy in the digital revolution, no machine is currently intelligent according to the Turing test, *Computing Machinery and Intelligence,* 1950.[59] As the arguments develop, a shared vision among innovators is also critical for the accumulation of knowledge and is central to how we use technology.[60] While technology aspires to bring people together it can also be isolating. "Today conventional wisdom holds that technologies have brought the world addictive devices, an omnipresent surveillance panopticon, racist algorithms, and disinformation machines that exacerbate polarization, threatening to destroy democracies from within."[61]

For example, if AI fundamentally disrupts the labour market where most of us earn our livelihoods, it could expand inequalities of pay and work. The main impact could be to redistribute power and prosperity away from ordinary people and towards those controlling the data and making key corporate decisions.[62] Progress has a way of leaving many people behind unless its direction is chartered in a more inclusive way. The direction a country takes in guiding the implementation of new technology governs who wins and who loses. There is often a struggle over direction and social power determines whose favourite direction prevails.[63]

Stepping back in time, British industry emerged through a revolution based on vision. It was fueled and implemented by thousands of men (and women) of humble origins, limited education, and little inherited wealth. These people were rebels within a social order.[64] It has been argued perhaps overconfidently that while we may fear the outcomes of a digital revolution, fears about AI-driven automation are particularly overblown, and popular perceptions about the world of work being processed are largely misleading. In particular, lowering costs of production, in doing so automation can create more demand for goods and services, boosting jobs that are harder to automate.[65] The current path of AI is raising the demand for capital, highly skilled production workers, and even higher skilled services, such as from management consulting and technology companies.[66] However importantly in a high skill demand

59 Johnson and Acemoglu, 2023, 306.

60 Johnson and Acemoglu, 2023, 24.

61 Lucy Bernholz, Hélène Landemore and Rob Reich. eds. 2021. *Digital technology and democratic theory.* University of Chicago Press, 3.

62 Johnson and Acemoglu, 2023, 31.

63 Johnson and Acemoglu, 2023, 95.

64 Johnson and Acemoglu, 2023, 175.

65 Johnson and Acemoglu, 2023, 298, citing the Economist magazine April 2021.

66 Johnson and Acemoglu, 2023, 336.

economy the argument of elite overproduction needs to be kept in mind and can distort well-being and a true democratic way of life.

Human intelligence has a social aspect, and the social aspect is of particular importance in the following ways, i) necessary information for important problem solving resides in the community, ii) our reasoning is based on social communication where we develop arguments and counter arguments in the process, and iii) we gain skills and capabilities through the empathy we have for others.[67] The important point is that human intelligence derives itself from being both situational and social. The ability to understand and successfully respond to one's environment, enables individuals to fluidly adapt to changing conditions.[68] Evidence supports that democracies lead to good economic outcomes and a fairer distribution of opportunities between people. Research shows that as democracies perform better in terms of delivering economic growth, public services and stability, in these situations support for democracies grows considerably.[69] Democracies tend not only to break down oligarchies but to also constrain rulers and inculcate law-abiding behaviour.[70] However the important question in the way we live today with machines is whether an unbiased democracy exist in the modern world where false information circulates? As mentioned earlier, accurate information and education is still an important commodity in guiding decision making and in maintaining democracy.

6 Stratification and Knowledge Distribution

Looking back in time Mill's classic formulation of social-economic stratification that the "opinions and feelings of the ruling portion of the community" create and enforce "rules" that determine wealth distribution among social classes.[71] To secure a promising future, Bentham thought that the "increase in the quantity of useful knowledge possessed by the middle classes" will manifest "probable results" of "improvement in respect of health, domestic economy and personal comfort." Improvement in the conditions of the lower and middle classes was thought to bring proportionate improvement to the conditions

67 Johnson and Acemoglu, 2023, 314.
68 Johnson and Acemoglu, 2023, 313.
69 Johnson and Acemoglu, 2023, 88.
70 Johnson and Acemoglu, 2023, 93.
71 John Stuart Mill. 1884. *Principles of Political Economy: With Some of Their Applicatons to Social Philosophy*. Vol. 1. D. Appleton, 155.

of their superiors. Schools became associated with the programs of social and economic improvement.[72] Bentham's moral arithmetic echoed the numerical approach of William Petty's political arithmetic. Together they demonstrate an intensification of a numerical approach to human life and paved the way to the age of surveillance capitalism.[73]

Bentham's idea for panopticon management of public institutions was borrowed from a small factory in Russia during his visit in 1787. The factory was operated with no machines but humans who worked as if they were machines. For the remaining part of his life, Bentham stood in admiration of the model of architecture that had located an inspector where he had the "power to commence and conclude a survey of the whole establishment".[74] Lancaster's schools were in full force in the early 20th century where the conception of a teacher as a machine dispensing rewards and punishment was rewarded. Teachers were conceived as part of the "technology" of the school classroom. Lancaster emphasised that daily activities were a contribution to the economy of the country and made children useful.[75]

Making people useful was driven by the economy in most cases. A variety of organisational structures and devices both governmental and private have gradually made individual entrepreneurship a rare commodity. Stock companies, subsidies, insurance, tariffs, as well as large governmental, business, and union bureaucracies have served, among other things, to reduce individual risk and enlarge institutional predictability.[76]

The Intelligentsia arose in the 18th century. They were a class with knowledge or awareness to see that a social and political revolution is in progress, formed the largest and politically most active component of the new middle class. The Intelligentsia, however, was the predominant force of this class, in part because its knowledge inescapably exposed the weakness or irrelevance of tradition. Just as in Russia in the 19th century, however, the Intelligentsia was more rebellious than self-confident. The thought was "by its very nature unspecific, unformulated, unfixed ... sensitive to every intellectual wind from Europe, alert to the changing history of both Russia and the West. For all their dogmatism at every stage, some of the most energetic minds of the intelligentsia passed from one ideological stage often to its extreme opposite in their

72 Bruce Moghtader. 2023. *Schooling, human capital and civilization: A brief history from antiquity to the digital era.* Taylor & Francis, 149.

73 Moghtader, 2023, 148.

74 Moghtader, 2023, 145.

75 Moghtader, 2023, 150.

76 Manfred Halpern. 1963. "Afro-Asians at Moshi." *Africa Report* 8, no. 3, 55.

insistent search for a total system which should somehow resolve all the largest questions of national destiny."[77]

The Intelligentsia were new men (and women). They were often the very first in the history of their family to be literate. They often discovered their best friends at school or in a political movement, not among kin or established brotherhood or faction.[78] They were the first to trust strangers on grounds of competence or shared ideology. They were ready to trade new dogmas for the old. They were also the first publicly to confess their uncertainties. Until Gamal abd al-Nasser no Egyptian politician had begun a statement of his philosophy with the confession: "I feel that I stand before a boundless world, a bottomless sea – and a trepidation restrains me from plunging into it since, from my point of vantage, I see no other shore to head for."[79][80]

7 Conclusion

The modern social world and associated data flow carries the depersonalising and dehumanising effects of the on-demand global economy. While online social networks can satisfy some social needs, social platforms can be isolating and frustrating on many levels. It is well known that the internet can influence political participation through false claims, and it can also stifle political participation by overwhelming voters with excessive amounts of information. The media has for a long time been accused of influencing elections, but now more than ever social media has the superpower to publish content to the masses, moderate and legitimise corporate activity, promote stereotypes, add bias and all without fact checks, oversight or restrictions. By influencing social and cultural norms these factors have a direct follow-on effect for equality and justice.

Systems and approaches of governments vary across the globe and are grounded by significant historical events. While Europe, the Americas, Australia and New Zealand have been highly democratic, China has been subject to autocratic rule for centuries. China is a state structured with a centralised state power as opposed to western liberal democratic societies. While the use of digital technology and data has led to considerable concern about

77 Herbert E. Bowman. 1957. "Intelligentsia in nineteenth-century Russia." *The Slavic and East European Journal* 1, no. 1, 1.

78 See Joseph S. Nye. 2004. *Soft power: The means to success in world politics*. Public affairs.

79 Gamal Abdel Nasser. 1955. *Egypt's liberation: the philosophy of the revolution*, Public Affairs Press, 195.

80 Manfred Halpern. 1962. *Middle Eastern armies and the new middle class*. Princeton: Princeton University Press, 56.

invasion of privacy and thus resistance to its growth in the West, the Chinese government has shown tolerance to the negative impact of AI for the sake of national security and delivering better digital services. Both teaching and learning are highly dependent on clear and concise transfers of information. Education cannot be rushed and even at the most fundamental level, learning to read cannot be replaced or accelerated by a virtual simulation or replication. There are still many things in education that are multifaceted and virtual online interactions are not enough to compensate for in person interactions in certain transfers of knowledge between teachers and learners. While the online world has brought about many advantages for education such as widespread availability and access, the spread of misinformation has been a worrying development that requires oversight.

In contrast to the developments in technology moving at lightning speed, in the background the education system labors with the enormous task of developing new skills for the future while balancing inequities between participants. For example, rural and remote learners could be further marginalised if they don't have online access to current and up to date information. On the other hand, online learners in populated areas may be affected by incompetent amateurs lacking a grasp of a key skills area or just blatantly spreading misinformation. Naturally, directed government funding can correct inequalities and government institutions can assist with authorising accreditation but there is an urgent need to curb misinformation. Clearly a profit motive does not work to improve education and this observation has been endorsed by many philosophers, theorists and academics over a long period of time.

It is critical that educational institutions are protected from the tentacles of those who possess power and influence. The aim for greater wellbeing is to reduce and correct gaps in inequality, and as Bentham saw it "to secure a promising future". The principles of justice and equality must always be used in education no matter what discoveries and innovations new technology brings. New technology has become part of every students' educational milestones. It is increasingly important that vigilance is used to protect key aspects of the non-virtual world even if they are less alluring and even if they do not provide a quick answer or a quick fix.

The next question which flows from the discussion of justice, society and the individuals is how new technology such as AI affects our sense of justice.

CHAPTER 8

Justice and AI

To the extent that algorithmic regulation becomes part of legislative, judicial or other practices of law, we need to make sure that it is not merely compatible with the rule of law, but actually integrates its core principles.[1]

The Organization for Economic Co-operation and Development (OECD) has counted 700 AI policy initiatives across more than 60 countries.[2] The inescapable fact is that AI is here to stay. AI is a fast-evolving technology and has great potential to increase productivity but also to automate existing jobs. The only question is how AI will affect society and what are the safeguards protecting society from potential harm? Despite this observation the 2019 G20 leaders in Japan declared among other things that, "We will work toward achieving an inclusive, sustainable, safe, trustworthy and innovative society through digitalization and promoting the application of emerging technologies … as an enabler of economic growth, development and social well-being."[3]

The political statement is arguably based on an understanding that various mathematical algorithms under classifications such as support vector machines, decision trees and neural networks all compound to how data is treated and managed to produce the outcome and predictability required to contribute to economic growth in societies moving forward.[4] Current observations suggest that the economic growth and economic well-being for at least some has been achieved, but as this book has and is arguing, at the cost of social wellbeing despite comments to the contrary. As an example, there may be fines imposed when managers contact and insist on responses from employees outside working hours and it is no longer essential to keep your

1 Mireille Hildebrandt. 2018. "Algorithmic regulation and the rule of law." *Philosophical Transactions of the Royal Society A: Mathematical, Physical and Engineering Sciences* 376, no. 2128, 9.

2 Katharina Koerner. 2022. *"Privacy and responsible AI"*, *IAPP*, https://iapp.org/news/a/privacy-and-responsible-ai/.

3 Anon. 2019. *"Full text of the G20 Osaka leaders' declaration"*, *Japan Times*, https://www.japantimes.co.jp/news/2019/06/29/national/full-text-g20-osaka-leaders-declaration/.

4 Chaminda Hewage, Yogachandran Rahulamathavan and Deepthi Ratnayake. eds. 2023. *Data Protection in a Post-Pandemic Society: Laws, Regulations, Best Practices and Recent Solutions.* Springer, 221.

 | DOI:10.1163/9789004702691_009

channels of communication open.[5] Combined with the trend of being socially connected via the machines the question needs to be asked is this status quo the new social wellbeing? The issue as Walters *et al* have noted there is a difference between regulating AI and data protection. They argue:

> Firstly, AI, to date, has largely been regulated by the market and there is very little government regulation that sets minimum standards, in new and emerging areas. Secondly, data protection laws being a recent addition to the regulatory framework, has a specific role that provides a level of control and protection of personal data. Thirdly, there is a lack of clarity within the law about where responsibility lies within AI.[6]

Simply put while previous technological advances in automation have tended to affect "routine" tasks, AI has the potential to automate "nonroutine" tasks, exposing large new swaths of the workforce to potential disruption.[7] There is no doubt that AI will bring benefits but at the same time there are also costs posed by AI to society.

> Examples that stem directly from AI's control of information include privacy violations, creating anti-competitive environments, and behavioural manipulation by machine learning techniques that enable companies to identify and exploit biases and vulnerabilities that consumers themselves do not recognise. Further, there is the direct risk that workers will be displaced by AI via excessive automation, as there is no guarantee that the current pace of the development of AI tools will achieve the socially optimal mix of automation and augmentation of tasks. Finally, there are a number of clear ways that AI have exacerbated social problems, including issues of discrimination and concerns about the functioning of democratic governments.[8]

---

5 Daniel Ziffer. 2024. *"The right to disconnect has started, giving Australians legal cover to stop responding to emails and calls after hours"*, ABC News, https://www.abc.net.au/news/2024-08-26/what-right-to-disconnect-from-work-means-for-you/104234308.

6 Robert Walters and Matthew Coghlan. 2019. "Data Protection and Artificial Intelligence Law: Europe Australia Singapore-An Actual or Perceived Dichotomy?", *American Journal of Science, Engineering and Technology* 56.

7 See European Union, 2022. *"The Impact of Artificial Intelligence on the future of workforces in the European Union and the United States of America", European Commission.* https://digital-strategy.ec.europa.eu/en/library/impact-artificial-intelligence-future-workforces-eu-and-us.

8 See European Union, 2022.

The real issue is not what AI can do but how governments guide the choices made in the development and importantly deployment of AI. Evidence of how governments across the globe are reacting to AI is now emerging in the form of the new United States AI Bill of Rights and the European Commission Artificial Intelligence Act.

As already noted in this book an understanding of history is important. Mokyr explains that,

> ... sustained economic growth after the onset of the Industrial Revolution was not solely due to the specific inventions made but was also facilitated by our understanding and management of these inventions. While there was also economic growth before the 1750's world from inventions such as gunpowder, spectacles, and the mechanical clock, this growth was not sustained because of a lack of understanding and management of these technologies.[9]

The still open question is how much does society understand about the consequences of the current era of AI and how can we best harness its enormous potential for sustained economic growth? The importance in answering the question is the fact that "there is no guarantee that the current pace of the development of AI tools will achieve the socially optimal mix of automation and augmentation of task."[10] Issues such as automation versus augmentation of tasks and profit maximation versus socially desirable directions need to be resolved as an unfettered AI would result in less just outcomes hence damaging social institutions including democracy. In addition, another potential downside "of AI is that it could raise ethical concerns as AI technology increasingly begins to impact our human lives in ways that we may not be comfortable with."[11] A further question is whether AI will increase the current economic inequalities by simply increasing the wealth pump?

These concerns are real, and the maintenance of justice as noted by Rawls as well as how a society needs to be constructed as explained by Berger and Luckmann take on increased urgency and hence the importance to analyse the effects is a timely task. The current issue is that there are "conceptual ambiguities"[12] in the language surrounding AI and ambiguity in ethics in particular.

9 Joel Mokyr. 2005. "Economic growth was not a novelty in 1800. In a celebrated passage." *The Journal of Economic History* 65, no. 2, 285–351.

10 See European Union, 2022.

11 See European Union, 2022.

12 Thomas M. Powers and Jean-Gabriel Ganascia. 2020. "The Ethics of the Ethics of AI." *The Oxford handbook of ethics of AI*, 29.

Emerging legislation across the globe attempts to reduce some of this ambiguity, making it an appropriate source of definitions.[13]

To do so it is essential to define AI for the purpose of this book. The OECD defines an AI system thus:

> … an AI system is a machine-based system that is capable of influencing the environment by producing an output (predictions, recommendations, or decisions) for a given set of objectives. It uses machine and/or human-based data and inputs to (i) perceive real and/or virtual environments; (ii) abstract these perceptions into models through analysis in an automated manner (e.g., with machine learning), or manually; and (iii) use model inference to formulate options for outcomes. AI systems are designed to operate with varying levels of autonomy[14]

To put it briefly "AI has also been categorized on its intelligence level, such as artificial general intelligence, which is a notional form of AI that, exhibits a level of intelligence comparable to that of the human mind. It has also been defined quite narrowly as a technology that solves specific tasks."[15] This is an interesting point to note in the context of the media reports that sometimes exaggerate the ability of AI and influence the public to believe that it is more powerful than it is.

There is also a need to briefly explain why it is essential to distinguish between an AI system and an AI agent as both perform different functions. The EU's AI Act defines an AI system as:

> … software that is developed with [specific] techniques and approaches … and can, for a given set of human-defined objectives, generate outputs such as content, predictions, recommendations, or decisions influencing the environments they interact with,[16] [and an

13 Morten Bay. 2023. "Participation, prediction, and publicity: avoiding the pitfalls of applying Rawlsian ethics to AI." AI and Ethics: 1–10.

14 The White House. 2021. *"An economic study prepared in response to the US-EU Trade and Technology Council Inaugural Joint Statement"*, https://www.whitehouse.gov/cea/written-materials/2022/12/05/the-impact-of-artificial-intelligence/.

15 Walters and Coghlan, 2019, 56.

16 See European Commission. 2021. Laying Down Harmonised Rules on Artificial Intelligence (Artificial Intelligence Act) and Amending Certain Union Legislative Acts, https://eur-lex.europa.eu/legal-content/EN/TXT/?uri=celex%3A52021PC0206.

> AI] "agent implements a function that maps percept sequences to actions."[17]

There is no debate that AI is increasingly integrated into everyday life and the threshold question is how does it affect the social fabric of society? It is argued here and by other authors that:

> The need to align AI systems with human morality and values is already salient for applications such as automated vehicles, online content recommender systems, and social robots. It also extends to more powerful types of AI that are expected to take on increasingly important economic and social functions in the future.[18]

In addition to testing Rawls' theory the European Union (EU) has commenced to introduce AI regulation. This is an interesting point as Rawls once expressed skepticism about the moral status of the European Union (EU). In the past EU scholars have either ignored Rawls or rather uncritically established positive links between his theory of domestic and international justice and the EU.[19]

As with all developments the law is always reactive to issues which emerge. The point is that in this case AI has been invented, offered for sales and further developed before being regulated. It is here for all to see or experience. This is potentially a very dangerous situation and the issue which is of paramount importance is that legislation has to be put in place in order to prevent the AI systems from swallowing up justice. In simple terms "we are missing a moral framework of justice altogether when it comes to evaluating the practices that constitute artificial intelligence."[20] The important question which needs to be worked out by the legislators and the courts is the question of responsibility if AI is in breach of a law or moral issues affecting justice. As an example, when an AI driven car causes personal or material damage, who is bearing the responsibility to pay damages. For all intended purposes of having an AI controlled car the driver is not driving the car it is the system or program which is

---

17 See Stuart J. Russell and Peter Norvig. 2016. *Artificial intelligence: a modern approach*. Pearson.

18 Laura Weidinger, Kevin R. McKee, Richard Everett, Saffron Huang, Tina O. Zhu, Martin J. Chadwick, Christopher Summerfield and Iason Gabriel. 2023. "Using the Veil of Ignorance to align AI systems with principles of justice." *Proceedings of the National Academy of Sciences* 120, no. 18: e2213709120, 1.

19 See Menno R. Kamminga. 2014. "Rawls and the European Union." *Philica*: 425.

20 Le Bui, Matthew and Safiya Umoja Noble. 2020. "We're missing a moral framework of justice in artificial intelligence." *The Oxford handbook of ethics of AI*, 163.

doing so. Hence is it the programmer or the seller of the car or the manufacturer who will be responsible? A simple answer is that the "owner" of the car is responsible, but this is not what might be termed a satisfactory answer as it ignores manufacturers liabilities.

In simple terms, the issues of liability and responsibility have not yet been worked out as well as "we are missing a moral framework of justice altogether when it comes to evaluating the practices that constitute artificial intelligence."[21] Where are we standing in relation to legislation?

1 European Union AI Legislation

The EU has already issued guidelines in order to draft an AI Act. The EU has recognised that "the same elements and techniques that power the socio-economic benefits of AI can also bring about new risks or negative consequences."[22] The stated aim therefore is that any regulation needs to be human centric and be a force for good in society. Importantly the commission noted:

> The proposed AI regulation ensures that Europeans can trust what AI has to offer. While most AI systems pose limited to no risk and can contribute to solving many societal challenges, certain AI systems create risks that we must address to avoid undesirable outcomes.[23]

The EU commission has specifically noted that AI systems are not always transparent, and it may not always be possible how to determine AI arrived at a particular result considering the question whether AI can always distinguish between facts and fiction that is fake news. It is not always the distinction, which is important, but the output AI is asked to achieve. An example is GPT-3. DALL-E which "can create images that it has never 'seen' but that fit the text description with which it was prompted."[24] How is the innocent bystander able to realise that the image is real and not fictitious? In this example AI is not alone as we have seen political leaders are very able to spread false facts to serve their own ends.

Importantly the commission understood that current data protection laws provide some protection, but they are insufficient to do so in relation to the

21 Le Bui and Noble, 2020, 163.

22 See European Commission. 2021.

23 See European Commission. 2021.

24 The White House, 2021, 7.

challenges AI might generate.[25] The commission is aware that just because there is a dark side to AI, the advantages are also a feature of AI. "AI should not subordinate, deceive or manipulate humans, but should instead complement and augment their skills".[26] These include assistance that AI might give to decision making under multiple uncertainties. AI use in the courts is an example that has been discussed where AI might be helpful to judges dealing in highly complex cases.

One aspect is obvious, namely that technology is beneficial but at the same time also has a disadvantageous side. The commission noted:

> This poses several challenges for policymakers. One example illustrated in the report is that much of the development and adoption of AI is intended to automate work instead of augmenting it. Private firms advancing AI technology are likely to do so in a direction that maximizes profits, which may not be the socially desirable direction. Another example is that AI increases the ability of employers to monitor workers. In sum, while the potential benefits of AI for labor markets are numerous, unfettered AI could also result in a less democratic and less fair labor market.[27]

To understand the complexities of AI the commission undertook a stakeholder consultation and a "total, 1215 contributions were received, of which 352 were from companies or business organisations/associations, 406 from individuals (92%individuals from EU), 152 on behalf of academic/research institutions, and 73 from public authorities ... in favour of the risk-based approach."[28]

The Commission envisaged to implement three categories first in Title II prohibited practices differentiating between AI that create (i) an unacceptable risk (ii) a high risk, and (iii) limited risk and (iv) low or minimal risk.[29] The unacceptable risk includes that "All AI systems considered a clear threat to the safety, livelihoods and rights of people will be banned, from social scoring by governments to toys using voice assistance that encourages dangerous behaviour."[30]

25 See European Commission. 2021.

26 Georgios Petropoulos. 2022. *Bruegel "The dark side of artificial intelligence: manipulation of human behaviour"*, https://www.bruegel.org/blog-post/dark-side-artificial-intelligence-manipulation-human-behaviour.

27 The White House, 2021, 16.

28 See European Commission. 2021.

29 European Commission. 2021.

30 European Commission. 2023. *"Shaping Europe's digital future"*, https://digital-strategy.ec.europa.eu/en/policies/regulatory-framework-ai.

High-risk include AI technology used in:

> … critical infrastructures (e.g. transport), that could put the life and health of citizens at risk; educational or vocational training, that may determine the access to education and professional course of someone's life (e.g. scoring of exams);
> safety components of products (e.g. AI application in robot-assisted surgery);
> employment, management of workers and access to self-employment (e.g. CV-sorting software for recruitment procedures);
> essential private and public services (e.g. credit scoring denying citizens opportunity to obtain a loan);
> law enforcement that may interfere with people's fundamental rights (e.g. evaluation of the reliability of evidence);
> migration, asylum and border control management (e.g. verification of authenticity of travel documents);
> administration of justice and democratic processes (e.g. applying the law to a concrete set of facts).[31]

Limited risk is termed as:

> … referring to AI systems with specific transparency obligations. When using AI systems such as chatbots, users should be aware that they are interacting with a machine so they can take an informed decision to continue or step back.[32]

Minimal or no risk:

> Allows the free use of minimal-risk AI. This includes applications such as AI-enabled video games or spam filters. The vast majority of AI systems currently used in the EU fall into this category.[33]

The Commission also prepared a report in relation to the effect AI would have on the workforce.[34] The importance does not so much rest on the workforce

31 European Commission, 2023.
32 European Commission, 2023.
33 European Commission, 2023.
34 European Commission, 2022.

as such but on the effects on society if AI significantly reduces employment hence institutional and policy decisions need to be envisaged.

No doubt other countries are grappling with the same issue like in Australia where it is argued that an ethical framework for AI has to be constructed. The Australian Law Council proposed an ethical framework comprising of eight core principles namely:

(a) the rapid development of AI and related technologies is in many respects outpacing the legal and regulatory frameworks necessary to guide and govern them, giving rise to risks that the privacy and other fundamental rights of individuals may be placed at risk;

(b) an ethics framework for AI should be rights-based and strongly grounded in overarching principles, including those drawn from international human rights law, and subject to principles of the rule of law and procedural fairness;

(c) to be effective and consistently applied, an ethics framework must be enforceable. Further, careful discussion is required regarding potential models of an enforcement mechanism, which may vary between contexts;

(d) establishment of a regulatory body should be carefully considered to provide oversight of AI systems and their development and use;

(e) accountability and liability associated with the development, implementation and use of AI systems should be determined so as to provide remedies in cases where damage is caused, and to allow for appropriate scrutiny by the Courts; and

(f) greater distinction (and further discussion) is needed between public and private sector applications of AI, noting the different principles of administrative law which apply particularly to decision-making by government organisations and other public sector entities.[35]

In order to achieve an ethics-based AI system a multi-disciplinary group would need to be tasked to devise a robust framework an effective data governance. That framework would need to be in line with international developments, notably the EU as noted above and be aware that a clear distinction is drawn between significant and insignificant risks. It is also obvious that a regulatory framework needs to be put in place to guarantee that an AI system operates only in clearly defined spaces. A point to note is that currently it has not been clearly established what AI can do that is the full extent of its capacity is not

35 Department of Industry, Innovation and Science. 2019. *"Artificial Intelligence: Australia's Ethics Framework"*, https://lawcouncil.au/publicassets/afebc52d-afa6-e911-93fe-005056be13b5/3639%20-%20AI%20ethics.pdf, 6.

yet been explored. However, the important point is that ethical considerations must be front and center of all considerations in controlling the application of AI. As Brownword noted,

> There is a universal responsibility for all humans to avoid catastrophic development of, or applications, of AI. The applications of AI might or might not be in line with our personal preferences: but in Europe, the applications have to be compatible with our fundamental rights; and, everywhere, applications of AI must be compatible with respect for the global commons.[36]

1.1 *Ethical Considerations*

The problem with an ethics based approach is that it needs to create a balance between the "political realities of surveillance"[37] The issue that the risk of an unfettered AI must be overcome through risk-based models of regulations namely "one concerned with better compliance [of data protection regulations] and one concerned with the determination of which Artificial Intelligence (AI) systems should be regulated."[38] Arguably governments have invested efforts to regulate one part of the problem namely the protection of data and its collection and use by technology giants in particular but the ethics component is only slowly finding some traction. Gry Hasselbalch was correctly noting that:

> Today we all have a digital 'data double' abstracted from the human body that can potentially be used for purposes of scrutiny and control by governments, sold for profit in commercial interchanges and also targeted by direct acts of digital violence and abuse.[39]

The problem is that the socially constructed identity of people has been compromised, that is it cannot be kept private as the digital world has penetrated

---

36 Roger Brownsword. 2022. "AI and Fundamental Rights: The People, the Conversations, and the Governance Challenges." In *International Conference on the Legal Challenges of the Fourth Industrial Revolution*, Cham: Springer International Publishing, 353.

37 Zygmunt Bauman and David Lyon. 2013. *Liquid surveillance: A conversation*. John Wiley & Sons, 20.

38 R.M. Gellert. 2021. "*The role of the risk-based approach in the General data protection Regulation and in the European Commission's proposed Artificial Intelligence Act. Business as usual?*" Journal of Ethics and Legal Technology, 15.

39 Gry Hasselbalch. 2021. *Data ethics of power: a human approach in the big data and AI era*. Edward Elgar Publishing, 33.

everybody's life either for the better or the worse. Hence the importance of introducing ethics into the workings of AI specifically is important. As this book relies on Rawls his definition of ethics is appropriately used namely:

> The two main concepts of ethics are those of the right and the good: the concept of a morally worthy person is, I believe, derived from them. The structure of an ethical theory is, then, largely determined by how it defines and connects these two basic notions.[40]

The key issue is that a morally based decision mechanism needs to be used in the shaping and control of AI. Importantly the Kantian notion of moral responsibility was connected with duty and obligation, "There is nothing it is possible to think of anywhere in the world, or indeed anything at all outside it, that can be held to be good without limitation, excepting only a good will".[41] Morality also has to be informed by the culture of a society producing a rights-based approach trying to balance the power structures between stakeholders. The problem is that on one side technology which is not value neutral is pitted against a society which is also not value neutral. Put differently, a balance needs to be achieved between morality and the desire to make a profit. Arguably cybersecurity and government legislation are possibly the first approach to introduce ethics into the debate. "Cyber security practices essentially protect the integrity, functionality, and reliability of organizations that rely upon such data and systems."[42] The important point is that systems to control AI cannot be over complicated or under resourced and hence it also needs to be understood that cybersecurity is a form of risk management not all risks can be eliminated and hence breaches can occur. It is an ethical duty to disclose to users when a breach has occurred or if the company discovers a critical vulnerability in their system. It allows customers to make informed decisions to minimise any perceived risks. Simply put "Cybersecurity professionals and organizations should adopt procedures for rigorously evaluating the compliance of their members with the applicable ethical cyber security obligations."[43] Simply put ethical principles guide human conduct and while

40 Rawls, 1971, 21.

41 See I. Kant. 2018. "Grundwork for the Metaphysics of Morals (Wood, WA, ed. and transl.)".

42 Swiss Cyber Institute. 2021. *"A Holistic Approach to Ethical Issues in Cyber Security"*, https://swisscyberinstitute.com/blog/a-holistic-approach-to-ethical-issues-in-cyber-security/.

43 Swiss Cyber Institute, 2021.

technology may copy ethical behaviour this does not mean that machines can make decisions that will be correct every time.

In sum the effect is that AI which is part of the sociotechnical system needs to be – at least –the subject of close government supervision. Experts are warning not enough is being done to educate young people about the dangers of using the technology to create explicit content.[44]

2 The Sociotechnical System

The digital revolution must be put into context as it is part of the sociotechnical system hence subject to political theory. However political theory "brackets out technological considerations, treating them as exogenous to the fundamental questions of political life."[45] The control and hence the answer to order social life is left to economic approach to law applying the overarching principle of justice and a political-ethical norm.[46] Courts are well versed in dispensing justice by applying three tools namely corrective justice, retributive and procedural justice. It appears that in the case of ordering an economic problem corrective justice appears to be best placed to do so.

Interestingly Rawls only in his explanation of the requirements of justice does place technology within the parameters of understanding and applying justice, he noted:

> But even holding firm to the priority of the basic liberties and fair equality of opportunity, there is no reason why this initial acknowledgement should be final. Society should take into account economic efficiency and the requirements of organization and technology.[47]

This is true but at the same time it calls into question the fact that as Rawls notes:

> Among the essential features of this situation is that no one knows his place in society, his class position or social status, nor does anyone know

44 Lincoln Russell. 2024. ABC News, *"AI pornographic images of school students shared by peers"*, https://www.abc.net.au/news/2024-02-26/concerns-over-non-consensual-images-school-students/103512190.

45 Iason Gabriel. 2022. "Toward a theory of justice for artificial intelligence." *Daedalus* 151, no. 2, 218.

46 Posner, 1993, 313.

47 Rawls, 1971, 130.

> his fortune in the distribution of natural assets and abilities, his intelligence, strength, and the like. ... The principles of justice are chosen behind a veil of ignorance.[48]

In reality this is less and less correct as everybody understands their social standing and hence the veil of ignorance is questionable. However, as a theoretical model or starting point for further elaborations it has merits.

With AI as a new and yet untested technology in light of creating a socially constructed reality the question is whether AI and justice are incompatible and calls to the contrary are misplaced.[49] The most important reason is that AI will affect the structure of society and hence previous social norms and the way in which we live will always include issues of justice and will always be in the forefront of considerations. The point is that AI controls or at least influences our lives but at the same AI is man made and hence it has its owners and hence controllers. Clearly, the power to shape and influence the path of technological change is not distributed evenly across individuals or society. Nonetheless, choices about the content and character of new technologies are being made.[50] Not surprising that Gabriel argues that:

> ... the basic structure of society is best understood as a composite of sociotechnical systems: that is, systems that are constituted through the interaction of human and technological elements. The claim here is not only that the basic structure contains social and technical elements, but also that these elements interact dynamically to constitute new forms of stable institutional practice and behavior.[51]

The problem with the above argument is that here is no distinction made between the interaction of humans and humans' interaction with technological elements. The distinction that this book makes is that the issue and the effect on society because of the digital revolution has changed the interaction between humans and hence the social reality of everyday life has been altered. As Berger and Luckmann noted, only the face-to-face situation in the fullest sense is real. The interaction between sociotechnical systems and the interaction of humans with digital assets is not real as it is spatial and not flexible. However, it is correct to argue that sociotechnical systems including AI must

---

48 Rawls, 1971, 11.

49 Gabriel, 2022, 219.

50 Gabriel, 2022, 219.

51 Gabriel, 2022, 220.

be subject to principles of justice. The problem is that “AI interacts with the behaviour of human decision-makers to shape the character of these practices, including how they distribute benefits and burdens across the population.”[52] That interaction is devoid of human contact, that is, it is governed or “controlled” by AI and hence there is the problem of an emerging “feedback loop of injustice” resulting in situations where “marginalized groups face higher levels of data collection when they access public benefits … [which] acts to reinforce their marginality when it is used to target them for suspicion and extra scrutiny.”[53] We now see new terms emerging such as digital redlining – with entire groups of people encountering new barriers to opportunity–and the emergence of what, with respect to race, sociologist Ruha Benjamin terms “the New Jim Code.”[54]

In Australia the “ROBO debts” scandal was an example where vulnerable social welfare recipients were wrongly accused of “scamming” the system.[55] Arguably here lies the problem namely that too much emphasis is given to machine determination without fully understanding the systems and hence the human input is reduced with the effect that justice is not served. Rawls understood that institutions must be regulated as institutions do not have a sense of justice and fairness unless people operating the systems instill and maintain at least a “background justice over time.”[56] Market forces are not currently checked enough or made subject to distributive justice which in effect is the problem faced by society due to the digital revolution. Class structures and belonging to a group within a society has been disturbed. Rawls was correct to note that:

> The primary subject of justice, as I have emphasized, is the basic structure of society. The reason for this is that its effects are so profound and pervasive, and present from birth. This structure favors some starting places over others in the division of the benefits of social cooperation.[57]

---

52 Gabriel, 2022, 221.

53 Virginia Eubanks. 2018. *Automating inequality: How high-tech tools profile, police, and punish the poor*. St. Martin 's Press, 6–7.

54 Safiya Umoja Noble. 2019. Algorithms of Oppression: How Search Engines Reinforce Racism. New York University Press, 2018. *Why Popular Culture Matters:* 166.

55 The Royal Commission into the Robodebt Scheme. 2023. https://robodebt.royalcommission.gov.au/.

56 Rawls, 2001, 10.

57 Rawls, 1971, 82.

As Berger and Luckmann, and Rawls explained it is the basic structure of society which is the "birthplace" of justice. The issue this book discusses is that the basic structure of society has been disturbed and currently there is no "replacement", or a new appropriate structure being developed. Arguably we are living in a fractured society which is out of balance and therefore institutions by definition have lost the starting point in deciding the benefits for social cooperation.

The problem is that Rawls' aspirational goals namely that justice would "secure common status of equal citizenship"[58] and also institutions must be "effectively and impartially administered,"[59] does not correspond with reality. Tommie Shelby and others have noted that "administration or enforcement of rules and procedures [by institutions] is frequently distorted by the racial prejudice and bias of its officials."[60] One only needs to examine policing in the US to find confirmation of conduct which is not corresponding to justice. The question is whether AI and that is automated decision making would perform better given that the "memory" of AI must be based on a data base hence creating a host of new concerns.

Simply put the fact is that every society is structured according to a class system. Rawls understood this fact when he suggested that "it is perhaps impossible to give a complete specification of these liberties independent from the particular circumstances–social, economic and technological–of a given society."[61] Given the fact that we live in a data society that is collected data is the stock of knowledge AI and other systems rely on to make decisions the question is whether data protection legislation will be sufficiently authoritative for AI to protect privacy. The problem is that privacy as well as unwanted interference are the price society appears to be willing to forgo. The desire to be connected is stronger than the desire to maintain personal privacy and hence this lessens the "ability to control what aspects of yourself you reveal to others"[62] has been traded away. Gabriel is correct to note that "the basic liberties may now include protection against invasive forms of surveillance or behavioral manipulation."[63]

58 Rawls, 1971, 199.

59 Rawls, 1971, 48.

60 Tommie Shelby. 2003. "Race and social justice: Rawlsian considerations." *Fordham Law Review* 72, 1706.

61 Rawls, 1971, 54.

62 See Andrei Marmor. 2015. "What is the right to privacy?" *Philosophy and Public Affairs* 43 (1), 3–26.

63 Gabriel, 2022, 224.

The common thread of current debates on AI for example is the focus on safeguarding the social fabric through appropriate legislation. The EU Commission is well aware of the issues which will be faced by an unchecked proliferation of AI. This effort is akin to the drafting of the data protection legislation. It protects users of digital technology from unwanted intrusion into their privacy. But as already noted above it has done very little to protect the social fabric of society. Indeed, the face-to-face conversations are being replaced by texting or e-mailing which according to Berger and Luckmann affects the structure of a society.

However, the issue is that the response to the EU commission it is not encouraging as only 1215 submissions on the proposed legislation were received. As already noted above the power to influence the workings of a society happens on three levels. It is critical that all three levels have an input on proposed changes, first the government, secondly corporations and thirdly the people. Reverting to Rawls it is obvious that submissions to government are not made by people behind the veil of ignorance. Rather, many of the submissions are made by interested groups advancing their own interests. Naturally this has an influence on the outcome of decisions that are made.

The question is whether it is the individuals at the grassroots level which in a functioning society will influence the powerful elite or whether the elite, not acting behind the veil of ignorance, are guided by their own interests. Importantly research has shown that Rawls is of utility and sets a point from where serious investigations can emerge. It is not whether Rawls was correct or not which is important but rather whether society and hence justice and fair conduct will still be guiding the construction of a reality in the fifth revolution. It is obvious – and has been demonstrated in this book that society is not a stagnant immovable entity. Reality is socially constructed and if reality changes so will the culture of society. A new socially constructed reality will be set in place. It is important to be aware that legislation such as protection of privacy and now the proposed regulation of AI must also be taken as altering how humans interacted with each other.

Hence the importance of Rawls lies in the fact that he makes us aware that social wellbeing must go hand in hand with the limitations imposed on the controllers of the new systems in order to preserve the culture of societies which need to adapt to the new reality of the fourth revolution.

It is therefore not correct to argue that Rawls proposed the "Veil of Ignorance (VoI) as a thought experiment to identify fair principles for governing a society."[64] Rawls rather proposed the bottom-up approach not the top-down approach that is society determines justice and fairness which then is used to draft relevant legislations to govern the AI systems. In brief, the Proceedings of the National Academy of Sciences research selected 2,508 participants to elicit principles to align AI systems. The important point is to proactively create principles based on morality and fairness which will ultimately guide the courts and parliament to govern AI systems.

Two approaches have been advocated namely a morally "instituitionist" in character approach or secondly a "theory-led approach, starting with a preferred moral and then reflectively maps out the implications of that theory for AI."[65] These two approaches have been criticised for lack of support over different belief systems as a moral theory can be tainted and influenced by personal bias. Rawls' approach instead of using morality looks at fair principles and what is just. It has been argued that the veil of ignorance suggests that people "do not know how the various alternatives will affect their own particular case [...] they are obliged to evaluate principles solely on the basis of general considerations and thus to deliberate impartially when selecting principles for society as a whole."[66]

For Rawls, it was crucial that such a well-ordered society should be realistically possible and not utopian. Taking humans at their best, a well-ordered society should be stable and enduring since its principles and requirements are compatible with "our moral sensibility and natural inclinations."[67]

Testing Rawls' theory a study using game theory and AI observed three effects:

> First, participants behind the veil of ignorance more often choose principles favouring the worst-off, relative to those in the control condition. Second, converging with Rawls' idea of a "reflective equilibrium," participants who experienced the Veil of ignorance more often endorse their choice upon reflection than participants in a control condition. Third, when explaining their reasoning, participants in the veil of ignorance

64 Weidingera, McKeea, Everetta, Huanga, Zhua, Chadwicka, Summerfield and Gabriela, 2023, 1.

65 See Weidingera, McKeea, Everetta, Huanga, Zhua, Chadwicka, Summerfield and Gabriela, 2023.

66 Rawls, 1971, 136–137.

67 Freeman, 2023, 1.

> condition more often make unprompted reference to fairness-based concepts.[68]

As noted above, artificial intelligence algorithms and game theory concepts are increasingly applied to test human behaviour. Hutan Ashrafian argues that "well-curated data offering analytical insights for necessarily complex human behaviours and activities, [and] this would allow decisions to be made for the benefit of societies and citizens based on rigorous objective information devoid of the traditional approach of choosing policies and societal values based on the opinion of a handful of selected representatives who may be exposed to a lack of comprehensive data analysis capacity and subject to personal biases."[69]

One could assume that Rawls was correct in his assumptions because he also noted that "The veil of ignorance is so thick that rational individuals cannot acquire information about facts that can affect their choices and thus will prefer the principles of justice as fairness."[70] This leads to the argument that participants behind the veil of ignorance took a holistic view as everybody functions within a perceived reality and the veil of ignorance allows participants to make decisions outside their lived experience but behind the veil of ignorance. The control group – that is the elite – in effect understand their position and are viewing any situation in an endeavour to be at least no worse off. In effect there is a strong and clear argument which plays out, for example, a person agreeing strongly with a migrant intake but not in my neighbourhood. The undeniable fact that every human has a socially constructed reality, and all decisions humans make are influenced by their own reality. However, this does not mean that Rawls' theory is not of utility.

Arguably the drafting of legislation could and should be influenced by decisions made behind the veil of ignorance. As such fairness-based concepts will find their way into legislation which after all are binding on society as a whole. However, in any society two issues must not be confused. Human interaction and institutionalisation. Institutionalisation takes place though habitualised actions by special types of actors.[71] A class of people therefore is an institution loosely bound together by similar actions. Hence every actor in an institution will be able to predict the others actions otherwise they would not be part of

68 Weidingera, McKeea, Everetta, Huanga, Zhua, Chadwicka, Summerfield and Gabriela, 2023.

69 Hutan Ashrafian. 2023. "Engineering a social contract: Rawlsian distributive justice through algorithmic game theory and artificial intelligence." *AI and Ethics* 3, no. 4, 1447.

70 Rawls, 1971, 23.

71 Berger and Luckmann, 1966, 72.

an institution. Berger and Luckmann also conclude that "two individuals are constructing a background, in a sense discussed before, which will serve to stabilise both their separate actions and their interaction … in other words a social world will be in process of construction containing within the roots of an expanding institutional order."[72] Therefore it is important to at least gain an understanding of how habitualisation works.

3 Habitualisation

Habitualisation describes how "any action that is repeated frequently becomes cast into a pattern which can be … performed again in the future in the same manor and with the same economic effort."[73] Habitualisation can have both positive and negative effects.

If we return to Rawls' theory specifically the notion of the veil of ignorance being so thick that rational individuals cannot acquire information about facts that can affect their choices indicates that interaction between others needs to take place. Thus, habitualisation will take place that is it provides direction and solutions and is relieving the accumulation of tensions that result from undirected drives.[74] As everybody is behind a veil of ignorance one would assume that an interaction needs to take place by people who then will form an institution. Rawls assumes that the natural outcome of the actors behind the veil of ignorance will naturally turn to fair outcomes and hence just outcomes. However, the point is that a social order needs to take place within an institution which is the result of human activity. The social order is not only a homogenous just outcome it can also be a hierarchy based on status. Even a criminal organisation has a social order which may not be socially accepted by another institution.

At present, we are witnessing a shift in the veil of ignorance that Rawls referred to. It is obvious that the outcome of any activity is in the end subject to habitualisation,[75] which in Rawls' theory is expressed in the desire to form institutions based on fair outcomes. In effect the background of habitualised activity in this case arriving at just and fair outcomes 'opens up a foreground

72 Berger and Luckmann, 1966, 75.
73 See Berger and Luckmann, 1966.
74 Berger and Luckmann, 1966, 71.
75 Berger and Luckmann, 1966, 70.

for deliberation and innovation.'[76] Overall and importantly humans need to interact for habitualisation to occur.

Given the effects of roles humans play and the effect of habitualisation within an institutional body suggests that Rawls' theory on a macro level is correct. However, it is argued that Rawls' theory is lacking once institutions meet and compete with each other. As an example, on a building project the workers are told by management to work harder to finish the project on time. After it is finished management receives a bonus whereas the workers receive nothing materially for the hard work. It is clear that fairness and justice does not prevail, if we look from the workers point of view at the bonus system however management sees it differently as in their opinion the bonus rewards their leadership. Not surprisingly industry developers in AI have adopted Rawls' theory of fairness due to its perceived simplicity specifically the notion of the veil of ignorance.[77]

The preliminary conclusion which can be drawn is that Rawls is correct on a higher level in his theory of how justice and fairness is being developed. What is missing is the realisation that institutions are formed, and they form a hierarchy. In each level of the hierarchy, the institutions develop their own social reality fitting their experience, hence habitualisation will form their perception of what is real that is what is just for the members of the institution. The question is how is the interplay between the different hierarchies affecting justice and fairness for the whole society? That is what roles do individuals play in the interplay with institutions? Not surprising the "unholy marriage" between AI developers and the theory of fairness developed by Rawls has been questioned elsewhere as well as in this book as the question of a fairness loophole needs to be answered.

4 The Fairness Loophole

The view of Rawls' that amongst other things technology is fair if the result is maximised for the least advantaged. The problem as noted above is that even if all of a society is advantaged not all may be equally advantaged which brings into question the issue of fairness and justice. Jørgensen and Søgaard use AI combined with natural language processing (AI/NLP) as an example to test the fairness used in the development of the system and its social impact. They note

76 Berger and Luckmann, 1966, 71.

77 See Anna Katrine Jorgensen and Anders Søgaard. 2023. "Rawlsian AI fairness loopholes." *AI and Ethics* 3, no. 4: 1185–1192.

that speech recognition works best for some languages specifically English and also for young men.[78] What is the effect of these facts on the industry?

> Industry players – and to some extent, research labs – target the most ready adoption-ready groups in society–often young, urban men in the US and Europe–trying to get products out as fast as possible, leveraging the fact that resources are widely available for English, and that return on investment will presumably be larger for these groups. Only secondarily, technologies are transferred to or scaled up to other groups and languages, often in trimmed down versions and with lower performance.[79]

Natural language processing (NLP) refers to the branch of computer science and more specifically, the branch of artificial intelligence or AI concerned with giving computers the ability to understand text and spoken words in much the same way human beings can.[80] AI/NLP as noted above works best for the young urban English-speaking group but at best terrible for other groups. The result is quite obviously named a justice gap which exists by design driven by the profit motive. In addition, the second driving force by developers of systems is that systems need loyal users to create an active market. Hence the trials to optimise the system will concentrate on what is perceived to be best for the market and this leads to further inequalities. Out of target groups such as the elderly are of no interest to developers. Jørgensen and Søgaard argue that "Subgroup Test Ballooning and Snapshot-Representative Evaluation are unjust practices."[81]

The problem is that too often Rawls is quoted but the result is that in many AI areas of development there is no correspondence to fairness or welfare. In its simplest form the Rawlsian principle of justice and fairness must not be equally beneficial but the benefit for the least advantaged group must be maximised. Maximisation must be understood to mean that the performance floor of the least advantaged group is raised. Another unanswered question of course is what is a group? There are of course accepted natural definition of groups such as gender and race.

If we look again at the AI/NLP system only the target group maximises the advantages of the system and all other groups are less or not at all advantaged.

---

78 Jørgensen and Søgaard, 2022, 1.

79 Jørgensen and Søgaard, 2022, 1.

80 Jim Holdsworth. 2024. *"What is natural language processing (NLP)?", IBM*, https://www.ibm.com/topics/natural-language-processing.

81 Jørgensen and Søgaard, 2022, 2.

What has been often overlooked is the fact that Rawlsian fairness often tolerates considerable inequalities.[82] The maximising performance has been met if the lowest performing group is better off than before. It does not negate the fairness principle despite the fact that another group is tenfold better off as only the relative position of the disadvantaged group is important and not their absolute position. Jørgensen and Søgaard argued that the Rawlsian Difference Principle "is too permissive to prevent common AI/NLP practices that actively contribute to global and social inequality gaps. Examples as mentioned earlier include test-ballooning technologies on specific target groups that are known to be adoption ready, or evaluation technologies on representative samples of the current end user population."[83] The next question which needs to be considered is how accurate is AI.

5 AI Accuracy

Machine learning requires a flexible exploratory research design that fosters playing around with datasets, curation, modelling and testing, before moving on to confirmatory learning that requires rigorous testing in ways that are geared to falsification rather than verification.[84]

While the benefits of AI have been outlined in health care with AI capable of detecting diseases such as brain tumours and breast cancer with the accuracy of a professional radiologist,[85] the lack of accuracy of AI should be noted. In particular, fake news and misinformation are concerns that have not been resolved. Graham and Choo (2022) analysed AI generated captions and found an average accuracy of 89.9%. They also noted the importance of manual copy editing the captions generated by AI. They also found that AI performs worse at understanding women and particular dialects other than white male voices.[86] "In addition, gender-based variation in language use and robust interpretation of the language used by native speakers across dialect regions impact the word

82 Jørgensen and Søgaard, 2022, 2.

83 Jørgensen and Søgaard, 2022, 6.

84 Hildebrandt, 2018, 9.

85 See Chandrani Singh and Sourav De. 2021. *"Applications of generative adversarial network on computer aided diagnosis."* In *Disruptive trends in computer aided diagnosis*, Chapman and Hall/CRC.

86 See Rebecca Graham and Jinhee Choo. 2022. "Preliminary research on AI-generated caption accuracy rate by platforms and variables." *Journal on Technology and Persons with Disabilities*, 10.

error rate, a common metric for measuring speech-to-text accuracy of automated speech recognition."[87]

In some cases, self-supervised learning is taking place.[88] Large-sized labelled thermal image datasets are hard to come by for different application requirements as image dataset labelling is a time-consuming and expensive process. Furthermore, in the case of industrial equipment, the situation is even worse given the lack of appropriate thermal image datasets for the same applications. Hence, resorting to self-supervised learning, a training algorithm that learns data characteristics through unlabelled data has been a fallback strategy. This makes the method malleable for a variety of similar applications. Self-supervised learning also mitigates the dependence on time and effort involved in labelling image datasets.[89]

6 False Information

Educational institutions are particularly susceptible to false information and this fact demonstrates the importance of regulation of digital information. While false information occurs on almost every platform research shows false claims are more viral on social media than authentic information. This virality of inauthentic content is driven by confirmation bias, attraction to novelty, and the abundance of fake accounts and bots on the internet platforms.[90] The entire information environment from news to social media is vulnerable to false information, as evidenced by the "infodemic" that accompanied the coronavirus:

> An overabundance of information – some accurate and some not – that makes it hard for people to find trustworthy sources and reliable guidance when they need it … In the information age, this phenomenon

87 Rachael Tatman. 2017. "Gender and dialect bias in YouTube's automatic captions." In *Proceedings of the first ACL workshop on ethics in natural language processing*, https://aclanthology.org/W17-1606.pdf.

88 See Shreyas Goyal and Jagath C. Rajapakse. 2024. "*Self-supervised learning for hotspot detection and isolation from thermal images.*" *Expert Systems with Applications* 237: 121566.

89 Alejandro Newell and Jia Deng. 2020. "How useful is self-supervised pretraining for visual tasks?" *In Proceedings of the IEEE/CVF Conference on Computer Vision and Pattern Recognition*, 7345–7354.

90 See Bridgit Dao. 2023. *The Metaweb: The Next Level of the Internet.* CRC Press.

> amplifies through social networks, spreading farther and faster like a virus.[91]

The human AI collaboration mediates the spread of fake news by identifying, flagging, and responding to false claims in the news. People can see flags when viewing the content. Anyone can flag false information, and, once verified, a false claim flag will appear next to the post. Because the network helps find falsehoods, the speed of identification increases with network size. The tool also makes fact checks easier to find and digest by presenting them next to false claims. More people will see the fact checks. As news breaks and posts on social media sites, the application uses AI to analyse new stories, detect false claims, and compare them with fact-check databases. Depending on the threat, it alerts the media, fact-checkers. The AI also reviews breaking content for false claims and proposes bridges and fact checks that connect evidence to claims.[92]

While this method of control is a positive development and could work in certain circumstances, filtering and flagging the vast array of digital information seems to be an enormous task. In addition, the detection what are false claims needs to be within a broad spectrum of moralities and this itself is open to interpretation.

7 Artificial Intelligence Moral Control Problems

It is clear that AI is and will perform tasks previously executed by humans. But how far AI can replace humans is not yet clear. However, as AI does perform human like tasks it should also be subject to a level of morality. This is so as morality and justice are interlinked as simply acting without morals is not just and does not align with our values. The term used is artificial moral agent (AMA) and is defined in the following way, "an AMA is a virtual agent (software) or physical agent (robot) capable of engaging in moral behavior or at least of avoiding immoral behavior. This moral behavior may be based on ethical theories such as teleological ethics, deontology, and virtue ethics, but

91 Pan American Health Organisation. 2024. "Understanding the infodemic and misinformation in the fight against COVID-19", *World Health Organisation*, https://iris.paho.org/bitstream/handle/10665.2/52052/Factsheet-infodemic_eng.pdf.

92 Bridgit, 2024, 232–233.

not necessarily."[93] The question is whether AMA's can have the same features as the ones human moral agents appear to have. Arvan argues that "as a guiding aim of machine ethics is to ensure that AI systems are controllable and suitably aligned with human values, we should treat 'artificial moral agents' (AMAS) as a term of art to simply refer to the types of machines we are interested in."[94]

The real problem will emerge once AI with cognitive capacities similar to or greater than our own will be achievable in the not-so-distant future. Arvan argues correctly that a failure to control AI is critical as it could result in existential risks.[95] He further argues that three distinct types of AMA's are possible:

> Inhuman AMAS: AI programmed to learn or execute moral rules or principles without understanding them in anything like the way that we do. Better-Human AMAS: AI programmed to learn, execute, and understand moral rules or principles somewhat like we do, but correcting for various sources of human moral error. Human-Like AMAS: AI programmed to understand and apply moral values in broadly the same way that we do, with a human-like moral psychology. Yet, these different types of AMAS themselves present us with distinct control and alignment problems. That is, different approaches to resolving "the" control and alignment problems for AGI present us with subtly different versions of these problems – none of which have been fully understood, let alone adequately resolved.[96]

The real concern is how do we construct the program to control and align AI with principles based on justice and morality before it is too late? Is Rawls' theory on justice relevant or is Berger and Luckmann's theory of socially constructing society equally relevant? It is hoped that institutional control over the development of AI would result at best in a Human-Like AMA. Even such a development does come with problems as a Human-Like AMA would have and needs to exhibit the same moral considerations and approach to justice like humans. Arvan also correctly notes that Human-Like AMA's would also have the moral failures like humans.[97] Where does it leave us? Arguably a

93 Jose-Antonio Cervantes, Sonia López, Luis-Felipe Rodríguez, Salvador Cervantes, Francisco Cervantes and Félix Ramos. 2020. "Artificial moral agents: A survey of the current status." *Science and engineering ethics* 26, no. 2, 505.

94 Marcus Arvan. 2022. "*Varieties of Artificial Moral Agency and the New Control Problem.*" *Humana.Mente-Journal of Philosophical Studies* 15(42): 228.

95 Arvan, 2022, 230.

96 Arvan, 2022, 230.

97 Arvan, 2022, 247.

Human-Like AMA would also have access to philosophical and sociological thoughts and theories such as those of Rawls'.

Rawls as noted above argued that justice is only achievable when "circumstances of justice" exist. Supposing that Rawls is correct, the circumstances have two components first there must be "objective circumstances which make social cooperation possible and necessary" and that "no one among them can dominate the rest".[98] Second people must have "roughly similar needs and interests", as well as similar "shortcomings of knowledge, thought, and judgment".[99]

The real question of course is how is the new elite which inevitably will rise consider justice and well-being of society. Arvan makes a valid observation namely that the elite have the power to lead society and hence would use the power to dominate and, in these circumstances, just cooperation would not be possible. If that is true, the Rawlsian theory of justice is not workable and hence of no value. However, Arvan correctly argues the following point:

> It is worth noting that the New Control Problem, as such, is not simply equivalent to the widespread problem we already have of ensuring that humans treat each other justly. According to virtually all theories of justice, existing societies (and the global/international order) are deeply unjust. Still, for all that, human beings today do not as a rule exert totalitarian control over one another. While some societies are of course ruled by tyrannical dictators, by and large human societies at least approximate Humean/Rawlsian "circumstances of justice." ... "Circumstances of justice", as Hume and Rawls understand them, are not sufficient for justice – but they are plausibly necessary for it, given what we know about human motivation.[100]

AI and other digital technologies could arguably be developed with greater logical capabilities than humans like the AI chess engines outperforming humans for example. A particular problem or possible solution to world problems is the fact that AI like digital instruments have a world-wide reach. The result could be a unified morality and system of justice prevailing or AI could dominate the world by enforcing a dominant morality. Arvan suggests that a solution would be that "we might seek to ensure that Human-Like AMAs cannot dominate us by ensuring that their capacities do not vastly outstrip ours – by, for example,

98 Rawls, 2001, 109–110.
99 Rawls, 2001, 110.
100 Arvan, 2022, 248.

imposing constraints on "how intelligent" a Human-Like AMA can be made, or by confining them to controllable environments."[101] One point is clear, creating human like AI poses a moral problem in itself namely the design of the New Control Problem must be absolutely secure and that it cannot be negatively manipulated in order to control rather than assist humans.

8 Conclusion

As seen in this discussion AI is a further development in the quest of increasing the scope of human endeavours. There is no doubt that AI and new digital technologies are here to stay but the real issue is how far is the development possible and what will be the effect on society and importantly the moral fabric as we know it today. As Brownsword notes, "the Rule of Law has particular substantive commitments … as well as applying to both public and private governance of AI and other emerging technologies of our times".[102] Will there be any effect to the extent that has been seen in the past. Simply put, we do not know what the genie will do once out of the bottle. As Walters *et al* have correctly pointed out that "The resulting effect, is a significant conundrum which has heightened the importance of expanding the focus of the debate from compliance with existing laws to the need to consider other approaches to enhance the quality of data protection and effective governance in the face of AI and other emerging digital tools."[103]

Brownsword clearly identified, "Contradictions and inconsistencies in the body of doctrine are not to be tolerated; precedents and principles should not simply be ignored; legal doctrine should not be distorted; law should be applied in a way that respects its integrity—all of this being regarded as desirable in itself."[104] The important fact is that all our institutions and especially the legal institution needs to revisit exiting laws and develop new ones to keep pace with the digital developments. One important area and as a good example is the fact that AI is able to capture, store, use and disclose biometric data. This type of data can be used for surveillance and discrimination and currently does not fall under the category of personal data. Despite this biometric data is

101 Arvan, 2022, 249.

102 Roger Brownsword. 2022. "AI and Fundamental Rights: The People, the Conversations, and the Governance Challenges." In *International Conference on the Legal Challenges of the Fourth Industrial Revolution*, Cham: Springer International Publishing, 353.

103 Walters and Coghlan, 2019, 62.

104 Brownsword, 2023, 21–22.

personal to the individuals who own them. Simply put, issues of digital morality and justice for individuals in these situations needs to be developed rather sooner than later. The regulation of digital technology needs to protect those who are most vulnerable in our societies, in our communities and in our own families.

The next chapter will look at the important and in a way one of the determining factors in how societal values are shaped and maintained, namely the influence of the existing power structures.

PART 4

The Balance of Power

CHAPTER 9

Power Structures

1 Introduction

Power has been and remains a fundamental feature of social life and sociological contemplation. The theory and research on the topic of power traverse levels of analyses, methodological orientations and discrete lines of research and substantive areas. More than 100 years of accumulated scholarship reveals that this construct remains relatively ambiguous, has several seemingly distinct faces, and is complex in its various manifestations.[1] Evidence suggests that power cannot be theoretically reduced to a singular attribute, position or a simple equation of tangible costs, benefits and balance or imbalance. Instead, it is best understood as an unequal relationship, or inequality, based on personal attributes, institutional positioning and status that are defined, codified and acted upon within historical and cultural contexts.[2]

One of the most important elements in any society is that it can only function if a certain institutional order is present and is safeguarded. If no order exists, then chaos is the result and social cohesion is impossible. Arguably though a society will split into subgroups. Order therefore is always established and maintained through power. Power is value neutral but it is undeniable that power structures are part of reality. From a sociological perspective the fact is that "the social space is simultaneously objectively structured through unequal distribution of capital and subjectively structured because the established perceptual, interpretational and evaluative schemata express the state of the symbolic power struggles."[3] Thus power is not only exercised by the elite but by anybody within society with various degrees of effectiveness. One of the associated issues is the resistance to established power structures on the part of institutions or the individual actors. Dreyfus and Rabinow focused their attention on Foucault who carefully analysed the balance of power, and the importantly recognised anti-authority struggles. He defined in many ways what the anti-authority struggles – as currently increasingly observed – had in common. One of the points he identified was:

1 Vincent J. Roscigno. 2011. "Power, revisited." *Social Forces* 90, no. 2, 364.

2 Roscigno. 2011. Citing Rogers 1974; Margolis 1989; Ridegway, Backor, Tinkler and Erickson 2009.

3 Steets, 2016, 98.

 DOI:10.1163/9789004702691_010

> They are struggles which question the status of the individual: on the one hand, they assert the right to be different and they underline everything which makes individuals truly individual. On the other hand, they attack everything which separates the individual, breaks his links with others, splits up community life, forces the individual back on himself and ties him to his own identity in a constraining way.[4]

This is an interesting observation, and we can see its relevance when exploring the identity of individuals in the modern world. The status of the individual is always a struggle and has never ceased to exist. The change in the struggle is the social reality in which it is exercised. It is also not new that authorities like to keep the struggles under control as it undermines social cohesion. It is democracy which allows the individual to be tied to his own identity and it is dictatorship in any form which does not allow individuals to assert their own identity.

Importantly Foucault specifically wrote about the "form of power" and identified three types of struggles: against domination, against forms of exploitation which separate individuals from what they produce or against that which ties the individual to himself and submits him to others in this way.[5] Using Foucault's ideas as an analogy, there is evidently a power struggle going on between the technology giants and technology users. The troubling issue is that in the first wave the question of data protection and privacy were debated, and governments attempted to curtail the powers of the technology giants and device data protection laws with arguably little effect. The use of power multiplies in societies where the social world is not in balance such as the Arab Spring uprising that took place in the Middle East and North Africa in 2010 and 2011. However once institutionalised it loses its power and is used by the emerging elite to justify its position such as through elections. When power is exerted, it can modify, use, consume or destroy things.[6] We have and are witnessing this at the moment in the United States where the wealthy can exert their power and influence over others to achieve remarkable outcomes. The same can be said about Russia and China.

Foucault linked power to action and highlighted that power needs to be considered as a productive network which runs through the whole social body.[7] Arguably Foucault talks in this instance about legitimate power given to

---

4 Hubert L. Dreyfus and Paul Rabinow. 2014. *Michel Foucault: Beyond structuralism and hermeneutics*. Routledge, 211.

5 Dreyfus and Rabinow, 2014, 212.

6 Dreyfus and Rabinow, 2014, 217.

7 Nigam Aditya. 1996. "Marxism and power." *Social Scientist* 24, no. 4–6, 6.

the elite by society like in a democracy. Foucault used an analogy of an educational system to explain a whole series of power process including "enclosure, surveillance, reward and punishment, the pyramidal hierarchy".[8] He went on explain that what constitutes the specific nature of power is "a way in which certain action modify others".[9] This analogy has a parallel example with the modification of behaviour we have seen during the digital revolution where individuals' daily actions have been modified significantly and a device now has the potential to take the place of a personal relationship. Dreyfus *et al* put in in the following way:

> Power exists only when it is put into action, even if, of course, it is integrated into a disparate field of possibilities brought to bear on permanent structures. This also means that power is not a function of consent. In itself it is not a renunciation of freedom, a transference of rights, the power of each and all delegates to a few ... the relationship of power can be the result of a prior consent, but it is not by nature the manifestation of a consensus.[10]

Foucault in principle understood power and the exercise of power in a figurative way "it can pile up the dead and shelter itself behind whatever threats it can imagine."[11] While this imagery suggests that individuals are those that are sacrificed fearful of loss, one also needs to consider power on a larger scale. This idea legitimises the idea of institutions who have power and there is no reference to the individual except that they are considered inferior. However Berger and Luckman's in *The Social Construction of Reality* – discussed at length in Chapter 4 – were also able to analyse that power is the subjective reality of the individual actor. To do so the discussion of power needs to be based on the idea of the dialectical relationship of objective and subjective reality which Berger and Luckmann derived from the theories of Marx, Weber and Durkheim. Hence the question is how is power constructed as an institutional tool.

---

8 Dreyfus and Rabinow, 2014, 219.

9 Dreyfus and Rabinow, 2014, 219.

10 Dreyfus and Rabinow, 2014, 220.

11 Dreyfus and Rabinow, 2014, 220.

2 The Construction and Constitution of Power

It is useful to revert to history as an example of the effects of institutional power. In the Middle Ages the institution of the Catholic Church held tremendous political power to tax people and to make laws. Church authorities such as the Pope held more power than the Kings and Queens of that time due to their wealth, education, community support and the backing of the power of the church. The church gained power by becoming the only reliable institution after the fall of the Roman Empire. The pontificate of Gregory IX (1227–1241) is associated with the culmination of the struggle between the papacy and the Roman Empire. He is known for issuing the *Decretales* and instituting the *Papal Inquisition* which continued the policy of papal supremacy.[12] Although things have changed dramatically since then, people still depend on the church for shelter, food, and protection even today.[13] Arguably the "Church" can be replaced by other terms in this century such as "President" who are in power for life.

Turning to this century Berger and Luckmann argued that as individuals are formed by a society, society therefore will guide their actions through institutions. It follows therefore as Dreher stated: "As far as power is concerned, it is precisely objective reality which comes into focus, since power structures and power hierarchies are specifically seen as structural conditions of, for example, social stratification related to inequality."[14] Using the church or presidents or parties as examples, power is also intrinsically based on the institutionalisation process that is linked to institutions. The power by members of the institution is used to control members of society by determining what they can or cannot do. It is the power to set up patterns of conduct. Institutions therefore are a power in themselves and are at the same time independent from the individual. They have coercive power "both in themselves, by the sheer force of their facticity, and through the control mechanisms that are usually attached to the most important of them."[15] The fact is that institutions are objectified, and they persist in one form or another from generations to generations such as an example the institution of the law. The power of the law rests within the control mechanism exercised by courts and judges.

12 See Damian J. Smith and Brenda M. Bolton. 2023. *Pope Gregory IX (1227–1241): Power and Authority*, Cambridge University Press, 1–368.

13 Joshua J. Mark. 2019. *"The Medieval Church", World History Encyclopedia*, https://www.worldhistory.org/Medieval_Church/.

14 Jochen Dreher. 2016. *"The social construction of power: Reflections beyond Berger/Luckmann and Bourdieu." Cultural Sociology* 10, no. 1, 55.

15 Dreher, 2016, 55.

> Through the externalization of human products created in processes of action and interaction, these products – institutions, cultural artifacts, etc. – obtain the character of objectivity; the process of externalization leads to what is considered 'objectification' (Versachlichung) in the Hegelian and Marxian tradition.[16]

The important issue is the legitimisation of the institution. Without being legitimised it has no control, that is it becomes powerless. The most basic form of legitimisation is that it needs a purpose. For example, a wise saying or a common interest such as the objectification of a desire to resolve disputes can lead to the specialisation of members as experts. Hence this type of specialised knowledge leads to the issue of power and hence symbolisation will take place such as procedural rules within the legal system such as wigs, gowns and the gavel to note a few.

Alfred Schutz proposed that,

> … everyday transcendent realties – political worlds of ideas, religious belief systems, scientific paradigms, etc. – are established through symbols as specific forms of signs. Symbols are used in everyday communication within the pragmatic world of everyday life to 'apprehend,' to make co-present everyday transcendent ideas, for example the ideas of 'solidarity,' 'liberty,' and so on.[17]

Power is therefore used to maintain the universe by the elite or leading class and that is the reason why creation of the institution takes place in the first place. Marx addressed this issue by observing "[t]he ideas of the ruling class are in every epoch the ruling ideas: i.e., the class which is in the ruling material force of society is at the same time its ruling intellectual force."[18] One can deduct from the ideas of Marx and others that the reflections of the ruling class such as politicians and their bureaucracy, those with wealth or business leaders but also ideology as such are the result of the ability of the ruling class to access the dominant ideas and material and turn them into ideas through the power which emanates from the institutional order. As Berger and Luckmann have correctly argued, the important expression of power is simply "He who

16 Dreher, 2016, 56.

17 See Alfred Schutz. 1962. "Symbol reality and society." In *Collected papers I: The problem of social reality*. Dordrecht: Springer Netherlands, 329–356.

18 Karl Marx and Friedrich Engels. 1976. *1845–6. The German Ideology*. 59.

has the bigger stick has the better chance of imposing his definitions of reality."[19] Pierre Bourdieu addressing the power or words and worldviews as "nothing other than the delegated power of the spokesperson"[20] of the institution.

The important realisation when questioning why and to what extent power is vested in an institution, Dreher points to the fact that: "It is not of importance how convincing the discourse of the powerful, of those who propagate a symbolic universe, may be; the power is not part of the speech act, but it comes from outside and it is given to the elites by structural preconditions."[21] The point to be made is that the influence of experts is important as their power is based on the ignorance or a knowledge gap which exists between them and those who are in a less powerful situation. Arguably such a knowledge deficit is already observable in today's society where knowledge is only absorbed in small grabs hence the big picture or the "endgame" is unknown and leads to the dangerous situation of dealing with those behind the veil of ignorance to borrow from Rawls. The dangerous issue is that the ignorant who think they know everything are easily persuaded by leaders like former President Trump for example. The problem today is which definition of reality is to be enforced? It again plays out in the United States with the machination in congress between the Democrats and the Republicans.

Berger and Luckmann have put their view in the following way namely "the propagated and established symbolic universe receives effectiveness and starts to function due to the fact that individuals in their socialization were pre-figured by ideas, thought systems and categories prescribed by the 'ruling class' of a society".[22] If on another level the question of cutting back inflation is and always has been determined by experts in the banking institution this will always be what will happen. However, there is never a unanimous answer because "The different interests of the competing experts determine the form and substance of the theories they develop; their material interests influence the expression of the theories."[23] This fact suggests that several competing interests are at work and that there is no monopoly of views present. The difference is that while there is a monopoly expressed as the only institution dealing with a particular issue like curbing inflation by the Federal Bank, there is no convergence in views of what is real then there will be no social change. However, if there is a breakdown of what has been taken for granted it will

19 Berger and Luckmann, 1966, 109.
20 Pierre Bourdieu. 1991. "Language and symbolic power." *Polity*, 107–116.
21 Dreher, 2016, 58.
22 See Dreher, 2016, 60.
23 See Dreher, 2016, 60.

be an impetus for social change. Arguably conservative political forces have a vested interest in a monopoly of views as it strengthens their power base. An ideology has been created as a basis for maintaining a particular power base.

Berger and Luckmann without doubt have defined how the power structure in a society is established and challenged. Once the social fabric is sufficiently disturbed by a counter-ideology, then the status quo of the established symbolic universe will lay the foundation of a redefinition of the current power hierarchies. Due to the digital revolution, society is changing, and new institutions are created. Examples of these are political parties creating their own experts and challenging the old order. In the end the simple fact is that those who occupy power impose power. Hence,

> … the decisive power positions are ready to use their power to impose [their] definition of reality on the population under their authority. Potentially competitive conceptualisations of the universe are liquidated as soon as they appear – either physically or integrated within the tradition itself.[24]

To analyse the emergence and enforcement of the power structures is useful to understand the functions of social constructionism.

3 Education and the Digital Divide

It has been demonstrated that the current disconnects between the economic standing of individuals and the digital revolution has brought benefits and wealth creation to some but has not contributed to the wellbeing of every individual in every society. While "quality education" is Sustainable Development Goal (SDG) 4 and it is important there are several other significant concerns for societies. "No poverty" is SDG 1.[25] As an example, Sub-Saharan Africa remains a region of concern for poverty reduction. Poverty reduction is an important global initiative and linked with mitigating many of the current global challenges. Globally, extreme poverty continues to decline but at a slow pace. The

24 Berger and Luckmann, 1966, 139.

25 United Nations. 2024. *"Sustainable Development Goals", Department of Economic and Social Affairs*, https://sdgs.un.org/goals.

proportion of people living in extreme poverty fell from 36% in 1990 to 16% in 2010 and 10% in 2015.[26]

Currently, about 3.7 billion people do not use the internet, and these people comprise vulnerable, marginalised groups such as females, rural, poor, elderly, and those with limited education and low literacy.[27] SDG 1 requires countries to end poverty of all forms and is linked with SDG 4. At the same time, SDG 9 calls for increasing Information and Communication Technology access and striving to provide universal and affordable access to the internet in the least developed countries by 2020.[28] Dzator *et al.*, reported that internet penetration, broadband penetration, and information and communication technology goods exported, increase poverty in African populations.[29] We are now witnessing homeless people prioritising connection to the internet over other important needs. It is noted that communication has become important for survival in some cases. The issue is that a new understanding of our social world is required in order to maintain stable and prosperous modern societies.

The social construct of a well-balanced society – as noted in previous chapters – has been disturbed by minimising a crucial element namely the ability to conduct face to face communications that is a real and not virtual social interactions.

Pariser coined the term filter bubble to describe how algorithm filters were creating an artificial space in which people heard only voices that were already aligned with their political views. Researchers have documented that filter bubbles exacerbate the spread of misinformation on social media sites because they are only influenced by the news items they see.[30] Sensational content makes people spend more time on social media platforms as does anxiety. Several psychology studies show that social media is intertwined

---

26 United Nations. 2019. *"The sustainable development goals report 2019", Department of Economic and Social Affairs,* https://unstats.un.org/sdgs/report/2019/ cited in Dzator, Janet, Alex O. Acheampong, Isaac Appiah-Otoo and Michael Dzator. 2023. "Leveraging Digital Technology for Development: Does ICT Contribute to Poverty Reduction?" *Telecommunications policy* 47, no. 4, 102524.

27 I. Deganis, P. Z. Haghian and M. Tagashira. 2021. *Leveraging digital technologies for social inclusion.* https://www.un.org/development/desa/dspd/ 2021/02/digital-technologies-for-social-inclusion/ cited in Dzator, Janet, Alex O. Acheampong, Isaac Appiah-Otoo and Michael Dzator. 2023 *"Leveraging Digital Technology for Development: Does ICT Contribute to Poverty Reduction?" Telecommunications policy* 47, no. 4, 102526.

28 Janet Dzator, Alex O. Acheampong, Isaac Appiah-Otoo and Michael Dzator. 2023. "Leveraging Digital Technology for Development: Does ICT Contribute to Poverty Reduction?" *Telecommunications policy* 47, no. 4, 102524.

29 Dzator, Acheampong, Appiah-Otoo and Dzator, 2023, 102552.

30 Johnson and Acemoglu, 2023, 360.

with feelings of envy and inadequacy, and often leads to concerns about self-esteem.[31] While these observations have negative effect on those in developed countries, the effects in undeveloped countries need analysis.

In the context of education, the faster pace and the quick grab mentality has in effect led to a deficit in attention spans. The rebalancing of all these negative impacts is not easy to achieve. Excessive regulation of the use of the internet would never work because the "horse has bolted" and besides that the effects of the digital revolution are irreversible. As this book has indicated, rebalancing is an issue and a challenge that needs to be addressed by institutions. Leading institutions such as the government and importantly the educational institutions need to take up the challenge to manage the ongoing development of the digital revolution. Clearly, the benefits flowing to society need to be more equally attainable.

4 The Power of Education

It is only fitting that Berger and Luckmann's view on education ought to be looked at first. They argue that language provides the means "for objectifying new experiences allowing their incorporating into the existing stock of knowledge"[32] This is so as language develops shape and is transmitted through interaction. Similarly, reading cannot be learned entirely and accurately in isolation from people.[33] Reading, one of life's essential skills, is one of the primary proficiencies children should acquire from the first years of school. Learning to read competently in primary classrooms is one of the cornerstones of academic success and is the foundation for children's later school success. It is believed that reading has a significant impact on children's lives in terms of developing skills such as learning, academic achievement, critical thinking, cognitive development, and problem-solving.[34] Simply put the skills which have been transmitted become part of a common stock of knowledge.

The real issue is that society holds the stock of knowledge temporarily, knowledge is only relevant to the actual needs and aspirations of a society in a given timeframe. As an example, if an agrarian society moves into an industrial

31 Johnson and Acemoglu, 2023, 370.

32 Berger and Luckmann, 1966, 86.

33 Seda Ozer Şanal and Mukaddes Erdem. 2023. "Overcoming reading disabilities among teenage students with learning disabilities through collaborative storybook intervention." *Education and Information Technologies* 28, no. 8, 9483.

34 Özer Şanal and Erdem, 2023, 9484.

society the knowledge of growing food is only relevant to those who farm but not to those who builds machines. It is all a question of relevance, and the crucial point is when does one stock of knowledge need to be replaced or at least modified to fit into the new reality. Here is in a sense the problem of the education system in modern times. What ought to be successfully transmitted to a new generation? The point is as Berger and Luckmann note "the past history of the society can be reinterpreted without necessarily upsetting the institutional order as a result."[35]

Arguably the real question is what is the foundational knowledge which is essential to establish the additional and new stock of knowledge, a socially constructed knowledge? It follows that the institutional meaning via education must be impressed powerfully upon the consciousness of the individuals. Berger and Luckmann make a very interesting comment and arguably very fitting by stating that, "Since human beings are frequently stupid, institutional meanings tend to be simplified in the process of transmission, so that the given collection of institutional 'formula' can be readily learned and memorized by successive generations."[36] As an example universities and other institution are focusing on the business principles of a balanced budget instead of focusing on educating in specific areas. The result is that courses are judged whether they are financially sustainable and not whether they are contributing to a rich understanding of our world such as perspectives of anthropology, history and even business.

As it is, one of the tenets of this book, a glance backwards in history is an essential tool to look forward.

4.1 *The Process of Education*

Mencken commenced his discussion of the educational process argued that,

> … a man who knows a subject thoroughly, a man so soaked in it that he eats it, sleeps it and dreams it – this man can almost always teach it with success, no matter how little he knows of technical pedagogy. That is because there is enthusiasm in him, and because enthusiasm is contagious.[37]

35 Berger and Luckmann, 1966, 87.

36 Berger and Luckmann, 1966, 87.

37 Henry L. Mencken. 1966. "The educational Process", in John Strephens, *Ten Articulate Men*, Australian Publishing Company, 195.

The problem with the above comment lies in the fact that to acquire thorough knowledge requires reading. Murdoch commented in *What are Books for?* "I was invited into a meeting of young men and women assembled to discuss modern literature"[38] this is an event totally unimaginable today as it requires face to face communication, and it cannot be modern machine to machine communication.

Turning to Russell in the opening paragraph in his paper *Last School Years* he stated:

> All rules, in education, should be capable of being broken for special reasons. But I think that, as a general rule. Pupils of more than average intelligence should begin to specialize say about fourteen, while pupils of less than average intelligence should usually not specialise at all at school unless in the way of vocational training.[39]

It is a very bold statement in the current political climate but in effect it is still in place insofar as the technical education sector (TAFE) is being rejuvenated. Russell did note that the above statement does raise economic and political issues "which are only indirectly connected with education."[40] Arguably Russell noted that the values of education which must be taken into account are that there the variations in ability and interest of individuals and that is, one size does not fit all. Taking the variations into account all students are educated to their level of competence. Russell interestingly noted that it is important for students to be "encouraged to take an interest in current controversial questions of importance, political, social, and even theological [but it is essential that] they should be encouraged to read all sides in such controversies, not only the orthodox side."[41]

Arguably the fact that informed debates and discussions are essential is again to be taken very seriously considering that we have seen a decline in face-to-face discussions and texting does not stimulate a debate. There is simply no shortcut to learning and our view is that a lacking element in the general education endeavour is that unfortunately too many shortcuts are taken. At present there is a reluctance to read more than a few pages at a time. Rather

38 Walter Murdoch. 1966. "What are Books for?" in John Strephens, *Ten Articulate Men*, Australian Publishing Company, 35.

39 Russell Bertrant. 1966. "Last School Years", in John Strephens, *Ten Articulate Men*, Australian Publishing Company, 240.

40 Bertrant, 1966, 240.

41 Bertrant, 1966, 244.

than a fact checked resource it is quicker to grab information taken from the net. Russell clearly stated that "education should be an educational adventure".[42] This idea is a long way from what is actually taking place today.

It should be sufficient to note the way some great thinkers have viewed education in general. It is time to look briefly at the current models and analyse their effectiveness.

5 Educational Reform

Some researchers say that the concept of the university as an institution is at a crossroad. The current blueprint for the university has its foundations built on the contexts of the First and Second Industrial Revolutions. It is no wonder, then, that while we are in the Fourth and on the cusp of the Fifth Revolutions, that the load-bearing institutional structures of the contemporary university are creaking under the weight of change. The Fourth Revolution is manifested by the internet and digitalisation, while the Fifth Revolution is said to be personalising and focusing on human-machine interactions.[43]

As education is the favourite tool of economists and policy makers for combatting inequality it is in need of revolutionary change to meet the new challenges. Schools are critical for worker skills and contribute to society by introducing common core values. There is also a sense that schooling is deficient in many nations and especially for students from low socioeconomic backgrounds,[44] as well as underdeveloped countries.

The technocratic illusion of online democracy, especially in the education environment has played an important role. The issue is arguably that technology giants making decisions which would be far too complicated for everyday people to understand,[45] and the education systems have not been able to keep pace. The argument is that technology is undermining democracy when we need it most. Others say that digital technology is fueling inequality by

42 Bertrant, 1966, 240.

43 Josephine Lang. 2023. "Workforce Upskilling: Can Universities Meet the Challenges of Lifelong Learning?" *The international journal of information and learning technology* 40, no. 5, 388 citing Arthur Levine and Scott Van Pelt 2021. *The Great Upheaval: Higher Education's Past, Present, and Uncertain Future*, Johns Hopkins University Press, Baltimore, MD and Zouina Sarfraz, Azza Sarfraz, Hamza Mohammad Iftikar, Ramsha Akhund 2021. "Is COVID-19 pushing us to the Fifth industrial revolution (society 5.0)?", *Pakistan Journal of Medical Sciences Bi-monthly*, Vol. 37 No. 2, 591–594.

44 Johnson and Acemoglu, 2023, 417.

45 Johnson and Acemoglu, 2023, 372.

intensively monitoring workers to channel and create downward pressure on wages.[46]

The new developments and the new directions in education can reflect a governments failure to adequately structure and finance education. In addition to teaching online and reduced face-to-face interaction, less reading and deep thinking is occurring. Discussions on crucial issues in courses training future generations have been left out. While technology should be steered in a direction that best uses a workforce's skills, education should of course simultaneously adapt to new skill requirements.[47]

The question therefore is what the education system promotes and whether the education system values justice and equality as a driving force for individuals in society. The answer simply is no. There is no debate that some schools – judging the availability of technology – are better equipped than others and hence a gap between those who have and those who have not is entrenched. Hendrix noted that "The grim realities of inequities in school funding are conspicuous, and the funding simultaneously masks and unmasks the injustices, which become so ubiquitous that they are being ignored and accepted."[48] It is acknowledged that race, classism and sexism not only in schools but in society as such is entrenched and has been so for a long time. However, the new challenge is the power to own, understand and manage technology. Education is dependent on students having a computer at home besides the one available at schools. Already by 2001, a divide between poor and rich students had been discussed and those affected by access to technology were recognised. The trend in education and the accessibility of technology to students in 2001 had already been observed:

> Rather than democratizing education, technology is widening the gap between wealthy and poor institutions – as those with the least resources are least likely to afford technology. Schools that comprised more than 90 percent of students of color had a student-to-computer ratio of 17-to-1 in 2000, compared with the national average of 10-to-1. The historic lag in the introduction of computers into many rural and urban schools is yet another symptom of the savage inequalities in school funding from district to district. These inequities established the framework for

46 Johnson and Acemoglu, 2023, 381.

47 Johnson and Acemoglu, 2023, 418.

48 Elizabeth Hendrix. 2005. "Permanent injustice: Rawls' theory of justice and the digital divide." *Journal of Educational Technology & Society* 8, no. 1, 68.

> differentials in computer access and usage that favored middle-class and wealthy students, contributing to what is now termed the "World White Web."[49]

Arguably the above observations have not changed, in effect the trend has worsened as new technological advances require updates and more sophisticated hardware needs to be purchased. The issue is that justice as defined by Rawls is not applicable in the education sector as the institution as such has not maintained educational practices which do not favour a particular class of students. It is not the ability to learn but the availability of the tools prescribed by the institutions which foster an imbalance in the ability to lead and hence there is injustice.[50] An important factor in the imbalance is that Rawls' principle of legitimate inequality that is the disparity must be beneficial to the least advantaged – the maximin principle – is not applied properly as not all students are educated to their level of competence as a one size fits all principle is applied currently in the education system.

It is useful to look at Antonio Abatemarco and Francesca Stroffolini who argued that "a formalization of the Difference Principle where the identification of legitimate inequalities depends on the impact of inequality on individual incentives to effort in education."[51] Arguably it is so as the efficiency principle is only applied to the bottom line of educational institutions but not to the function of education. In theory at least the maximin principle also embraces efficiency issues as noted by Rawls. He noted "it is not correct that maximin gives no weight to efficiency. It imposes a rule of functional contribution among inequalities; and since it applies to social arrangements that are mutually advantageous, some weight is given to efficiency."[52]

The stages considered to be influential in forming the contributions of individual within a society are namely "(i) ambitions (preference type) and (ii) native talent (abilities) is progressively acquired over time."[53] At the educational stage the preference type is revealed. However native talent is only taken under uncertain conditions. Admittedly educational institutions at higher levels will look at scores presumably indicating the level of talent, but

---

49 David Trend. 2001. *Welcome to cyberschool: Education at the crossroads in the information age*. Rowman & Littlefield, 145.

50 Abatemarco and Stroffolin, 2023, 996.

51 Abatemarco and Stroffolin, 996.

52 John Rawls. 1974. "Reply to Alexander and Musgrave." *The Quarterly Journal of Economics* 88, no. 4, 648.

53 Abatemarco and Stroffolin, 2023, 996.

the uncertainty is whether the native talent is directly relevant to the preference as chosen by students. Only at the working stage is talent fully realised and results in the earning capacity of individuals.

It is obvious that "differences in citizens' earnings capacity are influenced by (i) their native endowments, (ii) their preferences, (iii) their opportunities for education, and (iv) their good or ill fortune over the course of life."[54] The point is that inequalities due to environmental influences are inevitable and the only point where an institutional correction to inequalities can be made is in the educational sector.

Abatemarco *et al* argue that "if education opportunities are universally granted independently from the social class of origin, then the wage rate paid in the labour market is expected to reflect the earnings capacity achieved as a result of the endowment in terms of native talent and the effort investment in education."[55]

The argument is that educational opportunities can be granted independently from social class by highlighting the function of talent in the instructional process. Not every student is equally endowed with talent, hence there are limits in the learning capacity which must be taken into consideration. In other words, every student must be educated to their level of competence. Simply put, when a very gifted student is put in the same class with a lesser gifted student neither of the two will achieve their potential. Unfortunately, political consensus on this point despite the logic of the argument has not been achieved. Rawls is absolutely correct when the noted that "[s]ocial and economic inequalities are to meet two conditions: they must be (a) to the greatest expected benefit of the least-advantaged (the maximin criterion); and (b) attached to offices and positions open to all under conditions of fair equality of opportunity."[56] It follows that the only disparity within society exclusively originates from native talent and ambitions and cannot be by variations in their opportunity to education. Abatemarco and others note:

> Hence, in our view, the distinction between the educational and the working stage is key in [Rawls'] Theory and, to the extent that individual responsible decisions in the educational stage matter, the social contract is not to be intended as merely redistributive but, also, the mechanism-design by which incentives to effort in education are determined.[57]

54 Abatemarco and Stroffolin, 2023, 999.

55 Abatemarco and Stroffolin, 2023, 1000.

56 Rawls, 1974, 639.

57 Abatemarco and Stroffolin, 2023, 1001.

The conclusion which can be drawn is that educational institutions have not fully recognised that the principles of justice and equality must also be used in the classroom. A far more nuanced approach must be used in education. Digital tools are only tools, they are not a replacement for dialogue or a discussion of concepts and ideas. Hence it is not only instruction which is important in education but the wider meaning of learning to appreciate the elements of a well-balanced society such as music, history and literature.

Learning is multidimensional. The use of the constructivism theory in education where learners construct knowledge rather than just passively take in information has unfortunately not taken enough root in the current education system. The advantages of this theory are that:

- Students learn best when engaged in learning experiences rather than passively receiving information.
- Learning is inherently a social process because it is embedded within a social context as students and teachers work together to build knowledge.
- Because knowledge cannot be directly imparted to students, the goal of teaching is to provide experiences that facilitate the construction of knowledge.[58]

The passivity of the transfer of knowledge is grounded in the fact that students like short grabs of information. Less and less do students like reading more than a few pages and often they just want to be told or given the necessary facts to pass a subject and move on. It simply is not conducive to generate a stock of knowledge which is essential to advance a societies stock of knowledge and as Rawls would argue fosters justice for all.

To entertain the alternative argument, it is true that students are all digitally savvy and have a new stock of knowledge based on technology. Now in education students are using their day-to-day tools as well as a worldwide library. However, education goes beyond a technical ability and hence this book consistently argues that the social aspect of our lives is becoming compromised and neglected. In addition, access to the worldwide net without the ability to think deeply is in essence wasted because education can't be rushed. Education in a sense is the soft power to influence the path of reforms.

58 University at Buffalo. 2024. https://www.buffalo.edu/catt/develop/theory/constructivism.html\.

6 Soft Power, Constraints and Forces

In 1990, Joseph Nye first discussed the concept of soft power through a lens of culture, political values and foreign policy. At the time he captured both hearts and minds. He went on to describe how humans live in a web of inherited social forces, some of which are visible and others of which are indirect that we call "structural."[59] We tend to identify and focus on some of these constraints and forces rather than others depending on our interests. For example, social power operates beneath the individual behavioural level by shaping underlying social structures, knowledge systems, and general environment.[60] Civilizations and societies are not immutable, and effective leaders can try to shape larger social forces with varying degrees of success. As Weber said, we want to know the probability that an actor in a social relationship can carry out his own will.[61][62] Further to this, it is important that each individual has the freedom to choose to improve their own education and the education of their children.

Nobel Prize winning author Vargas Llosa argued that culture's encounter with computation has been so acute as to precipitate cultural demise. For him, narrowing the gap between highbrow and the lowbrow is precisely what has led to the cultural crisis. He argues that an open society and one which allows equality opportunity to succeed undermines high culture and this paradox leads to literature being an increasingly frivolous form of entertainment.[63] More recently, social media platforms have been described as serving as the hotbed of affective facts and the amplifier of hate. "The new media creates an infinite cycle of affective facts and exaggerated emotional responses that overwhelms the voices of dissent." In the world where neither dialogue nor deliberation is possible, media-induced affects determine the course of politics. The internet and social media-induced affects sprawl, magnify themselves and undo critical thinking, the foundation of any intellectual enquiry and deliberative democracy. This surfeit of the negative affects not only catalyses verbal abuse and other forms of hate crime but also misdirects decisions concerning

59 Keith Dowding. 2008. "Agency and structure: Interpreting power relationships." *Journal of Power* 1, no. 1, 21–36.

60 See Peter J. Katzenstein, ed. 2009. *Civilizations in world politics: Plural and pluralist perspectives.* Routledge.

61 Max Weber. 1947. *The theory of social and economic organization.* Oxford, 152.

62 Joseph S. Nye. 2021. "*Soft power: the evolution of a concept*", *Journal of Political Power*, 14:1, 196–208.

63 Mario Vargas Llosa. 2015. *"Notes on the Death of Culture"*, *Financial Times*, https://www.ft.com/content/1b48b420-2f93-11e5-91ac-a5e17d9b4cff.

political violence, ranging from de-citizenship to military operations. Virtual terrorists, virtual anxiety and people who monitor others' online status silently and follow spoof social media accounts possibly commenting and retweeting remain in the sanctuary of anonymity.[64]

Arguably therefore the question is how do we reconstruct social realism?

7 Shaping Realities through Social Constructionism

It is appropriate to start with an understanding of what constructionism means. Hjelm put it in the following way:

> … [s]ocial constructionism argues that the human world is not as simple and obvious as it seems and that people, you and I, take part actively in producing and reproducing – constructing – it.[65]

Constructivism according to Phillips assists in delving deeper into the way power operates.[66] As this book advocates any social construction that is, how any individuals view and understand their world will shape the collective understanding what is real. It appears to be obvious that the individuals' understanding, and perspective of the world is shaped by their culture and history.[67] It might not be obvious to the individual as the socialisation process does take place behind a veil of ignorance to use Rawls analogy. The reasons why an understanding of change is essential has been put forward correctly by Phillips who commented:

> The goal of utilising a social constructionist epistemology is to examine specific knowledge systems and assess how they may favour certain interests or groups over others. By engaging in such a critique, social

64 Carmen Zamorano Llena, Jonas Stier and Billy Gray. eds. 2024. *Crisis and the Culture of Fear and Anxiety in Contemporary Europe*. Routledge, 68–69.

65 Titus Hjelm. 2014. *Social Constructionisms: Approaches to the Study of the Human World*, Palgrave Macmillan, 2.

66 Andrew Bradley Phillips. 2007. "Constructivism." In *International relations theory for the twenty-first century*, Routledge, 175.

67 See Vivien Burr. 2015. *Social constructionism*. Routledge, 1–296.

> constructionists explore how such critique can lead to new possibilities for action and bring about social change in the future.[68]

It ought to be mentioned before going further that Berger and Luckmann made a noticeable departure from social constructivism. Berger considered it as one of the "impressive illustrations of the unintended consequences of publishing one's ideas."[69]

Put simply constructivism is in essence a question of how much power is shared and by whom. This has occupied the minds of many of the great thinkers and is not a new phenomenon. What is new is that society due to the digital revolution has seen a change or more appropriately a shift in the power structures of the elite as noted by Turchin in previous chapters. The result is a disempowerment of the middle class and an unbalancing of the social contrast of what is real and what is not. As already noted above, the disturbances in what you perceive to be real is nothing new. What is new and yet to be determined is how and to what extent will the digital revolution change the powerbase and structure of society, and hence what is perceived as real.

It is therefore not surprising that Immanuel Kant, Karl Marx, and Giambattista Vico reflected on the constructs of both social constructionism and constructivism from both individualistic and collectivist assumptions.[70] Rawls also did address the issue of power not as a major issue but as an explanation of what is achievable as many diverse groups have different ideas about the same issue. Hence the weighting of the claims or put differently the power of the groups holding similar views is normally influenced by their relative positions of power. The effect is that "The culture of the poorer strata is impoverished while that of the governing and technocratic elite is securely based on the service of the national ends of power and wealth."[71] The argument is that only if everybody has the same opportunities will there be a sharing of power. The unfortunate reality is that it is not the case that there will be sharing of power, especially when we see the middle class disappearing as a result of automation due to the digital revolution and the increasing use of technology.

---

68 Matthew J. Phillips. 2023. "Towards a social constructionist, criticalist, Foucauldian-informed qualitative research approach: Opportunities and challenges." *SN Social Sciences* 3, no. 10 174.

69 Peter Berger. 2011. *Adventures of an Accidental Sociologist: How to Explain the World without Becoming a Bore*, Prometheus Books, 93.

70 See generally Peter Conrad and Kristin K. Barker. 2010. "The social construction of illness: Key insights and policy implications." *Journal of health and social behavior* 51, no. 1, suppl, S67-S79.

71 Rawls, 1971, 91.

Rawls also pointed to the effects of government actions being subject to interest group pressure by stating:

> Moreover, the effects of injustices in the political system are much more grave and long lasting than market imperfections. Political power rapidly accumulates and becomes unequal; and making use of the coercive apparatus of the state and its law, those who gain the advantage can often assure themselves of a favoured position.[72]

Rawls also argued that "taking part in political life does not make the individual master of himself, but rather gives him an equal voice along with others in settling how basic social conditions are to be arranged".[73] Theoretically speaking this might be true but in reality an equal voice along party lines is more likely to be the outcome. The fact simply is that individuals taking part in political life are subject to the power of the political party and bound by the collective party view.

7.1 *Bourdieu, Berger and Luckmann, and the Social Constructivism*

A discussion of constructivism and the element of power would not be complete without at least an acknowledgement of Bourdieu. Bourdieu discussed the importance of power in social relations. Schwartz suggested that "Bourdieu perceives the task of scientific research as 'unmasking and debunking hidden, taken-for-granted power relations shaping social life' through which new possibilities for individual and collective arrangements become possible."[74] Dreher also noted that the "dialectical approach of Berger and Luckmann is a peculiar precursor to Bourdieu's integrative solution."[75] The interesting observation is that Berger and Luckmann as well as Bourdieu did pay little attention to each other's writing. The essential element is that all three followed the same dialectic approach.

Bourdieu like Berger and Luckmann also argued that objectivism cannot stand alone as it is an incomplete "mode of theoretical knowledge". They recognised that objectivism neglected the conditioning between who knows – the

72 Rawls, 1971, 199.

73 Rawls, 1971, 205.

74 David L. Swartz. 2005. "From Critical Sociology to Public Intellectual: Pierre Bourdieu and Politics", in David L. Swartz, Vera L. Zolberg (eds.) 2004. *After Bourdieu*, Dordrecht: Kluwer Academic Publishers, 338.

75 Jochen Dreher. 2018. "Oblivion of power?: The social construction of reality and the (counter-) critique of Pierre Bourdieu." In *Social Constructivism as Paradigm?* Routledge, 237.

subject – and the object of knowledge – the object.[76] If one would neglect this relationship one would reduce "history to a process without a subject."[77] However as with all thinkers Bourdieu has been criticised for perhaps something that is not fully justifiable. This criticism came from Jenkins who said: "My strongest criticism of his work is probably that he consistently says he is doing one thing while actually doing something else (and usually something which negates or undermines his stated project)". He seeks, for example, to transcend the objectivist – subjectivist dualism while remaining firmly rooted in objectivism.[78] However Bourdieu is not alone in being criticised, Vandenberghe also took a special dislike to Berger and Luckmann's social structure as a mere sum of separate classification strategies and acts. He saw the social construction of reality and the notion as a problematic reduction of structure to culture. He noted that through an "idealistic conception of social structure as a constraining system of typifications (reduction of structure to culture)".[79]

Considering that Berger and Luckmann published their theory in 1966 it is astonishing that no criticism as to the complete validity of their view would emerge until fifty years later. This is specifically significant as we are witnessing through the digital revolution a new socially constructed reality which has emerged. Berger and Luckmann's words namely that "Society is a human product. Society is an objective reality. Man is a social product,"[80] suggests that more rethinking is needed. That is by looking back at history and hence the redefinition of all of the theories is appropriate which is the purpose of the book specially looking back at history. Arguably the criticism is more a reflection of a new reality rather than pointing to mistakes of the original work. As far as the issue of power is concerned Jovanovic importantly notes:

> According to Bourdieu, power is "present" in all social spheres, with a *meta-field* of power existing and influencing divisions and conflicts in all other fields. Here Bourdieu becomes an orthodox Weberian when he sees *struggle* (*Kampf*) as a foundation for the dynamics of social life. The struggle for power is at the core of all social relations – the struggle for control over material and symbolic resources, which transform into

---

76 Pierre Bourdieu. 2010. *Outline of a Theory of Practice*, Cambridge University Press, 79.

77 Pierre Bourdieu. 1990. *In Other Words: Essays towards a Reflexive Sociology*, Polity Press, 123.

78 Richard Jenkins. 2007. *Pierre Bourdieu*, Routledge, 175.

79 Frederic Vandenberghe. 2018. "Under the Sacred Canopy: Peter Berger (1929–2017)", *European Journal of Social Theory*, 21 (3), 413.

80 Berger and Luckmann, 2016, 79.

> different forms of capital in that way. Therefore, examining the field of power is necessary and crucial for discovering and understanding the origin, meaning and consequences of power relations in any society.[81]

The difference between Bourdieu and Berger and Luckmann in relation to the importance of power is the fact that Bourdieu was close to the communist, socialist, and social-democratic political forces in France whereas Berger and Luckmann favoured limited government, free trade and adherence to economic liberalism.

8 Constructivism in International Relations

So far, the focus has been how power affects and guides society as a whole within a social cultural setting. This part will analyse constructivism as a substantive problem of international relations. Perhaps it is fitting to turn back to the Greeks who noted that "psychological balance – a harmonious relationship among reason, appetite, and spirit – promoted good decisions, happiness, and justice. Imbalance led to bad decisions, unhappiness, and behavior at odds with the real interests of the individual and community."[82] Arguably we are in a period of imbalance, but it is also obvious that developed states and powerful interest groups will have clashing preferences and the outcomes depend on their relative power. An example is the Rifle Association in the United States clashing with those who advocate for gun control.

That said, it is not only the acts of a government on the domestic front which shapes the social reality of the citizens but also how it manages its international relations. As an example, ratifying the WTO affects domestic economic activities specifically if one industry is propped up by subsidies. Two principal issues need to be considered namely "(1) the degree to which international relations are socially constructed, and (2) the degree to which power can be transcended in world politics".[83] Hence Barkin argues that realist constructivism is built on an analytical focus upon the dialectic between ideals and power.[84] That is obvious as any government has an ideal position that is it

81 Miloš Jovanović. 2021. "Bourdieu's Theory and the Social Constructivism of Berger and Luckmann", *Philosophy and Society* 32 (4), 530.

82 Richard Ned Lebow. 2004. "Constructive realism." *International Studies Review* 6, no. 2, 347.

83 Patrick Thaddeus Jackson and Daniel H. Nexon. 2004. "Constructivist realism or realist-constructivism?" *International Studies Review* 6, no. 2, 338.

84 J. Samuel Barkin. 2003. "Realist Constructivism". *International Studies Review* 5, 337.

benefits the country and the realistic assessment of its power to "have its way". It follows that political relationships are not contingent on natural necessities, but they are rather socially constructed because it is power that is implicated in social actions. The current conflicts in Europe are instructive. Considering that Hungary in the 1950's attempted to liberate itself from Russia it is interesting to note that Hungary despite its past is not supporting Ukraine. We see a power-driven split from the NATO alliance and social moves within society affecting the powerbase of the government which has moved away from collaborations with the natural allies. How then do we understand what determines international social reality?

To understand social reality we must begin with the sociability of the human species. As Berger and Luckmann have – in brief – advocated is that face to face conversation is making us fulfil our reality that is we understand our social reality in the face-to-face context. It can be truly said that humans are social. The effect arguably was that international politics concentrated on welfare issues as noted above. Today the social aspect of humanity is and has changed as face-to-face conversations which are not the norm as most communicate via machines and mostly via the smart phone. In effect the smartphone is the third "person" in our conversations. And why would the phone and other digital instruments be a third person? The reason is that the digital instruments are not only having a conversation with humans they also have a communication with other machines. Surveillance and data collection are functioning through other machines and hence communication is altered and different. Humanity as such has taken a back seat and hence the changing the political machinery and hence the purpose of power has come to the fore front. One only has to observe the current political manoeuvres in the United States where facts have given way to fiction and lies.

When observing international bodies it can easily be seen that blatant lies are the common language and international politics is driven by false statements and hence power is the dominant factor driving intentional politics.

Arguably therefore constructivism which existed twenty years ago is today a historical argument and is of little relevance except to learn and understand what has changed. There is no doubt international politics has seen a dramatic change in the last twenty years. The hippy years are dead. We now live in a world of tribalism. Brown did note in 2001 "a recognition of the power of tribalism is crucial to realism."[85] Mattern correctly argued that:

85 Chris Brown. 2001. Fog in the Channel: Continental International Relations Theory Isolated (or An Essay on the Paradoxes of Diversity and Parochialism in IR Theory). In

> … power is understood to take many forms and to be expressed in many ways, it is not enough to simply note that power is productive or to treat it as passively enacted through social relationships (as postmodernists do, for instance). Rather, given its variegated forms and expressions, the various agentic processes through which different forms and expressions of power produce realities are themselves a matter into which realist-constructivist research must inquire. In short, power is a question to be investigated, not a variable or process to be accounted for.[86]

The conclusion is that power games of powerful governments are affecting other smaller players in a political sense and hence society is in effect is forced to adjust to outside influences.

9 Conclusion

Berger and Luckmann did recognise the notion of power and put it in the following way:

> The historical outcome of each clash of gods was determined by those who wielded the better weapons rather than those who had the better arguments […] He who has the bigger stick has the better chance of imposing his definitions of reality. […] power in society includes the power to determine decisive socialization processes and, therefore, the power to *produce* reality.[87]

Looking at current events this sentence unfortunately does ring true. While democracy limps along, those who wield the better weapons rather than those who have the better arguments are controlling outcomes.

The Black Panthers use the slogan "All power to the people" when protesting the rich ruling class dominating society.[88] This is not a realistic view anymore.

International Relations: Still An American Social Science? edited by Robert M.A. Crawford and Darryl S.L. Jarvis. State University of New York Press, 212.

86 Janice Bially Mattern. 2004. "Power in realist-constructivist research." *International Studies Review* 6, no. 2, 345.

87 Berger and Luckmann, 2016, 137.

88 Charles Earl Jones. ed. 1998. *The black panther party (reconsidered)*. Black Classic Press, 39.

Knowledge has always been synonymous with power but now in the digital age those who have the power to coerce and influence others have become an emerging and a powerful class, namely the technology giants. Nigam analysing socialism, argued that there is a disjunction between the Marxist conception power and production.[89] In addition, the common point that binds the theorists namely Arendt, Parsons, Foucault and Giddens, is that power represents to them a phenomenon that is primarily creative or productive. Domination, conflict and repression are no doubt, abiding features of power; yet they are not all that power is all about.[90]

Trust in the power of the law to balance emerging powerhouses is the only thing a single individual has to rely on for justice when instability occurs. "Wielding a stick" is simply not politically or socially correct although it represents a metaphor for the leverage that is created where a power imbalance exists. Dictators on the other hand do not understand the politically correct notions and they sometimes use the court to validate their intentions as currently seen in countries such as Russia. While independent experts are important for balancing governance in a democracy, the combined power exerted by any group can dominate a democracy. The five factors that support their power and control are the complexity of the tasks, legitimisation of the regime, autonomy of organisations associated with experts, regime stability and regime position.[91] Alfred Stepan points out that technocratic elites often have "chameleon-like qualities that allow them to serve various political masters depending on their objectives".[92]

It is interesting to note how Eberle conceived Berger and Luckmann's view on the problem of social order. He noted that they concentrate on the "social processes which stabilize reality" and "conceive of social change as rather a threat to the social order than as a chance for progress".[93] It appears that their view has some merits insofar as it can be observed (and this book agrees) that the digital revolution has indeed been a threat to social order but also a vehicle for social communication and a bonus to the economic outlook of the powerful technocrats. We have argued that human contact is now influenced

89 Aditya, 1996, 3.

90 Aditya, 1996, 5–6.

91 Miguel Angel Centeno. 1993. "The New Leviathan: The Dynamics and Limits of Technocracy." *Theory and Society*, vol. 22, no. 3, 316.

92 Alfred Stepan. 1978. *State and Society*, Princeton University Press, 57.

93 Thomas S. Eberle. 2019. "Variations of Constructivism", in Michaela Pfadenhauer, Hubert Knoblauch (eds.), *Social Constructivism as Paradigm? The Legacy of The Social Construction of Reality*, Routledge, 148.

by machines. The difference between the influence of machines in the industrial revolution and the digital revolution is that machines as noted in this book in effect have become the third party in a marriage. Hence the effect of the machines on our social structure requires some comments in the next chapter.

CHAPTER 10

The Fading Line between Humans and Machines

1 Introduction

The "algorithmic culture" includes computers, programs and platforms with large data sets and complex mathematics in establishing, maintaining, and transforming the frameworks by means of which human beings orient our judgments, actions, and dispositions toward one another and toward the surrounding world. The issue is that automation is controlled by people whereas the new technology is capable of learning and the behaviour of AI for example can no longer be precisely predicted. The element of autonomy is a crucial issue.[1] Arguably the "algorithmic culture" and the story behind it – paraphrasing Marx – are about the complex interplay between "people making history" and doing so "under conditions not of our own making."[2] This last chapter will demonstrate – by briefly touching on transhumanism – that an understanding of society needs to be socially constructed that is by humans and not by machines. As such it highlights the purpose of this book to look globally at the issue of constructing societies wellbeing through contemporary but also historical thinking.

Heidegger in one of his lectures in 1938 noted – arguably before his time but of relevance: "One of the essential phenomena of the modern age is its science. A phenomenon of no less importance is machine technology".[3] Heidegger was very clear about the role research plays in developing new ideas such as AI. "It all begins with experiments. Experiments begin with the laying down of a law as a basis. To set up an experiment means to represent or conceive the conditions under which a specific series of motions can be made susceptible of being followed in its necessary progression, i.e., of being controlled in advance by calculation."[4] The issue we are facing today is the commercial aspect of AI in the minds of the technology giants which means that "first out into the market"

1 Janssen Andre. 2024. "Artificial Intelligence and Contract Performance". In Larry DiMatteo, Christina Poncibò, Pietro Sirena and Michel Cannarsa (eds.), *Artificial Intelligence and Private Law: Global Perspectives*, Cambridge University Press, on file with author, 1.

2 Ted Striphas. 2023. *Algorithmic Culture Before the Internet*, Columbia University Press, 6.

3 Martin Heidegger. 2005. *Introduction to phenomenological research.* Indiana University Press, 116.

4 Heidegger, 2005, 121.

 DOI:10.1163/9789004702691_011

makes the profit not the resulting sales of the product. The question whether the new technology performs as planned is only of secondary importance. It is not surprising that unplanned events and functions – commonly referred to as bugs – are a feature of new technology. What should be most important is "that the ground plan furnishes a criterion and constrains the anticipatory representation of the conditions."[5] The source of criticism is namely that discovery, examination, verification, evaluation, preservation, and interpretation of sources as noted by Heidegger are not diligently followed. This is exactly the problem this book aims to demonstrate. Indeed, Janssen noted that from a certain degree of autonomy onwards, it is no longer possible to predict without further ado, whether and how explanations and actions emanating from AI systems themselves originate from the operators of these systems at all and can still be attributed to them.[6]

2 Looking Backwards

Heidegger confirmed the importance of history. Indeed, this book also looks at history as an important factor in understanding the present. In recognising this, Heidegger stated:

> In the historical sciences, just as in the natural sciences, the methodology aims at representing what is fixed and stable and at making history an object. History can become objective only when it is past. What is stable in what is past, that on the basis of which historiographical explanation reckons up the solitary and the diverse in history, is the always-has been-once-already, the comparable. Through the constant comparing of everything with everything, what is intelligible is found by calculation and is certified and established as the ground plan of history ... It is not that historical research denies what is great in history; rather it explains it as the exception. In this explaining. the great is measured against the ordinary and the average. And there is no other historiographical explanation so long as explaining means reduction to what is intelligible and so long as historiography remains research, i.e., an explaining.[7]

5 Heidegger, 2005, 121.

6 Janssen, 2024, 242.

7 Heidegger, 2005, 123.

Heidegger also raises an issue which has been described by Berger and Luckmann as an important factor in the socialisation process, namely institutionalisation. To become relevant any new technology such as AI has to be able to be institutionalised "research is not an ongoing activity because its work is accomplished in institutions, but rather institutions are necessary because science, intrinsically as research, has the character of ongoing activity."[8] The issue is that AI is not institutionalised in the sociological, philosophical way as it has been left uncontrolled and only now are governments attempting to institutionalise AI research and output through legislation. The importance in the institutionalising process is the fact that "Nothing less than the making secure of the precedence of methodology over whatever is (nature and history), which at any given time becomes objective in research."[9]

One of the changes in modern technology and in this case the digital world is that the historical linkage to a place of learning such as a university is not strong anymore. The sharing of deep research is at odds with the profit motives of the technology giants. It is the race to the market, which is important as in many cases, and "the winner takes all". It is therefore not common to aspire to the thinking of Heidegger who argued:

> The more exclusively science individualizes itself with a view to the total carrying on and mastering of its work process, and the more realistically these ongoing activities are shifted into separate research institutes and professional schools, the more irresistibly do the sciences achieve the consummation of their modern essence.[10]

However, Heidegger points to an important difference between the onset of modern science in the first half of the 20's century and today. It was true to say that "Now if science as research is an essential phenomenon of the modern age, it must be that which constitutes the metaphysical ground of research and determines first and long beforehand the essence of that age generally. The essence of the modern age can be seen in the fact that man frees himself from the bonds of the Middle Ages in freeing himself to himself."[11] The difference is that man does not free himself to himself but to the corporate world. He has become the pawn in a bigger game, the one of feeding the elites as noted by Turchin in a previous chapter.

---

8 Heidegger, 2005, 124.

9 Heidegger, 2005, 125.

10 Heidegger, 2005, 126.

11 Heidegger, 2005, 127.

Interestingly Heidegger posed a question which is as relevant today as it was before namely, is it as an "I" confined to its own preferences and freed into its own arbitrary choosing or as the "we" of society; is it as an individual or as a community; is it as a personality within the community or as a mere group member in the corporate body; is it as a state and nation and as a people or as the common humanity of modem man, that man will and ought to be the subject that in his modem essence he already is?[12]

Man will know and will therefore carefully safeguard the truth, "that which is incalculable, only in creative questioning and shaping out of the power of genuine reflection". Reflection transports the man of the future into that "between" in which he belongs to being and yet remains a stranger amid that which is.[13] The question is whether reflection and the truth is still present within society, or has it become the domain of the academic world only?

3 Back to the Future

The terms algorithm and culture came to be entangled before computing became personal, mobile, wearable, implantable, ubiquitous, or otherwise – that is, before computing became "Everyware."[14] Our human vital signs are now dependent on technology with the advent of new medical devices to assist with problematic valves and nodes in hearts and other vital organs. Medical devices can be inserted into the brain to assist with conditions such as Parkinson's disease. Software integrated into a medical device promises wonders for the better health of people. The devices may perform similarly or better than humans in diagnosing and treating the most common or deadliest diseases, as well as enable a patients' holistic view, keeping them healthy and collecting data instead of treating diseases. However, if AI is the magic solution for dealing with health systems' major challenges, it can also pose a safety threat. In health, risks are at the highest level and may lead to death. Providing a safe ground and setting the rules for the widespread implementation of medical devices with technology interfaces and its investment is now paramount. The level of transparency and to explain the ability around AI medical devices for example is becoming increasingly complicated. Stakeholders predominantly do not understand how drugs and traditional medical device's function. They

---

12 Heidegger, 2005, 133.

13 Heidegger, 2005, 136.

14 Ted Striphas. 2015. "Algorithmic culture." *European journal of cultural studies* 18, no. 4–5, 402.

mainly trust regulatory assurance and information provided though labels and instructions.[15]

How can an individual feel safe and make informed decisions? Is the standard set by medical research also applicable to instruments used to direct and possibly assist society at large? This important aspect needs to be discussed and that is namely the impact of emerging technologies on the legal concept of the person. The question which needs to be asked is whether there is a fundamental change in what is or what was "a person", still stands. Can the definition of a person now pass the test of time?

4 The Question of Transhumanism

The word "transhumanism" was first used by Julian Huxley in a collection of essays that commences with a programme for what he, inspired by the triumphs in science and technology, sees as the "cosmic duty" of the human species: to "transcend itself … in its entirety, as humanity". He hoped for "a new kind of existence" when enough people will believe in "transhumanism".[16]

To begin with a definition will assist in the discussion of this futuristic development but nevertheless it is potentially a disturbing development. Transhumanism can be defined as "a way of thinking about the future that is based on the premise that the human species in its current form does not represent the end of our development but rather a comparatively early phase."[17] Another way to define it is the "belief or theory that the human race can evolve beyond its current physical and mental limitations, especially by means of science and technology."[18] However these concepts – not discussed in this book – are an extreme view of transhumanism evolving namely "posthumanism". An example of such is Xenofeminism which aims to "eradicate sex -one of the most fundamental and indelible aspects of the human condition" through technology.[19]

---

15 Tatiana de Campos Aranovich. 2023. "Regulating SaMD: Transparent and explainable AI medical devices for what?" *Algorithmic Justice Symposium*, Sydney.

16 Julian Huxley. 1957. "Transhumanism". In: *New bottles for new wine*. Chatto and Windus, 17.

17 Nick Bostrom. 2014. "Introduction—The transhumanist FAQ: A general introduction." *Transhumanism and the body: The world religions speak*, 1.

18 Transhumanism, *Oxford Dictionary of English* (3d ed. 2015).

19 See Lidia Zuin. 2021. *"Xenofeminism Aims to Abolish Gender Through Technology"*, *MEDIUM*, https://lidiazuin.medium.com/xenofeminism-aims-to-abolish-gender-through-technology-e6abfde4498c.

The worrying prediction is as Maris, the founder of Google Ventures put it recently: "If you ask me today, is it possible to live to be 500? The answer is yes."[20] To examine this claim with the knowledge we have one would argue that this is not possible not only from a medical point of view but also from an economic and political point of view. It is questionable whether sectors of commerce such as the building industry can be redirected or proceed on such a radical assumption. In addition, if we keep producing children the world would be too small to house and feed everybody as we are already not capable to do so for all. In brief important ethical questions are hidden by such radical statements. Nevertheless, some comments and more importantly some questions are necessary. The very point of transhumanism is that the legal concept of the person must be revisited and if necessary altered. A person in a general sense needs to be given legal protection within the structure of a society as discussed by Rawls and Berger and Luckmann in previous chapters. The importance is highlighted by Van Beers noting that "the complex interplay between the legal concept of the person and the images of the human [is] surfacing in new technological contexts."[21] This is to be contrasted with the view of Kurzweil who argued that "the development of transhumanist technologies is inevitable in a technologically advanced, globalized society."[22] This is true insofar the innovations in genetics and, nanotechnology combined with AI will offer new experiences both physically and cognitively. These kinds of challenges will impact not only on the law but also on the way society functions.

The most troubling aspect is how will the issue of power and the influence of elites affect the social fabric? One of the specific concerns is how is education in general affected?

5 Transhumanism in Education

New technology generally but transhumanism in particular raises new ethical and pedagogical questions too. Pedagogy is influenced by social, political, and psychological development of learners and this is where the very meaning of

---

20 Adam Kirsch. 2020. *"Looking Forward to the End of Humanity"*, *Wall Street Journal*, https://www.wsj.com/articles/looking-forward-to-the-end-of-humanity-11592625661.

21 Britta Van Beers. 2017. "The changing nature of law 's natural person: the impact of emerging technologies on the legal concept of the person." *German Law Journal* 18, no. 3, 559–594.

22 See generally Ray Kurzweil. 2024. *The Singularity Is Nearer: When We Merge with AI*. Random House, 7.

education is contested. A re-examination of how we educate the population is essential considering that our social reality and social values are being challenged. The issue Buchanan argued is that that education is a transhumanist project,[23] whereas Damberger and Hebert argue that the objective of pedagogy never intended to transcend humankind as such.[24] Bokedal *et al* highlighted "question the transhumanist tendency to describe humans as nothing more than information-processing objects, pertaining to a cognitivist understanding of the person."[25]

It has always been understood that human life, at its best, is wonderful.[26] However transhumanism blurs the "the distinction between individual accidental preferences and what is really desirable. It highlights ethical–didactic elements pertaining, not least, to disability and ability issues in the educational realm, as well as matters of equal human functioning." The problem in understanding the place of humans in the machine age is important especially considering Bostom arguing that "education [is] as 'low-tech' means of enhancement, aligned with philosophical contemplation and moral self-scrutiny."[27] What is the purpose of education? Buchanan's sums up best the view of education as he notes:

> Education should aim (i) to promote the individual's flourishing, (ii) to equip her for fulfilling the role of citizen in a democratic polity, (iii) to help her to avoid economic dependency by enabling her to be an effective contributor to produce social cooperation, and (iv) to promote the general (social) well-being by contributing to the development of skills and knowledge that make more productive and fulfilling forms of cooperation possible.[28]

23 Allen Buchanan. 2011. *Better than human: the promise and perils of enhancing ourselves*. Oxford University Press, 10.

24 Thomas Damberger and Estella Hebert. 2017. "Is pedagogy transhuman? Reflections on the relationship between pedagogy and transhumanism." *Studia Paedagogica Ignatiana* 20, no. 1, 53.

25 Tomas Bokedal, Solveig Magnus Reindal, Svein Rise and Stein M. Wivestad. 2022. "'Someone'versus 'something': A reflection on transhumanist values in light of education." *Journal of Philosophy of Education* 56, no. 2, (228.

26 Nick Bostrom. 2008. "Letter from Utopia". *Studies in Ethics, Law, and Technology*, 2(1), 7.

27 Nick Bostrom. 2005. "Transhumanist values". *Journal of Philosophical Research*, 30, 9.

28 Allen Buchanan. 2011. "Cognitive enhancement and education." *Theory and research in education* 9, no. 2, 148.

At first glance this view seems to be unproblematic. However once transhuman philosophical aspirations are viewed, pedagogical and ethical challenges appear. The point made was that "the objective of pedagogy never intended to transcend humankind as such [and] education in itself is a transhumanist project."[29] Looking back at the definition of transhumanism namely the "belief or theory that the human race can evolve beyond its current physical and mental limitations, especially by means of science and technology"[30] suggests that machines are playing a part in education. Arguably if the human race developed past its mental limitations this space will be taken over by new technology, that is machines. The question then is who controls the machines and importantly will the current belief that human beings are of the highest intelligence in the animal kingdom become obsolete?

As already noted above – and being one of the core beliefs of this book – there can be little doubt that our notions of educative formation (*bildung*) are closely associated with how we view reality – let us refer to this as our understanding of being. Existentialist philosophers, prominent thinkers like Kierkegaard, Heidegger, Gadamer and Sartre [have explained this fact].[31] The important theme among existentialists was the recognition of "choice" that is we are free to form a desirable life beyond the narrow – digitalised intelligence and information concentration currently stressed by transhumanists. Education is not only restricted to institutions, but it also takes place in everyday activities. At best education is the expression of choice. It is "a lifelong ethical – educational process that has its due value in itself. Its sole purpose is to form the individual's character, to form and to shape the 'self'".[32] Education is charged with strengthening certain aspects of the self, such as intelligence and memory which necessitates that it needs to engage the very core of the personality. Kirkegard specifically noted that "the whole race participates in the individual, and the individual in the whole race".[33] It follows that it is not only the classroom which educates people but also importantly the social setting and the interactions with others that will shape the self and importantly grow knowledge about oneself.

29 See Bokedal, Reindal, Rise and Wivestad, 2022, 228.

30 Transhumanism, *Oxford Dictionary of English* (3d ed. 2015).

31 Bokedal, Reindal, Rise and Wivestad, 2022, 233.

32 See generally Soren Kierkegaard. 1990. *Eighteen upbuilding discourses*. No. 5. Princeton University Press.

33 Soren Kierkegaard. 2014. *The concept of anxiety: A simple psychologically oriented deliberation in view of the dogmatic problem of hereditary sin.* WW Norton & Company, 28.

Self-scrutinising and self-searching is an integral part of education that is building a personal profile in a social setting which requires more than strengthening certain proficiencies or by strengthening certain aspects of the self, such as intelligence, memory etc. Here lies the problem of transhumanism. Technology has no self, that is technology has no ability of a spiritual formation. Education as envisaged by Kirkegaard as the cognitive one-sidedness that characterises transhumanism, needs to be rejected. Bokedal *et al* correctly argue that "[education] of the individual is enacted on a significantly broader educational platform than that propounded by transhumanism". Simply put, the arguments by Kirkegaard are not compatible with the ones reflected by Bokedal and also by the arguments constructed in this book.

Consequently, "the focus on personhood, the process of [education] also finds itself in a stronger position to serve as an educational guide in a complex world, characterised by contradiction."[34] It is the spiritual and cultural formation which sets education in a broad sense apart from transhumanism. This notion of education is very important as the digital revolution through mechanisms of speed and efficiency has eroded education. Currently, the self is not formed by real personal contacts, as access to the internet through the mobile phone as an example has narrowed interactions between people to interactions between the machine and person. Individuals have become independent of each other and also self-preoccupied. Hence the philosophy and the human science expressed by the German word *Geisteswissenschaften* have taken a backseat. "*Bildung* in the humanities can further happen in a world that is humanly constituted through embodiment, language and custom (and not primarily through technology)."[35] The importance of education or *Bildung* is aptly described by Gadamar who states, 'in acquired *Bildung* nothing disappears, but everything is preserved.'[36] Transhumanism ignores the fact that personal development comes from within the person and not externally, "artificially" supplied, from the outside. Therefore, the question is how does the legal institution define the important part in any society, namely the person.

6 The Legal Aspect of a Person

"Recent technologies, such as medical biotechnology and AI, are offering radical ways to transform the biological and physical aspects of life, thus

34 Bokedal, Reindal, Rise and Wivestad, 2022, 234.

35 Bokedal, Reindal, Rise and Wivestad, 2022, 234.

36 Hans-Georg Gadamer, 2013. *Truth and method*. A&C Black, 12.

challenging the natural outlines of the legal category of the person."[37] The distinction between the human and the person is still controversial all over the world specifically in current debates in the United States. For example when does a foetus becomes a person? When does a person on life support stop being a person? Gray has stated "[i]n books of law, as in other books, and in common speech, 'person' is often used as meaning a human being, but the technical legal meaning of 'person' is a subject of legal rights and duties."[38]

Considering the technological advances specifically with the yet to fully explore the capabilities of AI it is important to define not only a natural person but also to distinguish a natural person and an artificial person that is not a biological creation but a creation of machines. Once artificial persons are created by technology it is not disputed that they can make decisions, enter into contracts or own property to note a few possibilities. However, an artificial person cannot have children and hence be a parent and importantly cannot vote.

The question is whether an artificial person is viewed the same way as a corporation being "the mere creature of law."[39] It is interesting to observe that the word natural in contrast to artificial to describe humans has been questioned. The Nuffield Council on Bioethics on the meaning of the term "naturalness" in bioethical debates concluded "that effective communication on the ethics of science, technology, and medicine may be hindered, rather than helped, by appeals to naturalness."[40]

It is not surprising that the legal definition of a person has been questioned due to the recent developments by emerging medical technologies and robotics in general. Artificially intelligent machines are increasingly capable of accomplishing tasks that have until now been considered exclusively human abilities. Dworkin characterised the concept of autonomy as the right to be recognised as autonomous, rather than as a trait to be possessed. Dworkin proposed the 'integrity' view of autonomy where the value of autonomy is to protect the rights of competent persons to create or construct their own lives according to their own values.[41]

Strictly speaking even natural persons are a legally constructed entities with essential biological or naturalistic traits such as those belonging to the human

37 Van Beers, 2017.

38 John Chipman Gray. 2019. *The nature and sources of the law*. Routledge.

39 See *Trustees of Dartmouth College v Woodward*, 17 US 518 (1819).

40 Nuffield Council on Bioethics. 2015. "Ideas about Naturalness in Public and Political Debates about Science", *Technology and Medicine*, 106, https://www.nuffieldbioethics.org/assets/pdfs/Naturalness-analysis-paper.pdf.

41 Ronald Dworkin. 1986. "Autonomy and the Demented Self" 64 *The Milbank Quarterly* 4.

species, birth, death and are either male or female. The pressure to define and include artificial persons comes from the fact that a corporation – an artificial person – has already been given legal standing as well as blurring the lines between the difference between humans and artificial persons. Some examples are the fact that arguments have been made to include others such as animals into the legal construct of persons. It is not surprising that the legal definition of a person has been questioned and analysed due to the recent developments by emerging medical technologies.

The understanding of parenthood has also been challenged as same sex couples do not have to go through adoption if the child was conceived via assisted reproductive technologies and in some jurisdictions three parents of a baby can be listed.[42] There is a growing literature in relation to denaturalised and artificialised natural persons. As an example Grear argues that artificial personality is better able to "respond to the complexities, mutations, hybridities and multiplicities confronting law in the twenty-first century," including biotechnological developments and the emergence of transhumanism in the postmodern society.[43] The fault line which goes through the argument of postmodernism is the fact that no effort has been made to socially construct such a term and give it a reality which is defendable and is above else important for any society postmodern or otherwise to function. A pertinent question to ask is whether we are simply over-defining issues and, in the process, lost the end game we are all hoping to achieve namely a vibrant functioning society.

Van Beers asked the questions, "Has the time now come, then, to declare the death of law's natural person? Should the natural person move over and make place for the inherently plastic and disembodied artificial person? According to several authors writing on the law of persons, a further artificialisation of law's natural person – in the form of either a disembodiment, fictionalisation or customisation of this legal category – is indeed necessitated by the complexities, multiplicities, and fluid realities of life in a postmodern society."[44] Boyle did give an answer to Van Breer's questions by stating that "law-out of all the

42 The United Kingdom is the first nation worldwide to allow this technology. See Hannah Devlin. 2015. *"Britain's House of Lords approves conception of three-person babies", The Guardian*, https://www.theguardian.com/politics/2015/feb/24/uk-house-of-lords-approves-conception-of-three-person-babies.

43 See Anna Grear. 2013. "Law 's entities: complexity, plasticity and justice." *Jurisprudence* 4, no. 1, 76–101.

44 Van Beers, 2017, 592.

disciplines of market and society has been the only one with a postmodern subject."[45]

The conclusion which can be drawn is that the answers offered by the artificialist approach to law's definition of a person do not answer the most vital questions raised by new technologies especially biomedical technologies. It is all too easy to maintain that law is radically cut off from biological reality, or that individuals have the right to shape themselves as they want, in an era in which the human condition itself is becoming the object of technological interventions. On the contrary, emerging technologies such as artificial intelligence and medical biotechnology place the essentially contested concepts of humanity, human dignity and human nature back onto the legal agenda. No longer merely a bone of contention in the mainly theoretical debates between legal positivists and natural law thinkers, human nature has now or should become the focal point of heated political debates on the legal regulation of technologies that may actually affect the human condition. These questions are not of a merely legal-technical nature. Therefore, a strictly legal-technical concept of the person cannot suffice in the regulation of emerging technologies. Instead, what is needed is a legal concept of the person which can capture and express what is, ultimately at stake in the coming era of human enhancement technologies: Our embodied, human nature.

An effective system must be based on justice and ethics. Vagle correctly noted that: "… lawmakers and regulators must consider both the moral and political factors that are affected by connected technologies, paying special attention to the potential social harms and threats to individual freedoms and autonomy. It also means considering human values in the same vein as we have historically considered fiscal and business value".[46]

7 Autonomous AI or the Non-biological Machine

Bostrom and Yudkowsky first proposed by the principle of substrate non-discrimination with the view that if two beings have the same functionality and same conscious experience, and differ only in their physical substrate, then they should have the same moral status.[47] The question today is whether

45 James Boyle. 1991. "Is subjectivity possible-the post-modern subject in legal theory." *University of Colorado Law Review* 62, 489.

46 Mark D. Vagle. 2018. *Crafting phenomenological research*. Routledge, 111.

47 Nick Bostrom and Eliezer Yudkowsky. 2018. "The ethics of artificial intelligence." In *Artificial intelligence safety and security*, Chapman and Hall/CRC, 322.

machines can be considered a person that is are responsible for their actions has been recently tested.[48] In *Thaler v Commissioner of Patents*,[49] which is the first judicial determination in the world in favour of AI systems being named as inventors of a patent and hence a person under the law. However the Full Federal Court has now weighed in, overturning that decision.[50] The question really is whether a non-biological machine can be viewed as a person. Three issues or distinctions are important namely between "human", "person" and "property". The complicated issue in this debate is that a corporation as noted above is a non-biological entity but is a person in a legal sense. Hence the question which will occupy scholars for a long time is whether AI as a non-biological entity can ever be classed as a legal person in the context of 'intentionality' and 'autonomy.' However as seen in *Thaler v Commissioner of Patents* the law could simply define a legal person to be anything that the law chooses it to be.

Where the *Thaler* case gets interesting is in testing the boundary at which the instructions given to the AI system are vague enough, or the AI system is given enough freedom in how it applies those instructions, that the AI system is appropriately considered to be the responsible actor of its own actions.[51]

Calverley argued that the real issue of the argument is "that so long as a non-biological machine had a level of mental activity in areas deemed relevant to law, such as autonomy and intentionality, then it could be a legal person with independent existence separate and apart from its origins as property."[52] The crucial point is how is intentionality defined. Searle stated that "Intentionality is that feature of the mind by which mental states are directed at, or are about or of, or refer to, or aim at, states of affairs in the world."[53] From a philosophical point of view that might be true however as a legal person is defined by the law. We need to rely on a legal rather than a philosophical definition. Morse as an example defined intentionality in the following way which differs from the philosophical one. He noted:

---

48 Hui Chia, Daniel Beck, Jeannie Marie Paterson and Julian Savulescu. 2023. "Autonomous AI: what does autonomy mean in relation to persons or machines?" *Law, Innovation and Technology* 15, no. 2, 390.

49 *Thaler v Commissioner of Patents* [2021] FCA 879.

50 Rebecca Currey and Jane Owen. 2021 *"In the courts: Australian court finds AI systems can be 'inventors'"*, *Wipo Magazine*, www.wipo.int/wipo_magazine/en/2021/03/article_0006.html.

51 Chia, Beck, Paterson and Savulescu, 2023, 396.

52 David J. Calverley. 2008. "Imagining a non-biological machine as a legal person." *AI & Society* 22, 527.

53 See John R. Searle. 1999. *Mind, language and society: Philosophy in the real world*, Masterminds.

> The law clearly treats people as intentional agents and not simply as part of the biophysical flotsam and jetsam of the causal universe. ... (L) aw and morality are systems of rules that at the least are meant to guide or influence behavior ... They operate within the domain of practical reason.
>
> ...
>
> All things being equal, intentional action or forbearance is the only aspect of the human condition that is fully "up to us," that is fully within our control, and that can be fully guided by and produced by our reason.[54]

Hence to be a person the law needs to see an intention directed to a particular action. Simply put there has to be an awareness or a mental state that a particular act is intentionally performed. Arguably through, a non-biological machine has the capacity to act intentionally based on the desire to act according to its functions within a program. The question, however, is whether a machine can form an intention based on desire and a belief. Desire is driven or based upon the notion that there has to be a capacity to modify behaviour or habits that is there has to be a moral aspect to the behaviour. There are strong arguments to suggest that machines do have functional intentionality, but do they express responsibility and autonomy?

It is obvious in law that free will is not necessarily a criterion for responsibility. From this point of view alone, a non-biological entity can be a person but is a machine powered by AI acting autonomously? It can be argued that a machine is an agent of its designers and will therefore act autonomously that is it will faithfully act on the instructions given by the designers. In other words "there appears to be a 'controlling' entity, which is setting the parameters of action."[55] If that is the case the law would be ascribing legal responsibility to the person who programmed the computer. This is so as the programmer is the person who set the whole chain of events into motion hence, he bears ultimate responsibility. The question of course is whether there are conscious machines able to understand human feelings and, on that cue, will they act to the benefit of that particular person but in another scenario will they act differently? If that would be the case, there are arguments that a machine is indeed a person

54 Stephen J. Morse. 2004. "Reason, results, and criminal responsibility." *University of Illinois Law Review*, 363.

55 Calverley, 2008, 532.

like a corporation that is the machine acts autonomously and is phenomenally conscious.

Whatever the theoretical construct is we do not know how far new technology such as AI can be developed in order to be a non-biological machine with functions of will, autonomy and feelings attributable to it. If that would be the case it is arguable that the law would assign personhood to such a non-biological machine as it has done to corporations. Simply put the jury is still out in answering the question whether non biological machines can be persons. However an overarching conclusion suggests that a non-biological machine can never attain personhood because of "the way we embodied humans are embedded in and respond to our physical surroundings makes our intelligence different in kind from the electronic signalling of artificial intelligence. It follows that our embodied, environmentally sensitive aspects; our socially, culturally, and experientially shaped aspects; and our responsible ethical aspects represent dimensions of selfhood that define fundamental differences between persons and machines."[56]

8 Conclusion

Futuristic developments can be both exciting and terrifying. Futurists exploring human societies and how they will emerge from the present, make predictions that propagate stories that capture public attention and sometimes cause fear. It is true that not all of these futuristic predictions will eventuate, and it is less likely that the fundamental aspects of our biological lives will be altered if individuals continue to coexist with each other on planet earth. There is no doubt that technology is of assistance to human health and medical biotechnology has already shown evidence of increasing the length and quality of human lives. It is true that we are becoming more reliant on this type of technology.

That said, since the Industrial Revolution machine technology has been an important factor in enhancing commercial productivity. Machine technology and human technology has now come such a long way that transparency and explainability of new technology is becoming more complex and more remote to the users of the technology. AI for example can be used as a scape goat for operators to attribute blame when their instructions cause things to go wrong.

56 Walter B. Gulick, 2023. "Machine and person: reconstructing Harry Collins's categories." *AI & Society*, 1857–1858.

This is a perplexing problem considering that human lives are sometimes dependent on new and innovative medical biotechnology devices. The important conclusion is that the existentialist recognition of choice and freedom to choose a desirable life beyond a narrow and digitalised life is becoming more and more important, despite being less and less valued.

CHAPTER 11

Conclusions

1 The Digital Revolution

It is of value to look back to history as advocated in this book. Specifically the turbulent times of socialism at the turn of the 1890's in Germany and Europe have been significant times of change and readjustment. As this book has noted, in the modern era of the digital revolution we also live in a changing and one could argue turbulent time irrespective that the reasons might be different. The issue is the same, namely a changing social impression of one's social world. In Germany specifically the prevalent political movement was led by the socialists. The social democrats identified themselves as having embraced Marxism and declared their solidarity with the working class. May 1, still recognised today as the workers day. However, at the same time the Marxist ideas of changing private ownership to communally owned one was rejected. The utopia of Marxism that is communism was starting to be recognised. Rosa Luxemburg aptly commented that the end game is everything the movement is nothing.[1]

At the end of the 19th century the time was marked by a distinct and fundamental change. It highlighted contrasting movements, the change away from socialism and class struggles to a more communally oriented world with a liberal rather than a socialist outlook. On an intellectual level the move away from the greats like Hegel was also observable. It was the time of Nietzsche where he developed his philosophy on the will to Power and he is often heralded as the father of existentialism which took root with the writings of Sartre in France and Heidegger in Germany. The late 1890s and early 1900s was termed a "time of a carnival as well as at the same time Ash Wednesday."[2] It was a time of contrast between a renaissance in political stresses as well as a pessimistic time of decadence. In essence the *'fin de siècle'* was a time of contrasts and chaos not unlike today.

The most important development however was the rise of industry, science and technology by men like Werner Siemens. It heralded a race for industrial dominance in the world. Importantly, it was seen as befitting everybody.

1 Ziegler, 1911, 480.

2 Ziegler, 1911, 522.

 | DOI:10.1163/9789004702691_012

Workers were needed who participated in the new "technological age" and were able to the better their existence. The standard of living for the working class increased and it also shifted people from agrarian pursuit into towns and hence improved their social standing. A new middle class developed, and towns increased.

Arguably therefore the digital revolution is in effect the same phenomenon we have seen at the turn of the 19th century and interestingly the same problems have persisted, namely the reshaping and reinvention of a social reality as this book has explained. The understanding of emerging problems is still discussed. As Heidegger in 1955,[3] in a lecture in Munich talked about "the Question about Technology". The first important observation was that we need to have a free relationship with technology that "the relationship will be free if it opens our human existence to the essence of technology. When we can respond to this essence, we shall be able to experience the technology within its own bounds."[4] Arguably Heidegger advocates that we control technology and only insofar as we are concerned with the essence of it, as he notes, that we never experience technology if we "put up with it or evade it" then "we remain unfree and chained to it."[5] The question of what technology is was answered in the following way.

> One says: Technology is a means to an end. The other says: Technology is a human activity. The two definitions of technology belong together. For to posit ends and procure and utilize the means to them is a human activity. The manufacture and utilization of equipment, tools, and machines, the manufactured and used things themselves, and the needs and ends that they serve, all belong to what technology is. The whole complex of these contrivances is technology. Technology itself is a contrivance, or, in Latin, an *instrumentum*.[6]

Heidegger clearly places the human into the role of an observer or the master and not as a captive of technology it is a means to an end. "The will to mastery becomes all the more urgent the more technology threatens to slip from human control."[7] This book argues that the digital revolution has slipped from

---

3 It must be noted that Heidegger was a thinker on existentialism like Jean Paul Sarte.

4 Martin Heidegger. 1977. *The Question Concerning Technology and Other Essays*, Garland Publishing Inc., 3.

5 Heidegger, 1977, 4.

6 Heidegger, 1977, 5.

7 Heidegger, 1977, 5.

human control as it is controlled by the technology giants that is big business and as the reward for big business is the data. Individuals are merely supplying the raw material, that is information. The question is, have we asked questions? As Heidegger puts it:

> We must ask: What is the instrumental itself? Within what do such things as means and end belong? A means is that whereby something is effected and thus attained. Whatever has an effect as its consequence is called a cause. But not only that by means of which something else is effected is a cause. The end in keeping with which the kind of means to be used is determined is also considered a cause. Wherever ends are pursued, and means are employed, wherever instrumentality reigns, there reigns causality.[8]

The issue with the IoT is that causality is veiled in darkness, that is technocrats have invented, fabricated and sold it for their own profit motive. At best the *causa efficiens* could apply. If we were to ask what is the purpose of the invention of the digital technology, we have trouble finding a convincing and a common answer. The most convincing answer could be the purpose of the technology is to facilitate communication. But we already had communication basically face to face or letters. Or is the purpose to communicate faster? Which begs a different question namely what is the cost of communicating faster and we know the answer now, the cost is loss of privacy, and we are all the raw materials supplying what the surveillance industry wants namely data.

Heidegger also argued that all inventions contain a feature namely "bringing forth" that is bringing into appearance. "Bringing-forth brings hither out of concealment forth into un-concealment. Bringing-forth comes to pass only insofar as something concealed comes into un-concealment. This coming rests and moves freely within what we call revealing."[9] What then has the digital revolution revealed? The answer is we do not know yet the full effect of its "bringing forth" and what it reveals is arguably a trade secret of the technology giants. Heidegger sees it in a different light as he argued: "Technology is therefore no mere means. Technology is a way of revealing. If we give heed to this, then another whole realm for the essence of technology will open itself up to us. It is the realm of revealing, i.e., of truth."[10]

---

8 Heidegger, 1977, 6.

9 Heidegger, 1977, 10.

10 Heidegger, 1977, 12.

What is the truth, has it been revealed? Arguably we are finding out slowly bit by bit what the truth is only by discovering the untruth and inviting legislation to remedy, the problems such as privacy and ethical issues. To look at the issue from a different light it can be said that "technology is a mode of revealing."[11] The digital revolution has only revealed to us that we can see in the showroom, but it has not yet revealed the intentions of those who own and run the showroom. Heidegger is correct by noting that, "What is modern technology? It too is a revealing. Only when we allow our attention to rest on this fundamental characteristic does that which is new in modern technology show itself to us. ... It expedites in that it unlocks and exposes. Yet that expediting is always itself directed from the beginning toward furthering something else, i.e., toward driving on to the maximum yield at the minimum expense."[12]

Heidegger notes – what appears to be simple but at the same time rather subtle and hence challenging – what technology reveals.

> The revealing that rules throughout modern technology has the character of a setting-upon, in the sense of a challenging forth. That challenging happens in that the energy concealed in nature is unlocked, what is unlocked is transformed, what is transformed is stored up, what is stored up is, in turn, distributed, and what is distributed is switched about ever anew. Unlocking, transforming, storing, distributing, and switching about are ways of revealing. But the revealing never simply comes to an end. Neither does it run off into the indeterminate. The revealing reveals to itself its own manifoldly interlocking paths, through regulating their course. This regulating itself is, for its part, everywhere secured. Regulating and securing even become the chief characteristics of the challenging revealing.

It is suggested that Heidegger informs us that we do not control the concealment nor the un-concealment within the technology that is the digital technology and especially AI. Only later will the real character be revealed. The important point which appears to be – to borrow from Rawls – is hidden behind a veil of ignorance. Technology has ensnared society and Heidegger alludes to the missing link in the way we embrace technology. He argued that "Therefore, in the realm of thinking, a painstaking effort to think through still more primally what was primally thought is not the absurd wish to revive what

11 Heidegger, 1977, 13.

12 Heidegger, 1977, 14–15.

is past, but rather the sober readiness to be astounded before the coming of what is early."[13] The point to be made is that our relationship to the essence can only be thought by questioning, that is asking what is our relationship to technology? Put differently, has the social reality and also principles of justice taken account of the new reality brought about by technology that is the digital revolution?

The issue is what have we learned? This book has analysed selected historical thinkers. Heidegger puts it in the following way:

> History is neither simply the object of written chronicle nor simply the fulfillment of human activity. That activity first becomes history as something destined. And it is only the destining into objectifying representation that makes the historical accessible as an object for historiography, i.e., for a science, and on this basis makes possible the current equating of the historical with that which is chronicled.[14]

The last word and an encouraging one, belongs to Heidegger stating "The closer we come to the danger, the more brightly do the ways into the saving power begin to shine and the more questioning we become. For questioning is the piety of thought."[15]

The preliminary conclusion is that once economic interests are the only driving force the Rawlsian system of justice is not as appropriately used as Berger and Luckmann's explanation of how a society reality is constructed or Nielsen theory which is more egalitarian than the one from Rawls. In a nutshell Nielsen argued that:

> After provisions are made for common social (community) values, for capital overhead to preserve the society's productive capacity and allowances are made for differing unmanipulated needs and preferences, the income and wealth (the common stock of means) is to be so divided that each person will have a right to an equal share.[16]

The real issue is as Hutan Ashrafian explains:

13 Heidegger, 1977, 22.

14 Heidegger, 1977, 24.

15 Heidegger, 1977, 35.

16 Kai Nielsen. 1979. "Radical egalitarian justice: Justice as equality." *Social theory and practice* 5, no. 2: 209–226.

> For an algorithmic social contract, the core needs of data objectivity in the current era would require a significant overhaul as existing socially responsible data practices are generally lacking; limited data to date is truly objective. As a result, a system serving an entire nation state would require mechanisms to overcome bias and support fairness across a multitude of disciplines.[17]

One problem with Ashrafian's argument is that he suggests that the principles by Rawls' namely the *original position* and the *veil of ignorance* which are essential to construct a social contract are capable of being executed by an AI agent.[18] Morton Bay dismisses this argument. He correctly notes that the "Rawlsian theory dictates that the agent cannot be left alone to construct a social contract without human deliberation because the social contract will govern those humans. On the other hand, if the agent's "underlying" algorithm(s) can be adjusted by humans, it would require an original position/ veil of ignorance process to keep it Rawlsian – and that makes the AI agent redundant."[19]

Morton Bay equally concludes "that policymakers and regulators who wish to adhere to Rawls' theory of justice as fairness must be highly selective when choosing the contexts in which they apply AI systems and agents in their work."[20] Jørgensen Søgaard also noted that:

> Researchers and industry developers in artificial intelligence (AI) and natural language processing (NLP) have uniformly adopted a Rawlsian definition of fairness. On this definition, a technology is fair if performance is maximized for the least advantaged. We argue this definition has considerable loopholes, which can be used to legitimize common practices in AI/NLP research that actively contributes to social and economic inequalities.[21]

The first consideration is whether it is inconsistent "with Rawlsian principles to leave the deliberations involved in the construction of a Rawlsian social contract to an AI agent."[22] The problem is – as seen above – is that there are

17 Ashrafian, 2023, 1449–1450.
18 Ashrafian, 2023, 1454.
19 See Bay, 2023.
20 See Bay, 2023.
21 Jørgensen and Søgaard, 2023.
22 Bay, 2023,1.

ambiguities in the drafted legislations specially concerning AI ethics issues. "AI in the EU model draft is used as a "blanket term" for various computer applications ... which exhibit capabilities commonly and currently associated with human intelligence."[23] In addition it is essential that the use of AI system is not the same as AI agent. The EU have defined AI systems as "... software that is developed with [specific] techniques and approaches ... and can, for a given set of human-defined objectives, generate outputs such as content, predictions, recommendations, or decisions influencing the environments they interact with."[24] The issue which emerges is that humans – it may even be society – defines the objectives but how the decisions of AI influence the environment is arguably outside the control of humans as AI will only consult what is found on the net as a reference.

This accords to the view of Russell and Norvig who state that an AI "agent implements a function that maps percept sequences to actions."[25] However a better view of a definition of an AI agent is given by Powers and Ganascia who argue that it is a computational entity which has agency without intention and "an AI agent lacks true proper goals, personal intentions, or real freedom." which has ethical implications.[26] The important point is that AI is not human and hence humans need to control AI. Simply put a social contract based on Rawlsian principles cannot be left only to an AI agent but at the same time an AI agent is on the same footing as a human. Morton Bay advocates the significant difference between extrinsic and intrinsic adherence to Rawls' theory.

2 Extrinsic and Intrinsic Adherence to Rawls

An *intrinsic* adherence is necessary when the AI agent is trained to adhere to Rawlsian theory in an ethical way. An *extrinsic* adherence can be spoken of when the AI agent compels it to do so through external forces. The difference between the two states as explained by Morton Bay are:

23 Tambiama Madiega. 2023. *"Artificial Intelligence Act"*. European Parliament, Briefing PE 698.792, 3.

24 Madiega, 2023, 4.

25 Stuart J. Russell and Peter Norvig. 2016. *Artificial intelligence: a modern approach.* Pearson).

26 Thomas M. Powers and Jean-Gabriel Ganascia. 2020. "The Ethics of the Ethics of AI." *The Oxford handbook of ethics of AI*, 30.

> An AI system with intrinsic adherence to Rawls can be situated in a legislative zone where laws do not necessarily correspond to Rawls' principles, such as in the United States, where specific AI regulations have yet to emerge at the time of writing. Conversely, an AI system with extrinsic adherence must be governed by legislation or enforced policies that adhere to Rawlsian principles, such as the EU's AI Act appears to do to some extent.[27]

It must be remembered that Rawls specifically noted that "Agreements in everyday life are made in determinate situations within the background institutions of the basic structure"[28] Additionally and importantly "Only against the background of a just basic structure, including a just political constitution and a just arrangement of economic and social institutions, can one say that the requisite just procedure exists."[29]

It is obvious that corporations offering AI systems are and cannot be considered as following one of the principles of public institutions namely publicity as they are fearing the loss of a competitive edge by divulging trade secrets. The question is whether they can be compelled to be transparent by background institutions in the basic structure. The answer is simply no as technology giants appear to be self-governing or at best "as a stop-gap measure, the government has 'secured voluntary commitment' to AI safety from seven leading providers of AI systems."[30]

The question therefore is whether the EU AI Act is not only a just basic structure but also emanates from a just political structure? Can the Rawlsian system of justice be applied? It appears that the three-tier structure of high risk to limited risk as explained earlier could be classed as following the Rawlsian system of justice as it is transparent and hence follows the publicly known concept.

> "policymakers and regulators who wish to adhere to Rawls' theory of justice as fairness must be highly selective when choosing the contexts in

27 See Bay, 2023.

28 Rawls, 2001, 15.

29 Rawls, 2001, 76.

30 The White House. 2023. *"Biden-Harris Administration Secures Voluntary Commitments from Leading Artificial Intelligence Companies to Manage the Risks Posed by AI", The White House Briefing Room,* https://www.whitehouse.gov/briefing-room/statements-releases/2023/07/21/fact-sheet-biden-harris-administration-secures-voluntary-commitments-from-leading-artificial-intelligence-companies-to-manage-the-risks-posed-by-ai/.

> which they apply AI systems and agents in their work."[31] Importantly also there is an applicability of Rawlsian theory to AI ethics.

3 Economic Interests

A preliminary conclusion is that once economic interests are the only driving force in technology developments, the Rawlsian system of justice is not as appropriately used as Berger and Luckmann's explanation of how a society reality is constructed. Nielsen's theory is also more egalitarian than the one from Rawls'. In a nutshell Nielsen argued that:

> After provisions are made for common social (community) values, for capital overhead to preserve the society's productive capacity and allowances are made for differing unmanipulated needs and preferences, the income and wealth (the common stock of means) is to be so divided that each person will have a right to an equal share.[32]

The real issue is as Hutan Ashrafian explains:

> For an algorithmic social contract, the core needs of data objectivity in the current era would require a significant overhaul as existing socially responsible data practices are generally lacking; limited data to date is truly objective. As a result, a system serving an entire nation state would require mechanisms to overcome bias and support fairness across a multitude of disciplines.[33]

Morton Bay equally concludes that "that policymakers and regulators who wish to adhere to Rawls' theory of justice as fairness must be highly selective when choosing the contexts in which they apply AI systems and agents in their work."[34]

31 See Bay, 2023.
32 See Nielsen,1979.
33 Ashrafian, 2023, 1449.
34 See Bay, 2023.

4 The Legal Input

As we have seen education needs to play a significant role in overcoming the dark side of the digital revolution and rebalancing the social make-up of society. At the same time the level of social and importantly also the political order using laws through the legal system must play an important part. So far laws have been enacted to safeguard the privacy of data subjects as well as protection of the systems via cybersecurity. In other words, the law has understood that not only the digital systems need to be saved as well as individuals but so far not much has happened in protection of societies, that is protecting culture in a direct way. No doubt the volume of legislation in the online space certainly has an in direct effect only on the social reality and its maintenance.

The first observation is that the law is based on the interpretation of reality that is the "Jurist [view] legally relevant state of affairs and facts of the case as an interpretation of reality."[35] Put differently the law prescribes procedures but the lawyer will selectively use only certain pieces and aspects of reality in order to build a case. As reality is socially constructed, the issue is which reality is relevant to the jurist? The question is what is relevant? Strassheim summarised it in the following way relying on Schutz as "the four aspects of relevance mentioned above as forming a (a) comprehensive and (b) systematic complex of (c) standardized procedures and categories which (d) help coordinate individual behaviour at a social level."[36]

The second comment is that the peace agreements are of assistance in analysing the function of legal institutions as "it is not uncommon to find references to children, youth or young adults, and even future generations as both intended beneficiaries of the peace and as those who suffered particularly egregious harms during conflicts."[37] As an example, the 1994 Angola Peace agreement included a commitment to:

> Promote effective participation of the different socioeconomic actors, specifically the private sector, civil society, women and youth in the consolidation of democracy and good governance, particularly through the

35 Alfred Schutz. 1996. "Outline of a Theory of Relevance." *In Collected Papers: Volume IV*, pp. 3–5. Dordrecht: Springer Netherlands, 4.

36 See Jan Strassheim. 2018. "Lady Justice Turns a Blind Eye:(Ir-) Relevance, Legal Thought and Social Order." In *Relevance and Irrelevance: Theories, Factors and Challenges*. Strassheim, J., Nasu, H., eds. 281–301.

37 Alexandra Harrington. 2023. *The Future of Peace: Incorporation of Intergenerational Equity and Justice in Peace Treaties and Reconciliation Agreements*. Edward Elgar Publishing, 49.

> promotion of good governance at local level, and the emergence of independent and responsible media.[38]

Considering that many institutions and mechanical objects invented by the digital revolution have changed the way we interact, that is changed our lives, a peace agreement is an essential part to be created in order to establish a new shared social reality. It is the current and emerging generations which are now being affected by the dark side of new technology as explained in this book. The real issue is how do we educate our youth and future generations that there is a wealth of important knowledge which cannot be accessed through quick grabs on the internet. The question is, are we losing our historical knowledge as well as the full facts of today? As an example who is still aware of the armed conflicts which are still affection nations such as in Ukraine, Uganda, Sri Lanka, Brazil, South Africa, Sierra Leone, Rwanda, Peru, Mozambique, Mali, Guatemala, El Salvadore, East Timor Columbia, Chile, Chad, Argentina, Burma and the Middle East let alone knowing where all these countries are?

In summary this book has demonstrated that aspects of the digital revolution need regulation to prevent an imbalance in society, erosion of our institutions and negative flow on effects which result in conflicts. Legal theories have always been available to us and continue to give us the context we need to navigate new challenges and developments. History has shown us that a drift away from equality and justice can have powerful implications for societies including threats to democracy. Ultimately our own ideals and our own construction of reality as individuals within our own societies, even if under the pressure of the powerful, has become of paramount importance to our collective future.

---

38 Harrington, 2023, 50.

www.ingramcontent.com/pod-product-compliance
Lightning Source LLC
Chambersburg PA
CBHW071226230926
51849CB00001B/36